Exploring Applied Psychology:
Origins and Critical Analyses

Master Lectures in Psychology

Exploring Applied Psychology:

Origins and Critical Analyses

Master Lecturers

Anne Anastasi
David C. Berliner
Frank J. Landy
Kurt Salzinger
Hans H. Strupp

Edited by
Thomas K. Fagan
and Gary R. VandenBos

AMERICAN PSYCHOLOGICAL ASSOCIATION
WASHINGTON, DC 20002

Published by the
American Psychological Association
750 First Street, NE
Washington, DC 20002

Copies may be ordered from
APA Order Department
P.O. Box 2710
Hyattsville, MD 20784

Typeset in Cheltenham by Easton Publishing Services, Inc.,
Easton, MD

Printer: BookCrafters, Inc., Chelsea, MI
Technical/production editors: Peggy Schlegel and
    Cynthia L. Fulton

Library of Congress Cataloging-in-Publication Data

Exploring applied psychology : origins and critical analyses /
    edited by Thomas K. Fagan and Gary R. VandenBos.
        p.   cm.
    Includes bibliographical references.
    ISBN 1-55798-206-6
    1. Psychology, Applied—History. I. Fagan, Thomas.
II. VandenBos, Gary R.
BF636.E84   1993
158′ . 09—dc20   93-17321
                                                          CIP

Printed in the United States of America
First edition

CONTENTS

PREFACE

H istory is a hard sell. Despite admonitions that those who ignore history are destined to see it repeated, too often the history of psychology is perceived as dull and irrelevant to contemporary theory and practice. With few exceptions, applied psychologists avoided discussing the history of their field until psychology was more than a half-century old. Early historical discussions were typically of directions in experimental psychology (e.g., Boring, 1929), of organizational growth and trends (Fernberger, 1932, 1943), and only occasionally of changes in applied and professional psychology (Brotemarkle, 1931; Cattell, 1937; Louttit, 1939). By the 1930s, professional and applied psychology had evolved from an expanding knowledge base in general psychology to specializations defined largely by settings and clientele, in which generic titles such as psychoclinicist, consulting psychologist, or clinical psychologist were often used. Educational and school psychologists served children primarily in public school settings. Clinical psychologists served children as well as adults but mainly in correctional, court, charitable, community, hospital, and university-based clinics. Counseling psychologists, then often referred to as guidance or personnel counselors, served in a mix of the settings in which school and clinical psychologists were employed, especially academic settings. Industrial and organizational psychologists, then referred to as industrial and business psychologists, sought to apply psychology in business and industry, including the military. The commonality of some groups and the uniqueness of the industrial and business psychologists were revealed in a study by Darley and Berdie (1940). They indicated that clinical, school, and educational psychologists were quite similar in functioning, compared with industrial and business psychologists, and that regardless of titles and functions, most applied psychologists had virtually identical training. A study several decades later continued to reveal the similarities of clinical and counseling psychology, their proximity to school psychology, and the uniqueness of the industrial/organizational (I/O) group (Educational Testing Service, 1983).

The reorganization of the American Psychological Association (APA) in 1944–1945 gave distinctive organizational status to several applied and professional fields of psychology. Divisions 12 through 19 of the original 19 divisions were "assigned" to applied and professional fields, whereas the first 11 divisions had titles related to content areas of the field (e.g., 5—Evaluation and Measurement; 6—Physiological and Comparative; 7—Childhood and Adolescence; 9—Personality and Social Psychology). Of course, overlapping divisional interests were present, and in 1946, Division 11 (Abnormal Psychology and Psychotherapy) merged with Division 12 (Clinical Psychology). The divisional structure of the APA followed earlier organizational recognition of generic clinical psychology in the American Association of Clinical Psychologists (1917–1919), which became the APA Division on Clinical Psychology in 1919. The American Association of Applied Psychologists, founded in 1937, had sections for educational, clinical, business and industry, consulting, and military psychologists (English, 1938). Thus, by the end of World War II, there were several specialized fields of applied and professional psychology represented in the reorganized APA. The expansion of APA divisions in the past 48 years has been along lines of specialized content areas and applications (e.g., 26—History of Psychology; 29—Psychological Hypnosis; 40—Clinical Neuropsychology), settings (e.g., 42—Independent Practice), clients (e.g., 43—Family Psychology), and issues (e.g., 44—Society for the Psychological Study of Lesbian and Gay Issues). The present structure of 48 divisions reflects the continuing diversification of psychology. Our history has included many psychology groups other than the APA. Information on the historical development and diversity of psychological organizations is provided in Hilgard (1987), VandenBos (1989), and Fagan (1993).

Since the historic reorganization of the APA, there have been more retrospective analyses of applied and professional psychology (e.g., Brotemarkle, 1947; Fryer & Henry, 1950; Glover & Ronning, 1987; Reisman, 1966; Shakow, 1969). Although there are many contemporary books on the history of psychology, for the most part they have not given comprehensive coverage to applied and professional psychology. Treatments of applied and professional psychology have often been published separately (e.g., Canter & Canter, 1982; Glover & Ronning, 1987; Reisman, 1966, 1976; Webb, 1962). The comprehensive treatment of psychology's history by Hilgard (1987) is a notable exception. Another characteristic of such treatments is their practice of lumping together applied and professional psychology as interchangeable terms. For much of our history the distinction has been blurred. However, with the evolution of accredited and credentialed professional specialties in psychology, greater distinction has emerged. The writings of the past decade also reveal a shift in historical analysis from what Furumoto (1988) referred to as "concentrating on 'great men and great ideas'" (p. 12) to concentrating on a more critical analysis of such aspects of psychology's history. Some of the critical history has been spurred by the analyses of social scientists and historians taking an outsider's perspective (e.g., Burnham, 1988; Napoli, 1981). Thus, contemporary historical treatments of psychology and psychologists have not been as kind and accepting of our history as were earlier accounts. These recent studies serve to remind us that there is no such thing as *the* history of psychology. Rather, history is a matter of author perceptions and interpretations of people, events, movements, ideologies, and theories.

The history of psychology was, of course, contextual. It occurred within the broader context of society, and its interpretation was influenced by the contemporary context within which the author wrote. When the latter contextual influence overshadows the former, we encounter revisionist positions that fail to grasp the proper context of the former period; that is, history is interpreted too much in terms of the contemporary context. An example would be condemning early psychologists for advocating particular viewpoints that are no longer tenable. Overemphasizing the historical context, however, may fail to draw contemporary relevance from our history. Perhaps this failure is the basis for some perceptions of history as dull and irrelevant. Furthermore, historical writing is unavoidably influenced by the personal characteristics of the author. For all practical purposes, there are as many histories of psychology as there are historical authors.

As part of this context, it should be noted that our field itself has expanded. The early period of psychology was characterized by a far more limited number of persons, ideas, events, and content areas than in more recent times. This is readily observed in the applications of psychology. When a field emerges from a commonality of applications to a high degree of specialization of applications in just one century, interpreters encounter the problem of trying to explain each specialization's origins with greater specificity than may be possible. It is like trying to explain the differences among every contemporary Christian church by going backward and describing presumably independent contributions of a few early religious figures. In this time of great diversity, historical writers are faced with the challenge of discerning contemporary relevance from a time when such diversity did not exist.

Even though specialized fields of applied psychology were discernible in American psychology's first half-century, the primary contributors to these varied fields had several things in common. They were often educated in conjunction with Wundt's laboratory in Leipzig, Germany; they were recognized leaders in psychology; and many were elected to the APA presidency. Most pursued primarily academic careers, starting with traditional experimental psychology and later developing applied interests. The career paths are reminiscent of Napoli's (1981) insight that among the professions, psychology is unique in having predominantly academic roots. The founders of applied psychology were most often men whose principal contributions were made during the period from 1890 to 1930, and many of their descendants were also well-known psychologists. Moreover, the founding persons often knew one another personally or were aware of one another's work and may have been educated or worked together; their contributions were made to several applied fields of psychology concurrently.

These aspects can be observed in this book in the chapters by Landy and Salzinger regarding the contributions of Hugo Münsterberg or in the chapters by Anastasi and Landy discussing Cattell and Thorndike. The influence of Cattell and Thorndike could be seen in educational, school, and I/O psychology. Terman's adaptations and extensions of the Binet–Simon scales had widespread implications as well. Brotemarkle's (1931) text commemorating the career of Lightner Witmer in "clinical psychology" demonstrated the range of fields in which Witmerian conceptualizations were applied. In their quests to apply traditional psychology to real-world problems, these pioneers were, in effect, bootstrapping themselves in uncharted territory. They had not emerged from training programs in applied psychology. Instead, they were training themselves and others "on-the-job." Another characteristic was that their contributions were often along lines of applications that would help to sort, classify, or select people. In this book, this is most obvious in the chapters by Anastasi, Berliner, and Landy, but also applies to the research efforts described in Salzinger and Strupp.

There are many ways to approach the history of applied and professional psychology. One can deal with specific aspects of the field—noteworthy movements, events, or persons; or one can take a comprehensive look at psychology without undue attention to a particular specialty or orientation. The challenge is to make historical aspects of psychology relevant to contemporary psychological practitioners. This is no easy task. The writer must be familiar with the history of the field as well as the contemporary practice of the field.

In this book, we have gathered together the perceptions of distinguished scholars in applied psychology about the field's history and its relevance to contemporary practice. The five chapters are derived from the Master Lecture Series presented during the 1992 APA Centennial Convention in Washington, DC. In each lecture, the task of the presenter was to discuss historical aspects of an applied psychology field and to draw contemporary relevance from its history. Anne Anastasi addresses this concern from the outset by taking a historical approach to the question, "How can we improve the understanding and use of psychological tests?" She traces the development of the testing movement from the 19th-century interests of Galton to those of Cattell, Terman, and others in the intelligence test movement, and into a variety of other areas of testing. Her discussions of validity, context and cultural issues, modern day computer applications, and the evolution of standards for tests and their users continue to be strong areas of interest in the testing community. Her chapter appears first because it provides a framework for better understanding the measurement origins of many fields of applied psychology. The genesis of and major developments in educational psychology are described by David Berliner, who skillfully compares and contrasts the contributions of well-known psychologists such as G. Stanley Hall, William James, E. L. Thorndike, and John Dewey. Although the chapter concentrates on the development of educational psychology, similarities to the origins of developmental and school psychology are discernible. Berliner challenges the field of educational psychology to overcome the darker side of its Thorndikian legacy and to rebuild relationships with educators around real-world issues and problems of education. The chapter by Frank Landy provides a unique perspective on the major early contributors to industrial and organizational psychology, identifying their primary contributions and the shortcomings of the field that persisted for several decades. Hans Strupp and Kurt Salzinger depart from discussing specializations and, like Anastasi, describe the development of particular technological and methodological contributions to clinical psychology. Strupp discusses the importance of process and outcome research in psychotherapy and the development of training methods in psychodynamic psychology at Vanderbilt University. Salzinger identifies various approaches along lines of traditional experimental and behavioral psychology and their contributions to the study of abnormal psychology and the therapeutic process. The discussion reveals the proximity of applied psychology to experimental psychology and the importance of animal models of experimentation. Salzinger reminds us of the relevance of approaching the therapeutic process from an experimental perspective.

As you read these chapters, you will find yourself thinking about how we still do some things the old way, how we may explain some contemporary circumstances from earlier circumstances, or how almost nothing under the sun seems completely new. Perhaps you will question the significance of technology and methodology to the advancement of science and the directionality of that relationship. How important was the intelligence test to the conceptualization of intelligence or the segmentation of schoolchildren into classrooms based on intelligence? Would such conceptualizations and applications have occurred anyway, perhaps as a result of different technology? To what extent is progress in psychology a blend of technology and having the right people in the right place at the right time? Were Hall, Cattell, Münsterberg, and others discussed in this book critical to our history or did they just take advantage of a vacuous window of opportunity?

Is history relevant? It really has no choice except to be. Although Wundt's lab or Cattell's "mental tests" may seem distant from the interests of contemporary applied psychologists, these pioneers provided the methodological rigor and conceptualizations on which some psychologists built, and against which some psychologists rebelled, to create new methods and conceptualizations. Everything we are now doing is premised to some extent on our history. That history may be longer for some aspects of psychology than for others, but it is relevant nonetheless. Perhaps you will come to recognize that we are all a part of that history. In our own small and seemingly insignificant ways, we are creating the history of psychology for the next generation, while practicing in the context of our history from the last generation.

THOMAS K. FAGAN, PhD

References

Boring, E. G. (1929). *A history of experimental psychology*. New York: Appleton.

Brotemarkle, R. A. (Ed.). (1931). *Clinical psychology: Studies in honor of Lightner Witmer to commemorate the thirty-fifth anniversary of the founding of the first psychological clinic*. Philadelphia: University of Pennsylvania Press.

Brotemarkle, R. A. (1947). Clinical psychology 1896–1946. *Journal of Consulting Psychology, 11*, 1–4.

Burnham, J. C. (1988). Psychology and counseling: Convergence into a profession. In N. O. Hatch (Ed.), *The professions in American history* (pp. 181–198). Notre Dame, IN: University of Notre Dame Press.

Canter, S., & Canter, D. (Eds.). (1982). *Psychology in practice: Perspectives on professional psychology*. New York: Wiley.

Cattell, J. M. (1937). Retrospect: Psychology as a profession. *Journal of Consulting Psychology, 1*, 1–3.

Darley, J. G., & Berdie, R. (1940). The fields of applied psychology. *Journal of Consulting Psychology, 4*, 41–52.

Educational Testing Service. (1983). *Job analysis of licensed psychologists in the United States and Canada*. Princeton, NJ: Author.

English, H. B. (1938). Organization of the American Association of Applied Psychologists. *Journal of Consulting Psychology, 2*, 7–16.

Fagan, T. K. (1993). Separate but equal: School psychology's search for organizational identity, *Journal of School Psychology, 31*, 3–90.

Fernberger, S. W. (1932). The American Psychological Association: A historical summary. *Psychological Bulletin, 29*, 1–89.

Fernberger, S. W. (1943). The American Psychological Association: 1892–1942. *Psychological Review, 50*, 33–60.

Fryer, D. H., & Henry, E. R. (Eds.). (1950). *Handbook of applied psychology*. New York: Rinehart.

Furumoto, L. (1988). The new history of psychology. In I. S. Cohen (Ed.), *The G. Stanley Hall Lecture Series* (Vol. 9, pp. 9–34). Washington, DC: American Psychological Association.

Glover, J. A., & Ronning, R. R. (Eds.). (1987). *Historical foundations of educational psychology*. New York: Plenum Press.

Hilgard, E. R. (1987). *Psychology in America: A historical survey*. New York: Harcourt Brace Jovanovich.

Louttit, C. M. (1939). The nature of clinical psychology. *Psychological Bulletin, 36*, 361–389.

Napoli, D. S. (1981). *Architects of adjustment: The history of the psychological profession in the United States*. Port Washington, NY: Kennikat Press.

Reisman, J. M. (1966). *The development of clinical psychology*. New York: Appleton-Century-Crofts.

Reisman, J. M. (1976). *A history of clinical psychology*. New York: Irvington.

Shakow, D. (1969). *Clinical psychology as science and profession: A forty-year odyssey*. Chicago: Aldine.

VandenBos, G. R. (1989). Loosely organized "organized psychology." *American Psychologist, 44*, 979–986.

Webb, W. B. (Ed.). (1962). *The profession of psychology*. New York: Holt, Rinehart & Winston.

ANNE ANASTASI

A CENTURY OF PSYCHOLOGICAL TESTING

ORIGINS, PROBLEMS, AND PROGRESS

ANNE ANASTASI

A nne Anastasi, Professor Emeritus of Psychology at Fordham University, was born December 19, 1908, in New York City.

She attended Barnard College, receiving an AB in 1928. Two years later, after completing doctoral studies, she was granted a PhD by Columbia University. In October 1967, she received an honorary LittD degree from the University of Windsor (Canada). In June 1971, she received honorary degrees from Villanova (PaedD) and Cedar Crest College (ScD). A second ScD was awarded by Fordham University (1979), and a third by LaSalle College (1979). In 1977, she was the recipient of the annual Educational Testing Service Award for Distinguished Service to Measurement; in 1981, she received the Distinguished Scientific Award for the Applications of Psychology from the American Psychological Association (APA); in 1983, the American Educational Research Association Award for Distinguished Contributions to Research in Education; and in 1984, the E. L. Thorndike Medal for Distinguished Psychological Contributions to Education from the APA Division of Educational Psychology. The American Psychological Foundation Gold Medal was awarded in 1984. In 1987, she received the National Medal of Science from the president of the United States.

Anastasi taught at Barnard from 1929 to 1939, then was appointed assistant professor and chairman of the department of psychology at

Queens College (CUNY). In 1947, she joined the faculty of Fordham University, where she was designated full professor of psychology in 1951. She served as chairman of the psychology department from 1968 to 1974. In 1979, she was designated Professor Emeritus.

Anastasi lectured at the University of Wisconsin during the 1951 summer session and at the University of Minnesota in 1958; she served as research consultant for the College Entrance Examination Board (CEEB) from 1954 to 1956. She has at various times served as a research consultant for such organizations as the U.S. Office of Education, Office of Economic Opportunity, U.S. Air Force, several state civil service commissions, American College Testing Service, and NYC Board of Education. In the summer of 1968, she served as a consultant for the Ford Foundation in Brazil.

Anastasi was president of the Eastern Psychological Association from 1946 to 1947, president of the Division of General Psychology of the APA from 1956 to 1957, president of the Division of Evaluation and Measurement from 1965 to 1966, recording secretary of the APA from 1952 to 1955, and a member of its board of directors from 1956 to 1959 and from 1968 to 1970. In 1970, she became president-elect of the APA and succeeded as president in 1971. She is also a member of Phi Beta Kappa, Sigma XI, the Psychonomic Society, and the American Psychological Society.

Anastasi served as a trustee of the American Psychological Foundation and was its president from 1965 to 1967. From 1973 to 1990 she was a trustee of HumRRO. She has served as chairman of the Research and Development Committee of the CEEB and as a member of the Advisory Committee on Science Education of the National Science Foundation. From 1977 to 1979, she served as a member of the Congressional Panel for the Review of the Regional Laboratories and Research and Development Centers supported by the National Institute of Education. From 1977 to 1980, she was a member of the newly constituted College Board Committee on the Scholastic Aptitude Test.

Her major publications include *Differential Psychology* (1937, 1949, 1958) and *Psychological Testing* (1954, 1961, 1968, 1976, 1982, 1988), both published by Macmillan; and *Fields of Applied Psychology* (1964, 1979), published by McGraw-Hill. In addition, she edited three other books: *Individual Differences* (Wiley, 1965), *Testing Problems in Perspective* (American Council on Education, 1966), and *Contributions to Differential Psychology* (Praeger, 1982). She is coauthor of other books and has published more than 200 articles and monographs on research.

Anastasi is listed in *Who's Who in America, Who's Who in Frontier Science and Technology, Who's Who in American Women, The World Who's Who of Authors*, and *American Men and Women of Science*, among other directories. She is married to a psychologist, John Porter Foley, Jr.; they occupy a renovated brownstone in midtown Manhattan.

ANNE ANASTASI

A CENTURY OF PSYCHOLOGICAL TESTING

ORIGINS, PROBLEMS, AND PROGRESS

The basic question I am addressing in this chapter is, How can we improve the understanding and use of psychological tests? In an effort to answer this question, I look first at the historical origins of testing, the social context and theoretical climate within which modern testing developed. I next consider the chief sources of test misuse today and what is being done to prevent such misuse. I then turn to major current developments in both testing technology and relevant behavioral science that the test user should know about. I give special attention to those developments that are gaining momentum and are hence likely to characterize the future of testing.

Origins and Present Scope of Testing

Let me begin with the historical origins of psychological testing. Why should we consider this historical background? One reason can certainly be found in the growing interest in all aspects of the history of psychology. As the American Psychological Association (APA) celebrates the centennial year of its founding, it is especially fitting to take cognizance of the antecedent developments that led up to the current status of *any* field of psychology. Apart from this scholarly and—if you will—

sentimental motive, however, there are other, more compelling reasons for examining the history of testing. Knowledge about the settings in which tests were developed, the specific influences that contributed to their development, the practical problems encountered, and how these problems were solved should advance our understanding of what's good and what's bad in testing today. We can profit from the false starts as well as the astute observations of our predecessors.

Early Examples of Testing

Psychological historians have unearthed some fascinating examples of early uses of tests (Bowman, 1989; Doyle, 1974; McReynolds, 1975, 1986; see also Anastasi, 1965, pp. 1–11). A frequently cited example concerns the use of tests in Greece some 2,500 years ago, especially as described in the works of Plato and Aristotle. Testing served both as an adjunct to the educational process and in the selection of persons for state service (Doyle, 1974). Achievement tests were employed to assess mastery of literary and mathematical subjects and of such specialized areas as music, astronomy, and medical practice. Aptitude tests for personnel selection also covered general reasoning and learning skills, and appropriate character traits. Tests for military service were designed to sample physical, mental, and character traits deemed essential for military prowess. In all testing, attention was given to content analysis of the desired performance, to standardized observational procedures, and to reliability of ratings. There also seemed to be an awareness of the essential nature of a test, namely, a short performance sample observed under carefully controlled conditions that yielded an estimate of performance over longer periods in relatively uncontrolled real-life conditions.

Another favorite example is provided by the system of civil service examinations prevailing in the Chinese empire as many as 2,000 years ago (Bowman, 1989; DuBois, 1970). Covering a wide range of factual knowledge and literary skills, these tests were highly competitive and followed a long and arduous period of education. An all-to-familiar note is sounded by the lively controversies reported to have centered on such questions as the "effects of social class on test performance, the use of examinations to provide opportunities for social mobility, personal recommendations as an alternative to formal examinations in personnel selection, social protest against the nature of the examinations, the use of geographical units in allocating quotas of candidates to be passed, and the need to measure applied problem solving and reasoning" (Bowman, 1989, p. 578). There is also mention of such practical problems as the prevention of cheating and examiner bias.

The Testing Movement: Multiple Sources

Ebbinghaus has been credited with the remark that psychology has a long past but a short history (Boring, 1929, p. vii). This is equally true of psychological testing. It was not until the last decade of the 19th century that the psychological testing movement as we know it today took shape. The development of this movement can be traced through several strands from a variety of sources.

Measuring Individual Differences

The English biologist Francis Galton[1] was largely responsible for launching the testing movement. In the course of his varied approaches to the study of human heredity, Galton soon realized that he needed to measure the characteristics of related and unrelated persons. Only in this way could he discover, for example, the exact degree of resemblance between parents and offspring, siblings, cousins, or twins. With this end in view, he gathered extensive data on children in several schools and on adults who visited his anthropometric laboratory in London. Galton devised most of his own tests, which included measures of visual, auditory, tactual, and kinesthetic discrimination, muscular strength and coordination, reaction time, and other simple sensorimotor functions. Reflecting the influence of Locke, Galton believed that sensory discrimination tests could serve as an index of a person's intelligence. Thus, he wrote, "The only information that reaches us concerning outward events appears to pass through the avenue of our senses; and the more perceptive the senses are of difference, the larger is the field upon which our judgment and intelligence can act" (Galton, 1883, p. 27). This conviction was further strengthened by his observation that extremely retarded persons were often unable to discriminate heat, cold, and pain.

Another major contribution was Galton's development of statistical methods. Adapting several techniques from mathematics, he put them in such a form as to facilitate their use by mathematically untrained investigators in the quantitative analysis of test results. This phase of his work was carried forward by several of his students, the best known of whom was Karl Pearson.

An especially prominent position in the development of testing is occupied by the American psychologist James McKeen Cattell. In Cattell, the newly established science of experimental psychology and the still newer testing movement merged. After obtaining the PhD at Leipzig with

---

[1]For references on the history of the testing movement, see Anastasi (1965, pp. 1–44, 1988b, chap. 1). Major excerpts from publications by Galton, Cattell, and Binet are reproduced in Anastasi (1965, pp. 13–44).

Wundt, Cattell went to London, where his extensive contact with Galton led to a continuing interest in testing. On his return to the United States, he was active both in the establishment of psychological laboratories and in the development of a series of tests administered individually to college students. These tests were modeled partly on Galton's sensorimotor instruments but were expanded to include tests of memory and other simple mental processes. Cattell's test were typical of those independently developed in several countries in the 1890s. Attempts to evaluate these early tests proved disappointing. Performance showed little correspondence from one test to another and exhibited little or no relation to estimates of intelligence from school achievement or other real-life criteria.

Intelligence Testing

Among the psychologists of this period who were exploring various ways of measuring intelligence was Alfred Binet. Eventually he became convinced that the most promising approach was through the direct—albeit crude—measurement of complex intellectual functions. An opportunity to put this idea into practice arose in 1904, when the French Minister of Public Instruction appointed Binet to a commission for the study of educationally retarded schoolchildren. The immediate result was the development of the first Binet–Simon scale in 1905. This was followed by two subsequent revisions and by many translations and adaptations in several countries, including Terman's Stanford–Binet, first published in 1916.

At this point, Binet's work on schoolchildren merged with an earlier strand that originated in the early 19th century and dealt with the classification and training of severely mentally retarded individuals. Seguin, who introduced sense-training and muscle-training techniques for the severely retarded, developed procedures that were subsequently incorporated into performance tests of intelligence (Anastasi, 1988b, p. 6). Such tests are still in use to supplement the more academic, verbal types of intelligence tests. They also played an important part in the rise of so-called culture-free tests, because many could be administered without the use of reading, writing, or even spoken language. Empirical results, however, showed this application to be another false start. Tests cannot be culture free, because human behavior is not culture free. Actually, this type of test proved to be largely measuring spatial aptitudes, and it showed little correlation with the verbal and numerical skills required for schooling and other significant real life activities. Moreover, performance on spatial aptitude tests also varies with cultural background (Anastasi, 1988b, pp. 359–360).

Another major contributor to the strand of work involving mental retardation was Goddard (Cravens, 1987; Zenderland, 1987). While at the Vineland Training School, Goddard developed his own adaptation of the Binet–Simon tests. This revision was soon outdistanced by Terman's more psychometrically extensive and refined version. Nevertheless, Goddard's work was influential in promoting the acceptance of intelligence testing by the medical profession. It arrived at a propitious moment to meet the urgent need for a standardized measure for the diagnosis and classification of mental retardation. Another interesting feature of Goddard's career was the significant change in his theoretical position from an extreme hereditarian stance to a more moderate view that incorporated the role of environment. This change paralleled his move from the mental retardation setting at Vineland to a juvenile delinquent setting at the Ohio Bureau of Juvenile Research.

Group Tests and Special Ability Tests

The next steps in the testing movement are generally familiar. World War I gave us group testing. Derived from a psychometrically crude instrument that was developed under urgent time pressure, group intelligence tests spread rapidly after the war, for use with both children and adults. The popularization of these tests far outran their technical quality. When they failed to meet unwarranted expectations, skepticism and hostility toward all testing often resulted. The testing boom of the 1920s probably did more to retard than to advance the progress of testing.

Concurrent with the growth of intelligence tests, the development of special aptitude tests, chiefly in clerical and mechanical areas, was stimulated by the demands of vocational counseling and of personnel selection and classification for industrial occupations. At the theoretical level, factor analysis further focused attention on multiple aptitudes, including the verbal and numerical aptitudes covered by most intelligence tests. The period of multiple aptitude batteries was ushered in, complete with a controversy with the defenders of general intelligence, the IQ, and the g factor.

In the meantime, traditional school examinations were undergoing several technical improvements (Caldwell & Courtis, 1923; Ebel & Damrin, 1960). An important step was taken by the Boston public schools in 1845, when written examinations replaced oral interrogation by visiting examiners. Among the arguments offered in support of this innovation were that written examinations put all students in a uniform situation, permit a wider coverage of content, reduce the element of chance in question choice, and eliminate the possibility of favoritism by the examiner. All these arguments have a familiar ring: They were used much later to justify the replacement of essay questions by multiple-choice items.

Personality Tests

Personality testing, covering chiefly the affective or nonintellectual aspects of behavior, paralleled the development of ability testing but moved more slowly. In the late 19th century, it emerged primarily in work with neurotic and psychotic patients. World War I, along with its group intelligence testing, provided the prototype of self-report personality inventories in Woodworth's Personal Data Sheet. This inventory, too, was widely adopted for civilian use after the war, in both adult and children's forms. It also served as a model for the development of subsequent self-report inventories by empirical item selection and criterion-keyed scoring. This was the basic method originally followed in such well-known instruments as the Minnesota Multiphasic Personality Inventory (MMPI) and the Strong Vocational Interest Blank (SVIB).

Current Applications of Testing Methodology

Where are we today, at the end of all this history? It will come as no surprise that one of the features we share with earlier periods is the prevalence of vigorous controversy. The scope of this controversy is vividly portrayed by Sokal (1987). His procedure is to summarize the views of extremists on both sides, from claims that tests can do what they were never meant to do—and never should—to proposals that all testing be abolished. Much of the rest of this chapter is directed to an understanding of present controversies and of ways of solving the problems that underlie them.

At this point, however, I want to emphasize that, while the extremists continue to argue, the use of tests and of test-development methodology has been steadily rising and is spreading to new areas of application. There are signs of a growing psychometric orientation in fields that began with a qualitative approach, uncontrolled assessment procedures, and subjective interpretations (see Anastasi, 1988b, chaps. 16 & 19). Notable examples are traditional clinical practice, neuropsychological assessment, behavior therapy, and behavior modification. To this should be added the burgeoning field of health psychology, in which two of the most impressive illustrations include (a) the use of sophisticated psychometric methodology in developing scales to measure health status and the quality of life (Anastasi, 1988b, pp. 660–662; Kaplan, 1986) and (b) tests of behavioral toxicology, namely, the deterioration of human performance under adverse environmental conditions. This second example cuts across the needs of health psychology and of engineering psychology (Anastasi, 1988b, pp. 654, 660–662; Lane & Kennedy, 1990).

Role of the Test User

Increasing Focus on Uses and Misuses of Tests

A significant trend in mental testing today is the increasing recognition of the part played by the test user (Anastasi, 1990). Common criticisms of tests and popular antitest reactions are often directed, not to intrinsic features of the tests, but to misuses of the test by inadequately qualified users in education, industry, clinical and counseling practice, and other applied contexts. Many of these misuses stem from a desire for shortcuts, quick answers, and simple routine solutions for real-life problems. All too often, the decision-making responsibility is shifted to the test. The test user loses sight of the fact that tests are tools, serving as valuable aids to the skilled practitioner, but useless or misleading when improperly employed.

The test user, as contrasted to the test developer, is anyone who has the responsibility for choosing tests or for interpreting test results and employing them as one source of information in reaching practical decisions. Many test users serve both of these functions. Moreover, these professional functions are in addition to the more routine activities of administering and scoring tests, which in many cases are delegated to assistants who should function under careful supervision. Examples of test users are teachers, counselors, educational administrators, testing coordinators in school systems, personnel workers in industry of government, clinicians who use tests as aids in their practice, and many others in an increasing variety of real-life contexts. Anyone who chooses tests or uses test results needs some technical knowledge for the proper understanding of tests. If a test user, in this sense, lacks adequate background for this purpose, he or she should have ready access to a properly qualified supervisor or consultant.

The increasing awareness of the responsibilities of the test user is apparent in the successive editions of the test standards published by the APA and prepared jointly with two other national associations concerned with test use.[2] Each successive edition of these standards devoted increasing attention to test use; but this shift becomes especially prominent in the latest edition, published in 1985. The title has been changed from *Standards for Educational and Psychological Tests* to *Standards for Educational and Psychological Testing* (1985). The substitution of "testing" for "tests" in the latter title reflects the broadened scope of the *Standards*. It calls attention to the process of test use in addition to the technical qualities of the tests themselves. The organi-

---

[2]American Educational Research Association and National Council on Measurement in Education.

zation and content of the current *Standards* fully support this orientation. One section (including 5 chapters) covers technical standards for test construction and evaluation, whereas three sections (including 11 chapters) are devoted to standards for the use of tests in different professional applications and their use with special populations, as well as standards for test administration, scoring, and reporting, and for protecting the rights of test takers.

Test publishers, as well as test-related committees of national professional associations, have also been giving increasing attention to the key role of the test user. Some of the major test publishers are making special efforts to improve their communication with test users, to provide the necessary information for proper test selection and score interpretation, and to help guard against common misuses of tests. Steps are also being taken to spell out more fully in test manuals the necessary qualifications of test users for different kinds of commercially available tests.

A noteworthy event in this direction is the recently completed project of the Joint Committee on Testing Practices, sponsored by five national associations concerned with testing.[3] A special working group of this committee, comprising representatives of major test publishers and association members, was the Test User Qualifications Working Group, known by the delightful acronym, TUQWoG. The chief goal of TUQWoG was to develop an empirical, data-based set of essential qualifications for users of different types of tests, which test publishers could incorporate in their test purchaser qualification forms. Through 5 years of intensive, nationwide research, the TUQWoG project developed an impressive database. Some publishers have already begun to use the results in their purchaser qualification forms (Eyde, Moreland, Robertson, Primoff, & Most, 1988).

A second working group of the same committee was subsequently formed. Known by the modified acronym of TUTWoG (with a "T" for training), its purpose is to use the available TUQWoG database to develop guidelines and training materials for test users. The first product of this project is a casebook of test misuses to guard against (see Eyde et al., 1993). The cases are based on specific instances of misuses actually submitted from a variety of settings.

What Every Test User Should Know

It is generally recognized that the surest way to improve test use and to prevent misuse is through more and better training of test users

---

[3]American Association for Counseling and Development, American Educational Research Association, American Psychological Association, American Speech-Language-Hearing Association, National Council on Measurement in Education. Not all five associations were represented on the Joint Committee throughout the period of its operation.

Such training may be provided at different levels and in various forms. It includes college and graduate courses; in-service programs in school systems, industrial organizations, and other work settings; continuing education programs conducted by professional associations; and workshops provided by test publishers, either in conjunction with the introduction of their own new or revised tests, or more broadly oriented toward general testing problems.

What specialized knowledge do test users need? The appropriate use of tests and the correct interpretation of test results calls for knowledge about both the statistical properties of scores an the psychological characteristics of the behavior assessed by the tests. Apart from an understanding of different types of scores, such as percentiles, standard scores, and deviation IQs, the test user needs familiarity with such basic concepts as the standard error of measurement (SEM), which serves as a corrective against the tendency to rely unduly on a single measurement. So important is the SEM for this purpose that the College Board now includes data on the SEM and a simple explanation of its use, not only in brochures distributed to high school and college counselors but also in the individual score reports mailed to test takers. Even more important for test interpretation is the evaluation of score differences in multiscore batteries. Such evaluation requires data not only on the statistical significance of score differences but also on several other special questions, such as the differential validity of individual test scores and of score patterns (Anastasi, 1985a).

Besides correct statistical interpretation, the proper use of test scores involves an adequately informed substantive interpretation. The latter requires information about the behavior domain that the tests are designed to assess, including the conditions that influence the development of relevant cognitive and affective traits. It is in this connection, too, that we hear the often repeated caution that a test score cannot be interpreted in isolation; it needs confirmatory data from other sources as well as information about the individual's experiential history and about the particular contexts for which the individual is being assessed. Failure to observe this caution accounts for many current misuses of tests and for much popular mistrust of testing.

In the rest of this chapter, I describe some outstanding current developments in both statistical methodology and substantive psychological knowledge that every test user should know about.

Current Highlights in Testing Methodology

Evolving Approaches to Test Validation

One of the most significant innovations in test-construction methodology is a more comprehensive and theoretically based approach to test validation (Anastasi, 1986a). This change follows a trend discernible in psychology as a whole, namely, an increasing concern with theory and a movement away from blind empiricism of an earlier period. In psychometrics, theoretical orientation is exemplified by a growing emphasis on constructs in the analysis of personality and ability as well as by the increasing use of construct validation. The term *construct validity* was formally introduced into the psychometric vocabulary in the first edition of the *Standards*, published in 1954. The discussions of construct validation that followed for several decades served to make the implications of its procedures more explicit and to provide a systematic rationale for their use. In psychometric terminology, a construct is a theoretical concept closely akin to a trait. It is basically derived from empirically observed behavioral consistencies and interrelations. Constructs may be simple and narrowly defined, such as speed of walking or spelling ability; or they may be complex and broadly generalizable, such as mathematical reasoning, scholastic aptitude, neuroticism, or anxiety.

Tests published since the 1970s show increasing concern with theoretical rationales throughout the test development process. A specific example of the integration of empirical and theoretical approaches is provided by the assignment of items to subtests on the basis of logical as well as statistical homogeneity. In other words, an item is retained in a scale if it had been written to fit the construct definition of the particular scale and *also* was shown to belong in that scale through the statistical procedures of item analysis.

It is being recognized more and more that the development of a valid test requires multiple procedures, which are employed sequentially, at different stages of test construction. Validity is thus built into the test from the outset rather than being apparently limited to the last stages of test development, as in traditional discussions of criterion-related validation in test manuals. The validation process begins with the formulation of trait or construct definitions derived from psychological theory, previous research, or systematic observation and analysis of real-life behavior domains, such as job analyses. Test items are then prepared to fit the construct definitions. Empirical item analyses follow, with the selection of the most valid items from the initial item pools. Other appropriate internal analyses may then be carried out, including factor analyses of item clusters or subtests. The final stage includes validation and cross-validation of various scores and of interpretive score combinations through statistical analyses against external, real-life criteria.

The traditional concepts of context validity and criterion-related validity can be more accurately designated as content relevance and content representativeness for the first and predictive and diagnostic utility for the second, as proposed by Messick (1988, 1989). Actually, content analyses and correlations with external criteria fit into particular stages of comprehensive construct validation. They contribute to the process of both determining and demonstrating what a test measures. In certain practical situations, data obtained by these traditional procedures may be needed to answer specific questions. Nevertheless, even in such cases, information about constructs enriches the understanding of test findings. For one thing, constructs are more generalizable than particular tested variables, and some generalizability beyond the immediate testing context is nearly always implied in the use of test results. As for criterion-related validity, ideally both tests and criteria should be described in terms of empirically established constructs, and the correspondence between the two sets of constructs should then be investigated.

Explorations in Test Design: Computer Impact

My second example of innovations in test-construction methodology is probably the most conspicuous development of the 1980s and 1990s and one that is likely to have far-reaching effects on the future of testing. I refer to item response theory and computerized adaptive testing, which have already become widely known by their acronyms, IRT and CAT (Anastasi, 1988b, pp. 219–224, 314–317; Lord, 1980; Weiss, 1982; Weiss & Davison, 1981; Weiss & Vale, 1987). Statistical techniques of item analysis have played an important part in test construction since the early days of standardized testing. These techniques have traditionally been concerned with the measurement of difficulty level and discriminative value of items. The first is based on percentage of persons giving the correct response (or in noncognitive tests, the keyed response), which is usually converted to a sigma distance from the normal curve mean. The second is based on the difference in total test score (or score on some external criterion) between those passing and those failing the item.

It is apparent that both types of item measures are restricted to the samples from which they were derived and are generalizable only to populations adequately represented by these samples. For many testing purposes that require sample-free item measures, the procedure employed until recently was some variant of Thurstone's absolute scaling. This procedure requires the inclusion of a set of common anchor items across any two samples, in order to work out a conversion formula for translating all item values from one sample to another. A chain of linked sample values can be employed whereby all item values are expressed in terms of one fixed reference group. This was the procedure used in the College Board's Scholastic Aptitude Test (SAT) over several decades to express scores on each new form on a fixed score scale.

With the increasing availability of high-speed computers, more precise mathematical techniques are rapidly being introduced to provide sample-free measurement scales. These procedures were originally identified under the general title of *latent trait models*. There is no implication, however, that such latent traits exist in any physical or physiological sense nor that they cause behavior. They are statistical constructs derived from empirically observed relations among test responses. To avoid the excess meanings associated with the term *latent trait*, some of the leading exponents of these procedures have substituted the term *item response theory* (IRT), which is now gaining usage within psychology.

By whatever name, these procedures utilize three parameters: item discrimination, item difficulty, and a lower asymptote parameter corresponding to the probability of the correct response occurring by chance. Some simplified procedures, such as the Rasch model, use only one parameter, the difficulty level, on the assumption that item differences in the other two parameters are negligible or can be eliminated by discarding items. This assumption, however, must be empirically verified for each test.

One of the most important applications of IRT is to be found in computer-administered adaptive testing (CAT). Also described as individualized, tailored, and response-contingent testing, this procedure adjusts item coverage to the responses actually given by each test taker. As the individual responds to each item, the computer chooses the next item on the basis of the individual's response history up to that point. This procedure is essentially similar to what the examiner does when administering individual tests, such as the Stanford–Binet. CAT achieves the same objective in less time, with far greater precision, and without one-to-one administration by a trained examiner. By replacing Binet's examiner with an interactive computer program, it combines the advantages of individual and group tests.

Exploratory research on CAT has been in progress in several contexts. For example, it has already been successfully employed in a program for placing entering college students in remedial instruction groups (Forehand, 1986; Ward, Kline, & Flaugher, 1986). Its use is under investigation in several large-scale occupational testing programs, as in the Armed Services Vocational Aptitude Battery (Wiskoff & Schratz, 1988). Some first steps have also been taken toward the use of CAT in personality testing (Ben-Porath & Butcher, 1986; Butcher, Keller, & Bacon, 1985; Jackson, 1985, 1991). In this case, the choice of items to fit individual response histories is based, not on difficulty level, but on other appropriate parameters. In its present state of development, personality-test CAT is most readily applicable to classifying test takers into two or more descriptive categories rather than to measuring their locations on personality dimensions. For example, a preliminary routing test could identify broad behavioral categories in which the individual shows significant deviations from the test norms. This would be followed by increasingly more specific subsets of items, to narrow down the range of clinical groups into which the respondent can be classified. Subsequent items could then concentrate on intensive exploration of problem areas that are critical for that individual.

Dynamic Assessment in Education

Let me now turn to some testing innovations that put more emphasis on qualitative approaches and examiner interaction with individual test takers. the term *dynamic assessment* has been introduced to cover a variety of clinical procedures involving deliberate departures from standardized test administration; the object is to elicit additional qualitative data from the individual. Although skilled clinicians have been using such procedures for some time, this approach has gained popularity since the 1980s (Feuerstein, 1979; Lidz, 1987; Sattler, 1988, pp. 549, 551). It has been used as a supplementary source of data, not only in cases of specific learning disabilities but also with other children who have been experiencing difficulties with their schooling. The latter include those with moderate or mild mental retardation, commonly classified as educable mentally retarded.

One of the earliest of these qualitative adaptations of procedure is known as *testing the limits*. To obtain a score for normative interpretation, this procedure should not be applied until after the test has been administered under standard conditions. In testing the limits, additional cues may be provided by the examiner; or additional time may be given in a time-limit test; or the child may be asked how he or she set out to solve the problem and a different first step is then suggested by the examiner.

A more recently developed approach has been designated as *learning-potential assessment* (Babad & Budoff, 1974; Feuerstein, 1979; Lidz, 1987). The term *potential* in this label may carry an unwanted implication that the ability in question was always present and needed only to be "uncovered." Actually, these procedures involve a test–teach–test format, whereby the child is taught to perform a task that he or she was initially unable to carry out. Special attention has focused on the work of Feuerstein (1979) with his Learning Potential Assessment Device (LPAD). In developing his assessment and training program, Feuerstein identified many instances of ineffective attitudes, faulty work habits, and inadequate modes of thinking that interfere with both test performance and school learning. Examples include: unplanned and impulsive approaches to a problem; inadequacies in perceiving and defining a problem; an "episodic grasp of reality" as contrasted to seeking relations and organizing data; and scanty communication, on the assumption that what the individual thinks is already known to others (one wonders whether the endless repetition of "you know" in conversations by some persons is related to this orientation). Much of the training introduced in the LPAD involves study habits, problem-solving techniques, and the cultivation of effective cognitive skills. Assessment and remediation are closely linked, and the process may continue for 1 or 2 years through intensive personal interaction between the child and the teacher–clinician (Feuerstein, 1979, chap. 6; Feuerstein, Rand, Jensen, Kaniel, & Tzuriel, 1987).

The dynamic assessment techniques developed by Feuerstein and others offer promise in several directions: (a) for research on the modifiability of scholastic aptitude, (b) for the development of remedial programs, and (c) as an assessment aid to the qualified clinician. At their present stage of development, however, much more research is needed to establish the *generalizability* of both assessment conclusions and remediation effects to activities outside the program, especially real-life school performance (Brown & Campione, 1986; Campione & Brown, 1987). There is also the question of *transportability*, or the extent to which the procedures can be used effectively by other clinicians. In the hands of examiners lacking adequate clinical expertise, it is unlikely that this approach can provide either dependable quantitative data or constructive clinical insights.

From another angle, there is promise that dynamic assessment can be combined with sophisticated psychometric developments to provide an effective objective testing procedure. Specifically, Embretson (1987, 1988) has been exploring the use of IRT and CAT to assess each individual with items appropriate to his or her performance level. This procedure circumvents the technical difficulties of measuring change (Cronbach & Furby, 1970) because at this level, learning effects are largest and items yield the most reliable estimate of each person's performance. The entire testing procedure includes three stages: (a) CAT pretest; (b) computer-administered, individually targeted training session; and (c) CAT posttest. By applying the task-decomposition procedures developed in cognitive psychology, Embretson is able to vary systematically the specific cognitive processes required to perform each task. Diagnostic items can thus be developed that identify the individual's specific difficulties. Training content is targeted to these difficulties. The individual's learning potential is assessed from the improvement exhibited from pretest to posttest. Preliminary research with this technique demonstrates its applicability and promising validity in such areas as mathematical reasoning and spatial aptitude. Bringing together developments from such diverse fields as clinical psychology, cognitive research, mathematical statistics, and computer technology, this approach represents a significant achievement in psychometrics.

Clinical Assessment

My last example of testing methodology concerns the interpretation of test scores. In this connection, let me introduce and clarify the term *assessment,* which is sometimes used interchangeably with testing and other times used more broadly to refer to any information-gathering technique about individual behavior. At still other times, it is used in a more restricted sense, to mean what was formerly described as the clinical use of tests (see Anastasi, 1988b, pp. 511–517). The latter traditionally refers to the intensive study of an individual, in which test scores are considered together with all other relevant information about the person. Data sources may include intensive interviews; biographical history; reports by teachers, job supervisors, and other associates; and various special observational techniques for everyday-life behavior, as in behavior modification programs (Anastasi, 1988b, pp. 505–511; Tryon, 1983, 1985). To avoid confusion between the different usages of the term *assessment,* I am using *clinical assessment* to designate the clinical use of tests as just defined. It should be noted that this use of tests, that is, in combination with other relevant data in an intensive study of the individual, is not limited to clinical settings or to clients with psychological problems. These assessment procedures are also appropriate in other settings, such as schools, counseling centers, and industry (especially in the assessment of persons for high-level executive jobs).

In such an assessment process, the test user engages in a continuing cycle of hypothesis formation and hypothesis testing about the individual. Each item of information—whether it be a test score, an event in the biographical history, or an interviewee comment—suggests a hypothesis about the person that will be either confirmed or refuted as other facts are gathered. Such hypotheses themselves suggest further lines of inquiry. It should be borne in mind that even highly reliable tests with well-established validity do not yield sufficiently precise results for individual assessment. Hence, it is understandable that clinical examiners tend to be more receptive than other test users to psychometrically crude instruments, which may nevertheless provide a rich harvest of leads for further exploration.

From another angle, the availability of numerical scores from clinical instruments does not assure accuracy of interpretation; it may create only an illusion of objectivity and quantification. Such instruments are not designed for routine application but require test users with considerable psychological sophistication. The interpretative hazards inherent in clinical instruments are not limited to the misuse of tests by inadequately qualified examiners; they also occur in the rapidly proliferating computerized scoring systems that provide narrative interpretations of test performance (Anastasi, 1988b, 517–519; Butcher, 1987). First, these systems must demonstrate the reliability and validity of their score interpretations, through the publication of adequate supporting data. Second, they can serve only as aids to the trained clinician, not as a substitute for the clinician. The special problems presented by the commercially marketed computerized systems of narrative score interpretation have aroused widespread concern. Serious attention is being given to the formation of workable guidelines for the effective use of such interpretive services. A recent set is the *Guidelines for Computer-based Tests and Interpretations*,[4] published by the APA in 1986.

Some Psychology in Psychological Testing

Effective test users undoubtedly need to be well-informed and up-to-date regarding the statistical methodology of testing. They need "psychometric literacy" (Lambert, 1991), but this is not enough. As long ago as 1966, in my presidential address to APA Division 5 (Division of Evaluation and Measurement), my main thesis was that psychological testing was becoming dissociated from the mainstream of contemporary psychology (Anastasi, 1967). Psychologists specializing in psychometrics had been concentrating more and more on elaborating and refining the techniques of test construction, while losing sight of the behavior they set out to measure. As a result, outdated interpretations of test performance remained insulated from the growing knowledge base of behavioral research. I argued then—and I have continued to argue—that much of the criticism of testing stems from the isolation of psychometrics from other, relevant areas of psychology.

Evolving Concepts of Intelligence

What is human intelligence? Let me illustrate the effects of this isolation in two major areas. The first concerns the concept of intelligence. For several decades, the term *intelligence* was burdened by excess meanings that led to common misinterpretations of test scores and misuses of tests. A particular horror is the term *IQ test*. The IQ is neither a property of the organism nor a type of test. It is a kind of score that was discarded many years ago because of its insurmountable technical deficiencies (Anastasi, 1988b, pp. 88–90). Unfortunately, in response to the public demand for a simple numerical label to pin on a person, the term survived as a so-called deviation IQ. This is simply the familiar standard score arbitrarily expressed on some convenient scale—for instance, with a mean of 100 and a standard deviation of 15, as in the Wechsler scales. So rampant was the confusion about what intelligence tests do—and do not—tell about an individual, that such tests were officially banned in several school systems. Moreover, the word *intelligence* was eliminated from most newly developed or revised tests.

---

[4]Developed jointly by APA Committee on Professional Standards (COPS) and Committee on Psychological Tests and Assessment (CPTA).

More recently, there has been a revival of interest in more sophisticated redefinitions of intelligence and a growing recognition of the contribution that appropriate measures of intelligence can make to the solution of practical problems. Intelligence is not a single, unitary ability, but a composite of multiple functions. Human intelligence is that combination of abilities required for survival and advancement within a particular culture (Anastasi, 1986b). The specific abilities included in this composite, as well as their relative weights, vary with time and place. In different cultures and at different historical periods within any one culture, the qualifications for successful achievement differ. The changing composition of intelligence can also be seen within the individual's life span, from infancy to late adulthood. One's relative ability tends to increase with age in those functions that are reinforced by one's experiential context; it tends to decrease in those functions whose use is deemphasized.

Most well-known intelligence tests designed for children or adults largely measure verbal abilities; to a lesser extent, they also cover abilities to deal with numerical and other abstract symbols. These are the abilities that predominate in school learning. Such tests can therefore be regarded as measures of scholastic aptitude or academic learning. Their scores are both a reflection of previous educational achievement and a predictor of subsequent educational progress. Because the functions taught in school are important in modern, technologically advanced cultures, scores on tests of academic intelligence are also a partial predictor of performance in many occupations and other spheres of daily life. Much of our information about what available intelligence tests measure comes from practical studies of the utility of these tests in predicting educational and occupational achievement.

Contribution of factor analysis. At a more theoretical level, basic research on the nature of intelligence has been progressing apace. One approach is through the statistical procedures of factor analysis (Anastasi, 1988b, pp. 374–390). The controversy over Spearman's g versus the group factors or multiple aptitudes proposed by Thurstone and others flourished in the 1920s and 1930s. Recently, this controversy has been revived and has received considerable attention in the popular media.

In trying to work our way through the tangle of conflicting claims, we should consider *why* factor analysis is conducted. Factor analysis is no longer regarded as a means of searching for *the* primary, fixed, universal units of behavior, but rather as a method of organizing empirical data into useful categories through an analysis of behavioral consistencies. Like the test scores from which they are derived, factors are descriptive, not explanatory; they do *not* represent underlying causal entities. Interest has shifted to the conditions in the individual's learning history that lead to the formation of factors or traits. What brings about the particular relationships that lead to identifiable and differentiable ability constructs, such as verbal comprehension or numerical reasoning? (Anastasi, 1983, 1986b, 1988a).

Once we recognize the descriptive nature of factors, we see that the description could occur at different levels. More and more, we are coming to think in terms of a hierarchical model of factors or abilities. At the top is a general factor, which may be general only to the particular set of tests analyzed. At the next level are broad group factors, similar to some of Thurstone's primary mental abilities. These major group factors subdivide into narrower group factors at one or more levels. The factors specific to each variable are at the bottom level. Different theories focus on one or another level of this comprehensive hierarchical model. No one level, however, need be regarded as of primary importance. Rather, each test developer or test user should select the level most appropriate for her or his purpose.

Contribution of cognitive psychology. Another approach to the study of human intelligence is that of cognitive psychology (Embretson, 1983, 1986; Hunt, 1985; Simon, 1976; Sternberg, 1981, 1984; see also Anastasi, 1988b, pp. 159–161). From the standpoint of testing, the principal contribution of cognitive psychology is its focus on what the individual does when performing an intellectual task. Cognitive research concentrates on the *processes* rather than the *products* of thinking. In contrast, test performance typically assesses the products, as reported in test scores. Although interest in processes is not new in the history of psychometrics, cognitive psychologists have carried the techniques of process analysis to new heights of refinement and sophistication. Knowledge about the processes an individual uses in solving problems or performing intellectual tasks is especially useful in diagnostic testing, because it can help to pinpoint the sources of the person's difficulties. It is also highly relevant to the designing of training programs and other interventions to fit individual needs. Recognizing that what intelligence tests measure is not a fixed or unchanging entity within the person, psychologists in several countries have been investigating training procedures for improving intelligence (see Anastasi, 1988b, pp. 364–367).

Role of affective variables. Another relevant idea contributed by psychological research concerns the interrelations of different behavioral domains. We commonly think of different tests as assessing either abilities or personality—the latter covering such areas as motivation, emotion, interest, attitudes, and values. There is increasing evidence of mutual influence between these major behavioral domains (Anastasi, 1985b; 1988b, pp. 368–370). Nor is this influence limited to immediate performance, as when a person tries harder or persists longer on a task that interests him or in an activity that ranks high in her value system. The influence is also evident in the development of traits over the life span. One way that motivation and other affective variables may contribute to the development of aptitudes is through the cumulative amount of time the person spends on a particular kind of activity relative to other, competing activities.

The effect of sheer time-on-task is enhanced by attention control. What one attends to, how deeply attention is focused, and how long attention is sustained contribute to one's cognitive growth. The selectivity of attention leads to selective learning—and this selection will differ among persons exposed to the same immediate situation. Such selective learning, in turn, may influence the relative development of different aptitudes and thereby contribute to the formation of different trait patterns. From the standpoint of test-score interpretation, what all this means is that the prediction of a person's subsequent development can be substantially improved by combining information about motivation and interests with information about aptitudes.

Testing in Context

Context and the interpretation of test scores. The examples I have cited demonstrate that current knowledge about intelligence is certainly relevant to the proper use and interpretation of test scores. I now want to introduce one other topic that I consider even more important, which I call *testing in context.* Test scores tell us *how* individuals perform at the time of testing, not *why* they perform as they do. To find out why, we have to consider the test score within the person's *antecedent context.* We need to delve into the individual's reactional biography. In what environmental setting did this person develop? What conditions and events were encountered, and how did the person respond to them?

From another angle, we need to consider the test score within the person's *anticipated context.* What is the setting—educational, occupational, societal—in which this person is expected to function and for which he or she is being assessed? What can we find out about the intellectual, emotional, and physical demands of that context? Several concepts encountered in the recent psychological literature, such as functional literacy and the assessment of personal competence, arise from this approach to test interpretation (Sundberg, Snowden, & Reynolds, 1978). The full understanding and proper interpretation of a test score has both a backward and a forward reference to real-life contexts.

The concept of developed abilities. It is now coming to be widely recognized among psychometricians that all cognitive tests measure developed abilities, which reflect the individual's learning history. This is equally true of tests traditionally labeled *aptitude tests* and those labeled *achievement tests.* The two types of tests differ principally in the degree to which the requisite previous learning is specified and controlled (Anastasi, 1988b, pp. 411–415).

If we think of tests as measuring developed abilities, we can reformulate questions about test coaching in more meaningful terms. The basic question is not how much test scores can be improved by training but how such improvement relates to intellectual behavior in real-life contexts, such as performance on a job or in a course of study. To answer this question, we must differentiate between coaching that is test specific and coaching that affects the broader area of performance that the test is designed to assess, that is, the criterion we are trying to predict (Anastasi, 1981; 1988b, pp. 43–47). Any condition that alters test performance—for better or for worse—without correspondingly affecting criterion performance will simply lower the validity of the test and make it a poorer predictor of developed ability for the individual concerned. However, when coaching improves *both* test performance and criterion performance (or both test score and the construct being assessed), it leaves validity unchanged. Such broadly oriented type of so-called coaching could be more appropriately described as short-term, condensed education.

Test bias and cultural diversity. Reformulating the coaching question in terms of the relation between test performance and criterion performance is also helpful in examining the widely debated question of test bias. The goal is for tests to be free from cultural bias against any group with which the tests are used. This does not mean that there can be no group differences in test scores. Such differences could correctly reflect differences in antecedent development of the skills and knowledge covered by the test, which may also be required for the criterion performance that the test is designed to assess—in a course of study, a job, or other real-life context. Essentially, a test is free from bias and equally fair to two groups if it has the same validity for both groups and does not underpredict the performance of either group. In terms of the familiar regression model, this refers to the avoidance of slope bias and intercept bias of the regression lines (Anastasi, 1988b, pp. 193–201).

Even with equal validity, there can still be intercept bias if the two regression lines intersect the criterion axis at different points. This could mean that a minority person getting a lower test score than a majority person might perform equally well on the criterion. In other words, the minority test scores would underpredict criterion performance. Empirical studies have actually found the reverse. It is generally the group that scores higher on the test that tends to be underpredicted. There is sound statistical reason for this finding: As more tests are added to the battery, each of which has some predictive validity, the underprediction disappears (Linn & Werts, 1971; Reilly, 1973). The underprediction in the higher scoring group is likely to occur if the two groups differ in one or more additional variables that correlate positively with both test and criterion.

From a broader viewpoint, all testing should be considered within a framework of cultural diversity and evaluated within its appropriate context. No test is—or should be—culture free, because human behavior is not culture free. We live in a pluralistic society, not only within large, heterogeneous nations such as the United States, but also within the broader, worldwide society. Increasing international contacts require some reconceptualization of mental measurement. Each test should be fitted into this broad framework. For practical testing purposes, the most effective tests are likely to be those developed for clearly defined purposes and for use within specific contexts. Although these contexts will vary in breadth, none is likely to cover all testing purposes nor the entire human species. The important point is to identify the locus and range of cultural (or other experiential) context for which any given test is appropriate and then to keep both the use of the test and the interpretation of its scores within those contextual boundaries. In other words, when choosing or developing tests, and when interpreting scores, consider context. I shall stop right here, because those are the words, more than any others, that I want to leave with you: *Consider context.*

References

American Psychological Association. (1986). *Guidelines for computer-based tests and interpretations*. Washington, DC: Author.

Anastasi, A. (Ed.). (1965). *Individual differences*. New York: Wiley.

Anastasi, A. (1967). Psychology, psychologists, and psychological testing. *American Psychologist, 22*, 297–306.

Anastasi, A. (1981). Coaching, test sophistication, and developed abilities. *American Psychologist, 36*, 1086–1093.

Anastasi, A. (1983). Evolving trait concepts. *American Psychologist, 38*, 175–184.

Anastasi, A. (1985a). Interpreting results from multiscore batteries. *Journal of Counseling and Development, 64*, 84–86.

Anastasi, A. (1985b). Reciprocal relations between cognitive and affective development: With implications for sex differences. In T. B. Sonderegger (Ed.), *Psychology and gender* (Nebraska Symposium on Motivation, Vol. 32, pp. 1–35). Lincoln: University of Nebraska Press.

Anastasi, A. (1986a). Evolving concepts of test validation. *Annual Review of Psychology, 37*, 1–15.

Anastasi, A. (1986b). Intelligence as a quality of behavior. In R. J. Sternberg & D. K. Detterman (Eds.), *What is intelligence* (pp. 19–21). Norwood, NJ: Ablex.

Anastasi, A. (1988a). Explorations in human intelligence: Some uncharted routes. *Applied Measurement in Education, 1*(3), 207–213.

Anastasi, A. (1988b). *Psychological testing* (6th ed.). New York: Macmillan.

Anastasi, A. (1990). What is test misuse? Perspectives of a measurement expert. *Proceedings of the 1989 ETS Invitational Conference* (pp. 15–25). Princeton, NJ: Educational Testing Service.

Babad, E. Y., & Budoff, M. (1974). Sensitivity and validity of learning-potential measurement in three levels of ability. *Journal of Educational Psychology, 66*, 439–447.

Ben-Porath, Y. S., & Butcher, J. N. (1986). Computers in personality assessment: A brief past, an ebullient present, and an expanding future. *Computers in Human Behavior, 2*, 163–182.

Boring, E. G. (1929). *A history of experimental psychology.* New York: Appleton-Century-Crofts.

Bowman, M. L. (1989). Testing individual differences in ancient China. *American Psychologist, 44*, 576–578.

Brown, A. L., & Campione, J. C. (1986). Psychological theory and the study of learning disabilities. *American Psychologist, 41*, 1059–1068.

Butcher, J. N. (Ed.). (1987). *Computerized psychological assessment: A practitioner's guide.* New York: Basic Books.

Butcher, J. N., Keller, L. S., & Bacon, S. F. (1985). Current developments and future directions in computerized personality assessment. *Journal of Consulting and Clinical Psychology, 53*, 803–815.

Caldwell, O. W., & Courtis, S. A. (1923). *Then and now in education, 1845–1923.* Yonkers, NY: World Book.

Campione, J. C., & Brown, A. L. (1987). Linking dynamic assessment with school achievement. In C. S. Lidz (Ed.), *Dynamic assessment: An interactive approach to evaluating learning potential* (pp. 76–109). New York: Guilford Press.

Cravens, H. (1987). Applied science and public policy: The Ohio Bureau of Juvenile Research and the problem of juvenile delinquency, 1913–1930. In M. M. Sokal (Ed.), *Psychological testing and American society, 1890–1930* (pp. 158–194). New Brunswick, NJ: Rutgers University Press.

Cronbach, L. J., & Furby, L. (1970). How we should measure change—or should we? *Psychological Bulletin, 74*, 68–80.

Doyle, K. O., Jr. (1974). Theory and practice of ability testing in ancient Greece. *Journal of the History of the Behavioral Sciences, 10*, 202–212.

DuBois, P. H. (1970). *A history of psychological testing.* Boston: Allyn & Bacon.

Ebel, R. L., & Damrin, D. E. (1960). Tests and examinations. In C. W. Harris (Ed.), *Encyclopedia of educational research* (3rd ed.; pp. 1502–1517). New York: Macmillan.

Embretson, S. E. (1983). Construct validity: Construct representation versus nomothetic span. *Psychological Bulletin, 93*, 179–197.

Embretson, S. E. (1986). Intelligence and its measurement: Extending contemporary theory to existing tests. In R. J. Sternberg (Ed.), *Advances in the psychology of human intelligence* (Vol. 3, pp. 355–368). Hillsdale, NJ: Erlbaum.

Embretson, S. E. (1987). Toward development of a psychometric approach. In C. S. Lidz (Ed.), *Dynamic assessment: An interactive approach to evaluating learning potential* (pp. 135–164). New York: Guilford Press.

Embretson, S. E. (1988). Diagnostic testing by measuring learning processes: Psychometric considerations for dynamic testing. In N. O. Frederiksen, R. Glaser, A. M. Lesgold, & M. G. Shafto (Eds.), *Diagnostic monitoring of skill and knowledge acquisitions.* Hillsdale, NJ: Erlbaum.

Eyde, L. D., Moreland, K. L., Robertson, G. J., Primoff, E. S., & Most, R. B. (1988). Test User Qualifications: A data-based approach to promoting good test use. In *Issue in Scientific Psychology.* Washington, DC: American Psychological Association.

Eyde, L. D., Robertson, G. J., Krug, S. G., Moreland, K. L., Robertson, A. G., Shewan, C. M., Harrison, P. L., Porch, B. E., Hammer, A. L., & Primoff, E. S. (1993). *Responsible test use: Case studies for assessing human behavior.* Washington, DC: American Psychological Association.

Feuerstein, R. (1979). *The dynamic assessment of retarded performers: The Learning Potential Assessment Device, theory, instruments, and techniques*. Baltimore: University Park Press.

Feuerstein, R., Rand, Y., Jensen, M. R., Kaniel, S., & Tzuriel, D. (1987). Prerequisites for assessment of learning potential: The LPAD model. In C. S. Lidz (Ed.), *Dynamic assessment: An interactional approach to evaluating learning potential* (pp. 35–51). New York: Guilford Press.

Forehand, G. A. (1986). *Computerized diagnostic testing* (ETS Res. Mem. 86-2). Princeton, NJ: Educational Testing Service.

Galton, F. (1883). *Inquiries into human faculty and its development*. London: Macmillan.

Hunt, E. (1985). Verbal ability. In R. J. Sternberg (Ed.), *Human abilities: An information-processing approach* (pp. 31–58). New York: Freeman.

Jackson, D. N. (1985). Computer-based personality testing. *Computers in Human Behavior, 1*, 225–264.

Jackson, D. N. (1991). Computer-assisted test interpretation: The dawn of discovery. In T. B. Gutkin & S. L. Wise (Eds.), *The computer and the decision-making process* (pp. 1–10). Hillsdale, NJ: Erlbaum.

Kaplan, R. M. (1985). Quality-of-life measurement. In P. Karoly (Ed.), *Measurement strategies in health psychology* (115–146). New York: Wiley.

Lambert, N. M. (1991). The crisis in measurement literacy in psychology and education. *Educational Psychologist, 26*, 23–35.

Lane, N. E., & Kennedy, R. S. (1990). *Users' manual for the Automated Performance Test System (APTS)*. Orlando, FL: Essex Corporation.

Lidz, C. S. (Ed.). (1987). *Dynamic assessment: An interactional approach to evaluating learning potential*. New York: Guilford Press.

Linn, R. L., & Werts, C. E. (1971). Considerations for studies of test bias. *Journal of Educational Measurement, 8*, 1–4.

Lord, F. M. (1980). *Applications of item response theory to practical testing problems*. Hillsdale, NJ: Erlbaum.

McReynolds, P. (1975). Historical antecedents of personality assessment. In P. McReynolds (Ed.), *Advances in psychological assessment* (Vol. 3, pp. 477–532). San Francisco: Jossey-Bass.

McReynolds, P. (1986). History of assessment in clinical and educational settings. In R. O. Nelson & S. C. Hayes (Eds.), *Conceptual foundations of behavioral assessment* (pp. 42–80). New York: Guilford Press.

Messick, S. (1988). The once and future issues of validity: Assessing the meaning and consequences of measurement. In H. Wainer & H. Braun (Eds.), *Test validity* (pp. 33–45). Hillsdale, NJ: Erlbaum.

Messick, S. (1989). Validity. In R. L. Linn (Ed.), *Educational measurement* (3rd ed., pp. 13–103). New York: Macmillan.

Reilly, R. R. (1973). A note on minority group test bias studies. *Psychological Bulletin, 80*, 130–132.

Sattler, J. M. (1988). *Assessment of children* (3rd ed.). San Diego, CA: Jerome M. Sattler.

Simon, H. A. (1976). Identifying basic abilities underlying intelligent performance of complex tasks. In L. B. Resnick (Ed.), *The nature of intelligence* (pp. 65–98). Hillsdale, NJ: Erlbaum.

Sokal, M. M. (1987). Introduction: Psychological testing and historical scholarship—Questions, contrasts, and context. In M. M. Sokal (Ed.), *Psychological testing and American society, 1890–1930* (pp. 1–20). New Brunswick, NJ: Rutgers University Press.

Standards for educational and psychological testing. (1985). Washington, DC: American Psychological Association.

Sternberg, R. J. (1981). Testing and cognitive psychology. *American Psychologist, 36*, 1001–1011.

Sternberg, R. J. (1984). What cognitive psychology can (and cannot) do for test development. In B. S. Plake (Ed.), *Social and technical issues in testing: Implications for test construction and usage* (pp. 39–60). Hillsdale, NJ: Erlbaum.

Sundberg, N D., Snowden, L. R., & Reynolds, W. M. (1978). Toward assessment of personal competence and incompetence in life situations. *Annual Review of Psychology, 29*, 179–221.

Tryon, W. W. (1983). Digital filters in behavioral research. *Journal of Experimental Analysis of Behavior, 39*, 185–190.

Tryon, W. W. (1985). *Behavioral assessment in behavioral medicine.* New York: Springer.

Ward, W. C., Kline, R. G., & Flaugher, J. (1986). *College Board Computerized Placement Tests: Validation of an adaptive test of basic skills* (ETS Research Rep. No. 86-29). Princeton, NJ: Educational Testing Service.

Weiss, D. J. (1982). Improving measurement quality and efficiency with adaptive testing. *Applied Psychological Measurement, 6*, 473–492.

Weiss, D. J., & Davison, M. L. (1981). Test theory and methods. *Annual Review of Psychology, 32*, 629–658.

Weiss, D. J., & Vale, C. D. (1987). Computerized adaptive testing for measuring abilities and other psychological variables. In J. N. Butcher (Ed.), *Computerized psychological assessment: A practitioner's guide* (pp. 325–343). New York: Basic Books.

Wiskoff, M. F., & Schratz, M. K. (1988). Computerized adaptive testing of a vocational aptitude battery. In R. F. Dillon & J. W. Pellegrino (Eds.), *Testing: Theoretical and applied perspectives.* New York: Praeger.

Zenderland, L. (1987). The debate over diagnosis: Henry Herbert Goddard and the medical acceptance of intelligence testing. In M. M. Sokal (Ed.), *Psychological testing and American society, 1890–1930* (pp. 46–74). New Brunswick, NJ: Rutgers University Press.

DAVID C. BERLINER

THE 100-YEAR JOURNEY OF EDUCATIONAL PSYCHOLOGY

FROM INTEREST, TO DISDAIN, TO RESPECT FOR PRACTICE

D avid C. Berliner is professor of psychology in education and professor of curriculum and instruction in the College of Education at Arizona State University. He was professor and chair of the department of educational psychology at the University of Arizona (1977–1988), director of research at the Far West Laboratory for Educational Research and Development (1970–1977), and has held shorter appointments at universities in California, Massachusetts, and Oregon, as well as in Australia and Spain. His doctorate in educational psychology was from Stanford University in 1968.

In the area of research on teaching, Berliner has focused on teacher effectiveness, teachers' use of instructional time, and the differences between novice and expert teachers. He has written extensively on the implications of research on teaching for teacher education and has developed instructional material for use in programs of teacher education. He is active in educational policy at state and national levels and in disseminating educational research to practitioners. A central theme of his work is the role of research in understanding the complexity of contemporary classroom teaching.

Berliner is coeditor of the first *Handbook of Educational Psychology* (in press) and is coauthor of the text *Educational Psychology*, now in its fifth edition. He has edited the *Educational Researcher* and the *Review of Research in Education* and has coedited *Teaching and Teacher Education.* He is author of well over 100 journal articles and book chapters.

Berliner is currently president-elect of Division 15 of the APA, the Division of Educational Psychology, and is a fellow of the APA and the Center for Advanced Study in the Behavioral Sciences. He is past-president of the American Educational Research Association (AERA). His scholarship has been recognized with a Doctorate of Humane Letters, Honoris Causa, from the University of Massachusetts; the Medal of Achievement of the University of Helsinki; the Distinguished Service Award of the National Association of Secondary School Principals; two writing awards from the American Association of Colleges for Teacher Education; the Distinguished Educator Award from the Association of Teacher Educators; and the Award for Interpretive Scholarship from the AERA.

DAVID C. BERLINER

THE 100-YEAR JOURNEY OF EDUCATIONAL PSYCHOLOGY

FROM INTEREST, TO DISDAIN, TO RESPECT FOR PRACTICE

W e can date the emergence of the discipline of educational psychology to the same year in which Granville Stanley Hall called 26 colleagues to his study to organize the American Psychological Association (APA) (Hothersall, 1984). Thus, when the APA recently celebrated its centennial, we in the Division of Educational Psychology, Division 15, felt like the party was for us.

From the very beginning of the APA, psychoeducational issues were important to our leaders, and those issues influenced the growth of academic and scientific psychology. In what follows, I describe the founding years of both general and educational psychology, noting the important individuals of those times and their influence on our discipline. The time period for those events was approximately 1890 to 1910, the same years that saw American psychology separate from its European roots and grow into a uniquely American discipline. But, we should remember that our field began long before that time.

I wish to thank BethAnn Berliner for her editing and her coaching in historiography, as well as the two anonymous reviewers, who gave many thoughtful suggestions and additional references.

The Origins of Educational Psychology

Our field probably started unnoticed and undistinguished, as part of the folk traditions of people trying to educate their young. For example, the ancient Jewish ritual of Passover precedes the contemporary work of Cronbach and Snow (1977) by hundreds if not thousands of years, yet fully anticipates their scholarship into aptitude–treatment interactions. The leader of the Passover service is commanded to tell the story of Passover each year but is ordered to tell it differently to his sons, according to their individual differences. To the wise son, he teaches the entire story, with all the details and in all its complexity. To the contrary son, he teaches in a way that emphasizes belonging to a community. To his simple son, the leader responds in still different ways. It is likely that even before these times, from the emergence of Homo sapiens, whoever reflected on teaching probably had thoughts that we would now label as mainstream educational psychology. It could not be otherwise. To reflect on any act of teaching and learning demands thinking about individual differences, assessment, development, the nature of the subject matter being taught, problem solving, and transfer of learning. These psychological topics are vital to education and therefore are vital to human social life. Thus, issues central to our current interests have been the subject of discussion throughout the centuries.

In the fifth century B.C., Democritus, for example, wrote on the advantages conferred by schooling and the influence of the home on learning (Watson, 1961). A century later, Plato and Aristotle discussed the following educational psychology topics (Adler, 1952; Watson, 1961): the kinds of education appropriate to different kinds of people; the training of the body and the cultivation of psychomotor skills; the formation of good character; the possibilities and limits of moral education; the effects of music, poetry, and the other arts on the development of the individual; the role of the teacher; the relations between teacher and student; the means and methods of teaching; the nature of learning; the order of learning; affect and learning; and learning apart from a teacher.

During Roman times, Quintilian (35–100 A.D.) argued in favor of public rather than private education to preserve democratic ideals—a battle still being fought today. He condemned physical force as a method of discipline, commenting that good teaching and an attractive curriculum take care of most behavior problems—advice that is as appropriate today as it was 2,000 years ago. He urged that teachers take into account individual differences, suggesting that they take time to study the unique characteristics of their students. He also set forth criteria for teacher selection (Quintilian's *Institutio Oratoria*, translated by Butler, 1953; *Quintilian on Education*, translated by Smail, 1966; and Wilds & Lottich, 1964). Quintilian's arguments, although archaic in form, are still functional educational psychology. For example, in Book 1 of the *Oratoria* he wrote

> As soon as the child has begun to know the shapes of the various letters, it will be useful to have them cut out on a board, in as beautiful script as possible, so that the pen may be guided along the grooves. Thus mistakes such as occur with wax tablets will be impossible to make for the pen will be confined between the edges of the letters and will always be prevented from going astray. (Adapted from both the Butler and Smail translations)

A contemporary educational psychologist or psychologically trained special educator would probably now cite B. F. Skinner on error reduction but would give similar advice.

Comenius (1592–1671), a humanist writing at the beginning of the modern era, also influenced both educational and psychoeducational thought (1657; Broudy, 1963). He wrote texts that were based on a developmental theory and in them inaugurated the use of visual aids in instruction. Media and instructional research, a vibrant part of contemporary educational psychology, has its origins in the writing and textbook design of Comenius. He recommended that instruction start with the general and then move to the particular and that nothing in books be accepted unless checked by a demonstration to the senses (Broudy, 1963). He taught that understanding, not memory, is the goal of instruction; that we learn best that which we have an opportunity to teach; and that parents have a role to play in the schooling of their children.

The contributions of one of our many ancestors often are overlooked, yet Juan Luis Vives (1492–1540) wrote very much as a contemporary educational psychologist might in the first part of the 16th century (Vives, 1531/1913; Charles, 1987). He stated to teachers and others with educational responsibilities, such as those in government and commerce, that there should be an orderly presentation of the facts to be learned, and in this way he anticipated Herbart and the 19th-century psychologists. He noted that what is to be learned must be practiced, and in this way he anticipated Thorndike's law of exercise. He wrote on practical knowledge and the need to engage student interest, anticipating Dewey. He wrote about individual differences and the need to adjust instruction for all students, but especially for the "feeble minded," the deaf, and the blind, anticipating the work of educational and school psychologists in special education and the area of aptitude–treatment interaction. He discussed the schools' role in moral growth, anticipating the work of Dewey, Piaget, Köhlberg, and Gilligan. He wrote about learning being dependent on self-activity, a precursor to contemporary research on metacognition, where the ways in which the self monitors its own activities are studied. Finally, Vives wrote about the need for students to be evaluated on the basis of their own past accomplishments and not in comparison with other students, anticipating both the contemporary motivational theorists who eschew social comparisons and those researchers who find the pernicious elements of norm-referenced testing to outweigh their advantages. Thus, long before we claimed our professional identity, there were individuals thinking intelligently about what we would eventually call *educational psychology*. Our roots are deep within the corpus of work that makes up Western intellectual history.

In this brief reminder of our roots, we must note also the mid-19th-century philosopher and psychologist, Johann Friedrich Herbart (1776–1841). He not only may be considered the first voice of the modern era of psychoeducational thought, but his disciples, the Herbartians, played a crucial role in preparing the way for the scientific study of education. They wrote about what we now call *schema theory*, advocating a cognitive psychology featuring the role of past experience and schemata in learning and retention. Herbartians promoted teaching by means of a logical progression of learning, a revolutionary idea at the end of the 19th century. They promoted the five formal steps for teaching virtually any subject matter: (a) preparation (of the mind of the student), (b) presentation (of the material to be learned), (c) comparison, (d) generalization, and (e) application. It was the Herbartians who first made pedagogical technique the focus of scientific study, pointing the way, eventually, to the field of research on teaching, a very fruitful area of research in educational psychology.

Although the Herbartians oversold their ideas and claimed a scientific base that they did not have, the educational psychologists at the turn of the 20th century owed them a monumental debt. The Herbartians had played an important role in convincing the teachers and school administrators of America that education was a field that could be studied scientifically. To promote this radical idea, the National Herbart Society for the Scientific Study of Education founded a yearbook series under that name.[1] The yearbooks of that organization, and its successors, featured chapters about the emerging science of pedagogy by prominent educational psychologists.

Science and Education

We must remember that before the turn of the 19th century, experimental methods in education were brand new phenomena. These new

---

[1]As the Herbartian movement faded, the organizers of the Society changed their name to the National Society for the Experimental Study of Education and continued publishing yearbooks with a strong empirical and scientific base. Eventually, as experimental methods were finally and grudgingly accepted in education, they changed their name to the National Society for the Study of Education, and to this day they still publish high-quality yearbooks on educational issues.

methods were not accepted by all as appropriate to the study of educational topics. Ironically, although Herbart's name was invoked by those promoting the scientific study of education, he rejected the notion that one could have an experimental psychology. Herbart was an empiricist, dedicated to observational methods, and a developer of mathematical psychology. But he maintained that one could not experiment with the mind (Boring, 1950). Although Wundt, Ebbinghaus, and James were challenging those beliefs in the psychological laboratories that existed at the end of the 19th century, there was still opposition to psychological science in education at that time. This was based, in part, on the very strong belief that education is a moral and philosophical endeavor, and therefore, its problems cannot be solved by scientific study. Such beliefs permeated education because its leaders often came from religious backgrounds and training (Tyack & Hansot, 1982) rather than from the liberal arts or the emerging sciences. Breaking down the resistance to science as a means for the study of education and promoting the acceptance of scientific findings as a guide to educational policy were most important events in the history of our field. Although educators' refusal to use our science as a guide to policy and practice is not now as widespread a problem as it once was, barriers to the use of scientific findings have not disappeared completely. The research on retention in grade, corporal punishment, and bilingual education, for example, are contemporary cases of this historic resistance.

Paving the Way for Thorndike

It is customary to attribute the paternity of educational psychology to E. L. Thorndike, whose contributions are noted later. He was bright, brash, amazingly productive, and as he proceeded to organize the field, he revealed an unshakable faith that psychological science could solve many of the ills of society. But like another prophet, reformer, and founder 2,000 years before him, the way to the "true path" had to be prepared. In this case, the true path was science, not faith, and we should note those who served that role for Thorndike.

One of those who set the stage for Thorndike was the great muckraker and classroom observer Joseph Mayer Rice (1857–1934), the father of research on teaching. Rice endured great difficulties for his beliefs just a few years before the experimental psychology of E. L. Thorndike was deemed acceptable (see Rice, 1912). In 1897, in Atlantic City, New Jersey, Rice was asked to present his empirical classroom-based research on the futility of the spelling grind to the annual meeting of school superintendents. I do not think they were as polite as today's administrators, as they attacked the speaker, yelling the equivalent of "give him the hook." Leonard P. Ayres (1912) reports on the meeting as follows:

The presentation of these data threw that assemblage into consternation, dismay, and indignant protest. But the resulting storm of vigorously voiced opposition was directed, not against the methods and results of the investigation, but against the investigator who had pretended to measure the results of teaching spelling by testing the ability of the children to spell.

In terms of scathing denunciation the educators there present, and the pedagogical experts who reported the deliberations of the meeting to the educational press, characterized as silly, dangerous, and from every viewpoint reprehensible the attempt to test the efficiency of the teacher by finding out what the pupils could do. With striking unanimity they voiced the conviction that any attempt to evaluate the teaching of spelling in terms of the ability of the pupils to spell was essentially impossible and based on a profound misconception of the function of education. (p. 300)

The school administrators would not hear Rice's research because faculty psychology was still dominant, and thus it was clear to them that the spelling faculty needed exercise; besides, it was good for children to work hard and memorize, learning at the same time obedience, diligence, habits of concentration, and so forth. It was the process, not the outcome, that determined good teaching. Good teaching, a normative judgment, was more valued than efficient or effective teaching, terms that derive their meaning from empirical data. Educational issues, for these administrators, simply could not be decided by scientific work. Decisions about what was beneficial to children were best made by those with a religious background or philosophic training, called to the profession to take responsibility for educating the young. Obviously, a good deal of preparation was needed for our field to emerge as the dominant science in the world of education.

By 1912, however, the climate had undergone a change. At that year's meeting of the superintendents, 48 addresses and discussions were devoted to tests and measurement of educational efficiency. Underlying the addresses and discussions was the proposition "that the effectiveness of the school, the methods, and the teachers must be measured in terms of the results secured" (Ayres, 1912, p. 305). In 1915, the antiscience forces had their last chance to challenge the new science, and they lost. Charles Judd (1925) made the following remarks about that meeting of superintendents:

There can be no doubt as we look back on that council meeting that one of the revolutions in American education was accomplished by that discussion. Since that day tests and measures have gone quietly on their way, as conquerors should. Tests and measures are to be found in every progressive school in the land. The victory of 1915 slowly prepared during the preceding twenty years was decisive. (pp. 806–807)

The Grandfather and Granduncles of Educational Psychology

Three individuals prepared the way to that victory so decisively won, eventually, by E. L. Thorndike. These major figures were William James, his student G. Stanley Hall, and Hall's student, John Dewey. These three men—our grandfather and granduncles—distinguished themselves in general psychology as well as in educational psychology, fields that overlapped considerably at the end of the 19th century. I focus, particularly, on the science that these three men promoted. However, it was not their views of psychological science that were ultimately adopted by our field. It was the views of their successor, E. L. Thorndike, that conquered. I argue that Thorndike's version of science and his vision of educational psychology has led us to a narrower conception of our field than would have been true had the views of these three other ancestors gained prominence.

William James

William James (1842–1910) can be considered the central figure in the establishment of psychology in America. Compared with his contemporary, the great Wilhelm Wundt (1832–1920), German founder of experimental psychology, James was said to have had "the courage to be incomplete" (Boring, 1950, p. 516). His was a psychology of humility, humor, and tolerance, particularly when it is compared with the psychology of Wundt or, later, that espoused by his own very serious student, E. L. Thorndike. James's (1890) *Principles of Psychology*, published in 1890 after 12 years of labor, was the preeminent event in American psychology (Barzun, 1983), although Professor James did not think so at the time. When he finally sent the manuscript to his publisher, Henry Holt, he wrote

> No one could be more disgusted than I at the sight of the book. *No* subject is worth being treated of in 1000 pages! Had I ten years more, I could rewrite it in 500; but as it stands it is this or nothing— a loathsome, distended, tumefied, bloated, dropsical mass, testifying to nothing but two facts; 1*st*, that there is no such thing as a *science* of psychology, and 2*nd*, that W. J. is an incapable. (H. James, 1920, p. 294)

James's version of psychological science argued against the elementalism of the Europeans, giving us the notion that consciousness was continuous—a stream—and not easily divisible. Moreover, and still more startling, he said consciousness chooses—it controls its own attention. Thus, built into James's views of experimental psychology were cognitive and teleological conceptions of individuals, beliefs the nascent behaviorists chose ultimately to ignore. James did not believe that ignoring those attributes of humans might be bad for scientific psychology, as long as psychologists remembered that there were other legitimate ways to conduct inquiries about human consciousness and behavior. That is, he probably would have found nothing wrong with a scientific and strongly behavioral psychology if it helped the field make progress. But such a psychology, James thought, certainly would not provide a complete picture of humans. It would provide merely a glimpse of those complex beings.

The *Principles* also made much out of the role of nurture by emphasizing the plasticity of the nervous system, at least among the young. James called acquired habit "the enormous fly-wheel of society" (W. James, 1892, p. 21). It was habit, he explained, that keeps the workers of the most repulsive trades in their business. It keeps the fishermen and loggers, the miners and the farmers, all steadily working and not rising up and attacking the rich. It is early acquired habit that guides behavior and provides the glue that holds society together. Thus, James saw education as a crucial element of society, with the school a place for habits to be acquired by design, not willy-nilly. In his emphasis on habit, he provided the intellectual environment for his student E. L. Thorndike, who would more thoroughly explore habit formation in school and out. Sadly for us, the *Principles* marked the turning point after which philosophy rather than psychology was to dominate James's life. But in that philosophy he gave us another set of uniquely American views, called *pragmatism*, in which the test for truth was whether or not ideas worked for the individual. As a result, James took away the eternal verities of Aristotle and the revealed truths of religion and gave us social criteria for determining truth. Truth would thereafter be written with a small "t," because it became relativistic and personal. Testing whether ideas worked, whether they were functional for the individual or for an animal (the distinction between human and animal disappeared after Darwin), led to psychology's development of functionalism. This set of beliefs (see Angell, 1907) became the theoretical underpinning for growth in many areas of psychology, particularly educational psychology.

In 1891, Harvard's administrators asked James to provide some lectures on the new psychology to the teachers of Cambridge, Massachusetts. These talks were polished and expanded over the years and published in 1899 as the now famous *Talks to Teachers on Psychology* (W. James, 1899/1983). With that book, we have our field's first popular educational psychology text, including speeches first delivered in 1892 (see p. 3, W. James, 1899/1983).[2] The lectures of 1892 marked the beginning of a vigorous educational psychology presence in America. A scholar of international renown had now become associated with our field and provided intellectual grounding for its growth. The year 1892, then, may be used to mark the beginnings of both the APA and the field of educational psychology.

As we determine lineage, James may be thought of as our grandfather, but he did not have much respect for the teachers to whom he spoke. On teachers' comprehension of his lectures, he said

> A teacher wrings his very soul out to understand you, and if he ever does understand anything you say, he lies down on it with his whole weight like a cow on a doorstep so that you can neither get out nor in with him. He never forgets it or can reconcile anything else you say with it, and carries it to the grave like a scar. (W. James, 1899/1983, p. 241)

And, during his 1898 lecture tour to California, he wrote to his brother Henry that the tour ended in a blaze of glory

> With many thanks for having emancipated the school teachers' souls. Poor things they are so servile in their natures as to furnish the most promising of all preys for systematic mystification and pedantification on the part of the paedogogic authorities who write books for them, and when one talks plain common sense with no technical terms, they regard it as a sort of revelation. (W. James, 1899/1983, p. 241)

James's science was an eclectic one, and this he communicated in his talks to teachers. In one of his *most* quoted and *least* influential statements, conspicuously ignored by educational psychologists over the years, we find James saying

> You make a great, a very great mistake, if you think that psychology, being the science of the mind's laws, is something from which you can deduce definite programmes and schemes and methods of in-

---

[2]In the preface to *Talk to Teachers*, James wrote, "In 1892 I was asked by the Harvard Corporation to give a few public lectures on psychology to the Cambridge teachers." But in the history and the letters covering the origins of that series of lectures (p. 234, W. James, 1899/1983), it appears that James began them in the fall of 1891 and finished them in the winter of 1892. He appears to have forgotten some of the background to the origins of the lecture series when he wrote the preface, which was approximately 7 or so years later. He regarded the enterprise as forced labor and lamentable work (p. 234), so it is not surprising if some error of memory occurred.

struction for immediate school-room use. Psychology is a science, and teaching is an art; and sciences never generate arts directly out of themselves. An intermediate inventive mind must make that application, by using its originality. (W. James, 1899/1983, p. 15)

James recognized that psychologists could not tell educators precisely what to do:

A science only lays down lines within which the rules of the art must fall, laws which the follower of the art must not transgress; but what particular thing he shall positively do within those lines is left exclusively to his own genius. ... To know psychology, therefore, is absolutely no guarantee that we shall be good teachers. To advance that result we must have an additional endowment altogether, a happy tact and ingenuity to tell us what definite things to say and do when that pupil is before us. That ingenuity in meeting ... the pupil, that tact for the concrete situation, ... are things to which psychology cannot help us in the least. (W. James 1899/1983, pp. 15–16)

As will be shown, this was not the psychology or the science of Thorndike. In its time, it was also a direct slap at the "scientific" movement of the Herbartians, who were at the peak of their influence. James's comments on other aspects of the emerging scientific psychology were equally cautious, and, at least in public, he was very supportive of the wisdom of practicing teachers. He criticized the attempt to make over teachers into psychologists or scientists in the service of the child study movement. He said it was not a teacher's duty to collect scientifically rigorous observations, because to act as a scientist often conflicted with one's performance as a teacher. The teacher's approach to the child was necessarily ethical and concrete, whereas the psychologist's was necessarily abstract and analytical. These are not habits of mind that are easy to blend. James also believed that laboratory studies in psychology had to fail the test of usefulness for teachers because they did not treat the whole person in real contexts.

Man is too complex a being for light to be thrown on his real efficiency by measuring any one mental faculty taken apart from its consensus in the working whole. ... No elementary measurement, capable of being performed in a laboratory, can throw any light on the actual efficiency of the subject· for the vital thing about him, his emotional and moral energy and doggedness can be measured by no single experiment, and becomes known only by the total results in the long run. ... The total impression which a perceptive teacher will get of the pupil's condition, as indicated by his general temper and manner, by the listlessness or alertness, by the ease or painfulness with which his school work is done, will be of much more value than those unreal experimental tests, those pedantic elementary measurements of fatigue, memory, association, and attention, etc., which are urged upon us as the only basis of a genuinely scientific paedagogy. Such measurements can give us useful information only when we combine them with observations made without brass instruments, upon the total demeanor of the measured individual, by teachers with eyes in their heads and common sense, and some feeling for the concrete facts of human nature in their hearts. (W. James, 1899/1983, p. 82–84)

Clearly, William James would approve of the portfolio assessment movement of our times and support the ways in which Howard Gardner and Robert Sternberg have broadened our conceptions of intelligence. James consistently held a holistic view of human beings, and he understood the important distinction between the real world on the one hand and both laboratory and school tasks on the other. Despite his private comments about the pedestrian minds of teachers, he put faith in the classroom teacher to guide the young to acquire proper habits. In so doing he rejected those who saw the mission of the school as curriculum bound, with the teacher there merely to impart facts (Bowen, 1981). James also rejected the view that science could provide much advice to teachers about what to do in concrete situations. He did, however, see the study of psychology as useful in three ways: to provide the underpinnings for beliefs about instruction, to prohibit teachers from making certain egregious errors, and to provide intellectual support to teachers for some of their pedagogical decisions.

G. Stanley Hall

G. Stanley Hall (1844–1924), founder of the child-study movement that James worried about, was a promoter of psychology in ways that James must have found distasteful. Hall was APA's organizer and its first president. He was as much an educational psychologist as anything else we might label him, and that came to him naturally (see Ross, 1972). Hall's mother was a major influence on him, a schoolteacher who did something quite unusual for her time, or for any time. She kept detailed records of her students' developmental progress. Hall, in becoming our first developmental psychologist, eventually followed the paths that she had originally laid out. Hall's father had for a time also been a schoolteacher. Thus, it should come as no surprise that Hall also taught school on completion of his precollege education. After additional studies, some for the ministry, some in Europe, Hall eventually received the first doctoral degree in psychology in America (Ross, 1972). The granting institution was Harvard University, the year was 1878, and Hall's major advisor was William James. Hall promptly returned to study in Europe for 2 years, returning home without funds. This is when the famous president of Harvard, Charles W. Eliot, made the first of the two requests by the administration of Harvard that markedly influenced our field. In 1880, Eliot rode by Hall's house and, while still astride his horse, asked the impoverished Hall to deliver a series of public lectures on education, under the auspices of the university (Ross, 1972; Joncich, 1968). The delivery of that Saturday morning series of talks on psychology and education preceded James's by about a decade. It was such a smashing success that the president of the newly founded Johns Hopkins University, after ignoring Hall for many years, asked Hall to visit his institution and repeat them. Once again, the lectures on psychoeducational issues were a great success, and the persuasive, energetic Hall was offered a job as a professor of psychology and of pedagogy. Interestingly, E. G. Boring never mentioned the latter part of Hall's title in his classic *History of Experimental Psychology* (1957). Perhaps Boring, like Hall himself, kept the pedagogical work at a distance because of its low status (see Ross, 1972, for a description of Hall's fright at taking a professorship in pedagogy).

The research laboratory Hall founded at Johns Hopkins, as opposed to the one James had halfheartedly developed, was the first formal laboratory for the study of psychology in the United States. The laboratory also introduced, by courtesy of the university president, something unique in America—fellowships for graduate students. These attracted some other soon-to-be notable figures, John Dewey and James McKeen Cattell. Each of them profoundly affected the history of our field, and each of them found it difficult to work with Hall.

Hall is remembered at Hopkins by the APA for founding the first English language psychology journal, the *American Journal of Psychology*. But Hall also founded the second English language psychological journal in America, and it was an educational psychology journal. That came about after Hall went to Clark University as its first president in 1888. There he founded first a pedagogical seminary, or workshop, for the scientific study of education. Then, he provided it with a journal titled the *Pedagogical Seminary*, which is still published under a different name, the *Journal of Genetic Psychology* (Boring, 1950).

Hall placed the pedagogical courses in the psychology department at Clark University and had them taught by W. H. Burnham, a psychologist he brought with him from Hopkins. Burnham stayed at Clark 36 years, making it one of the first universities to have a genuine and continuous department of educational psychology, although it was not originally known by that name.[3]

With his study of the contents of children's minds, begun in 1883 among Boston kindergarten children, Hall is credited with starting American developmental psychology in general and the child study movement in particular. Like Piaget 50 years later, Hall inquired into children's conceptions of nature, including animals, plants, and the solar system. And like Robert Coles 100 years later, he questioned what children knew about numbers, religion, death, fear, sex, and their own bodies. By 1915, Hall, with his students and coworkers, had developed 194 questionnaires to determine what youngsters and adolescents knew (Hall, 1923).

Hall's influential views on science, however, are our primary interest here. His was a science that was open to common people, not removed from daily life and definitely not conducted in a laboratory. Hall (1897) wrote that the laboratory was not a place to learn about the real feelings and beliefs of individuals. The natural environment, using ordinary people as data collectors, was needed to establish his new science of child study. The Boston study that launched Hall's career was research of this type, carried out by the teachers of Boston. It was a brilliant educational psychology investigation, and because there had never been any studies like it in America, it may qualify as the first empirical educational psychology study that was widely disseminated, as well.

The teachers who collected the data learned that 80% of the children knew where milk came from, but only 6% knew that leather came from animals. They learned that 94% of the children knew where their stomachs were, but only 10% knew where their ribs were. Actually, although the United States was still a rural country, 20% of those youngsters had never seen a cow or a hen, 50% had never seen a pig or a frog, and 80% had never seen a crow or a beehive. Boring (1950, p. 568) informs us of the important moral that was derived from this research: "Show children objects, explain relationships to them, do not trust them to know meanings or referents of common words; they must be taught." This advice to urban educators dealing with children from many different language groups and cultures is as compelling today as it was 100 years ago.

Hall was a great organizer, popularizer, and teacher of psychology. In fact, in 1893, 11 of the first 14 PhDs given in American psychology

---

[3]A great deal of the subject matter of educational psychology had been taught, from 1863 on, at the normal school in Oswego, New York, in a child study course. That course probably was the model for the child study courses that spread to other normal schools after the Civil War (Watson, 1961). And those courses are the immediate predecessors to the courses on educational psychology that we see today in programs of teacher preparation. Courses *explicitly titled* "Educational Psychology" generally began just before the end of the 19th century (Charles, 1987). The first of these was apparently taught at the University of Buffalo in 1895, followed by one at the Normal school at Greely in 1896. The third course in the country with that particular title was taught by E. L. Thorndike at Teachers College, beginning in 1902 (Joncich, 1968).

were to Hall's students. By 1915, Hall's students numbered well over half of all PhDs in American psychology, a group that included H. H. Goddard, Lewis Terman, and Arnold Gesell,[4] all of whom profoundly influenced general, developmental, and educational psychology (see also Diehl, 1986, for Hall's paradoxical views on the education of women). So, Hall was arguably the most influential psychologist in the United States in the years just before and after the turn of the 19th century. But Hall's very popular science actually became more unscientific with each passing year. The samples he obtained were poorly described or unknown, the questionnaires he developed were not psychometrically sound, the data collectors were untrained, and the data were poorly analyzed. It is tempting to suggest, as well, that because he worked with people of low status—teachers—there was suspicion about his data from the scientific community.

Hugo Münsterberg was the psychology professor at Harvard hired by William James as he moved himself away from psychology and into philosophy. Münsterberg is generally acknowledged as the founder of applied psychology, particularly forensic psychology. Near the turn of the 19th century, he launched a particularly vicious attack on the child study movement (Münsterberg, 1898a, 1898b) and was joined by others. E. L. Thorndike (1898b), who was remarkably tolerant of their amateurishness, still called the child study movement "very poor psychology, inaccurate, inconsistent and misguided." He predicted that very few successful hypotheses and very little verification of their findings would occur. Ultimately, it appears that the child study movement failed because it was not good science and because Hall, who held it together, had developed some very strange views of education and child rearing. The legacy of the child study movement, however, was enormous (Siegel & White, 1982). These terribly imperfect, naturalistic studies that relied on teachers and parents as researchers, formed "the beginnings of a host of new areas focusing on the child, such as experimental child psychology, educational psychology, school psychology, physical education, social work, mental retardation, mental hygiene, and early education" (Davidson & Benjamin, 1987, p. 56).

So, we have a popular movement that accomplished at least three things. First, it presented a view that science could guide educational thought, paving the way for Thorndike, who would soon follow. Thorndike's second book, it should be noted, was titled *Notes on Child Study* (Davidson & Benjamin, 1987; Joncich, 1968). Second, the movement promoted the belief that anyone could be a scientist, that is, that reliable data could be gathered by minimally trained individuals. Finally, the movement promoted the idea that data from the natural environment

---

[4]It appears that the first person in the nation to hold the title of "School Psychologist" was Hall's student, Arnold Gesell (Kramer, 1987).

are at least equal to those of the laboratory. These are once again contemporary views in education, and the critics of those views today are not unlike those who condemned such work in the past. The question then and now is "What is the warrant for thinking thus and so, or for acting in such a manner?" Hall's answer to that question was not acceptable to the community of scholars of that time. Although Hall's science was not good science, it prepared a lot of people for better science and for a different view of science.

John Dewey

The contributions of another American giant, John Dewey (1859–1952), were, like James's, in three intertwined fields of study: philosophy, psychology, and pedagogy.

Dewey obtained his doctorate at Hopkins in 1884, with Hall as his advisor, although they appear not to have liked each other. Dewey wrote a psychology text in 1886, 4 years before James's *Principles* came out. Although well received, it was not a major intellectual event in the field. It was decidedly philosophical, which was perfectly natural for its time (Dewey, 1886). One of Dewey's very few empirical articles was published in 1894, the year he went to the then newly created University of Chicago. It was an article on the relative frequency of word use by young children, probably his own (Dewey, 1894). His first major article in psychology came out in 1896. It was on the relations between stimuli and responses, and it had a particular American flavor to it (Dewey, 1896). As with the work of James before him, it was against elementalism and in defense of a more holistic view of stimuli and their associated responses, including the context in which they occur. Dewey noted that stimuli and responses occur as part of previous and future chains, because that is the nature of experience. Therefore, we should really think of the stimulus and response as inseparable entities. Experience, as James had noted, is a stream. Dewey argued that what held together stimuli and their responses were the interpretations given to both, thus putting consciousness, attribution, and constructivist views squarely before the emerging stimulus–response (S–R) psychologists of that time.

Dewey's important psychological article (1896) had immediate educational implications. If it was the whole act that constituted the basis for learning, then the prevalent form of instruction at that time had to be inappropriate. Reciting lessons to students, where teachers acted like they were pouring knowledge into students' heads, had to be a mistake. Lessons of that type were, at best, emphasizing only one part of a system. Where was the emphasis on having children respond, on having them be active in some way? What was to be done about will, volition, and motivation? And where was there time allotted during teaching for interpretation, to the making of meaning out of what was presented? These concerns are as relevant today as they were 100 years ago when they were forcefully brought to the attention of educators. And lest we forget how radical these ideas were (and still are), we should note that powerful forces lined up against Dewey when he was introducing the "new" education in the first yearbook of the Herbartians (Dewey, 1895). For example, 2 years later in the third yearbook of that series, U.S. Commissioner of Education William T. Harris (1897) was still advocating traditional methods. He stated the four cardinal rules for efficient instruction: "The child must be regular [in attendance] and punctual [in assignments], silent and industrious. . . . It is this which 'builds character'" (pp. 59, 65). Obedience to authority was considered necessary for developing the child's personal sense of responsibility and duty (Monroe, 1952).

Dewey and his colleagues at the University of Chicago founded the functionalist school of psychology, a way of thinking about psychology that was strongly influenced by Darwin. Functionalists promoted a psychology interested in the purpose of behavior or the function of mind. That is, instead of describing some event, say a rat's pursuit of food or a child's acquisition of fear, psychologists should ask what would that behavior accomplish? What purpose would it serve? What is the behavior's function? Functionalism promoted the study of both animal psychology (for Darwin linked us to the animal world) and educational psychology (for Darwinian theory suggested also that societies evolve and that one of the most important means for doing so seemed to be education). Our field has its roots deep in the functional school of psychology that emerged at the turn of the 19th century, and that point of view continues to have contemporary followers (Berliner, 1990).

Before obtaining his doctorate with a thesis on the psychology of Kant, Dewey had been a high school teacher. Thus, more than most, he could fulfill the duties expected of him when he moved to Chicago to the Department of Philosophy, Psychology and Pedagogy. In fact, soon after his arrival, he founded an elementary school as a place to learn more philosophy, more social theory, and more psychology. His laboratory school began as a place to study how children learn, not as a site for teacher education, as some laboratory schools became later. Dewey, the pedagogue, was against imparting mere knowledge, believing that such information was either wrong or would soon be outdated. He was against rote learning and drill and practice approaches. He was for what we would call today the development of thinking skills and against the attainment of decontextualized, inert forms of knowledge. In the fullest functionalist tradition, he said that knowledge was a tool, not an end in itself (Dewey, 1910). He advocated allowing students to participate in the educational process because it was their personal needs that were the starting place of that process.

The principles of effort and interest were the guiding psychological principles of the day. But to Dewey, neither the motivating factors associated with effort nor the development of interest was the means by which education could best be accomplished. Those were external factors, under the direction and control of the teacher. He felt that the individual's internal processes must be understood. Most important were the urgent needs, impulses, and habits that each child possessed (Dewey, 1895, 1910). It was when the teacher found these and created an environment to free these qualities that the greatest and most meaningful learning took place. Dewey, therefore, believed in a personal and idiosyncratic curriculum for each child. Thus, the project method was advocated by the progressive educators who tried to put Dewey's ideas into practice. Our contemporary norm-referenced standardized achievement tests, which are based on the assumption of a common school curriculum for all students, would not be appropriate for the conceptions of schooling that were held by Dewey.

Dewey also recognized the uniqueness of the teacher's role as a fellow human being in a community of learners. In his presidential address to the APA in 1899, he (1900) chose to discuss educational issues, particularly psychology and social practice. He pointed out the failure likely to occur should educational psychology not recognize that the teacher

> lives in a social sphere—he is a member and an organ of a social
> life. His aims are social aims ... Whatever he as a teacher effectively
> does, he does as a person; and he does with and towards persons.
> His methods, like his aims, ... are practical, are social, are ethical,
> are anything you please—save merely psychical. In comparison
> with this, the material and the data, the standpoint and the methods
> of psychology, are abstract. ... I do not think there is danger of
> going too far in asserting the social and the teleological nature of
> the work of the teacher; or in asserting the abstract and partial
> character of the mechanism into which the psychologist ... trans-
> mutes the play of vital values. (p. 117)

In that speech in which he reminded psychologists about the nature of classroom teaching, Dewey asked also whether it was possible to have the educational psychologist on one side, acting as a legislator, and classroom teachers on the other, acting as a class of obedient subjects. He wondered, "Can the teacher ever receive 'obligatory prescriptions'? Can he receive from another a statement of the means by which he is to reach his ends, and not become hopelessly servile in his attitude?" (p. 110). His answer, of course, was that the pronouncements of psychologists with regard to classroom practice had to be tempered.

In addition to his basic democratic concern for building relationships between the educational psychologist and the classroom teacher on the basis of equality, Dewey would add another factor, particularly if the results to be disseminated were based primarily on laboratory work. That factor was tentativeness:

The great advantage of the psychophysical laboratory is paid for by certain obvious defects. The completer control of conditions, with resulting greater accuracy of determination, demand an isolation, a ruling out of the usual [means] of thought and action, which leads to a certain remoteness, and easily to a certain artificiality. When the result of laboratory experiments informs us, for example, that repetition is the chief factor influencing recall, we must bear in mind the result is obtained with nonsense material—i.e., by excluding the conditions of ordinary memory. The result is pertinent if we state it thus: The more we exclude the usual environmental adaptations of memory, the greater importance attaches to sheer repetition. It is dubious (and probably perverse) if we say: Repetition is the prime influence in memory. Now this illustrates a general principle. Unless our laboratory results are to give us artificiality's, mere scientific curiosities, they must be subjected to interpretation by gradual re-approximation to conditions of life ... The school, for psychological purposes, stands in many respects midway between the extreme simplifications of the laboratory and the confused complexities of ordinary life. Its conditions are those of life at large; they are social; and practical. But it approaches the laboratory in [that it is simpler]. ... While the psychological theory [c]ould guide and illuminate the practice, acting upon the theory would immediately test it, and thus criticize it, bringing about its revision and growth. In the large and open sense of the words psychology becomes a working hypothesis, instruction is the experimental test and demonstration of the hypothesis; the result is both greater practical control and continued growth in theory. (pp. 119–120)

So, Dewey also recognized a wholism, a concern for the life of teachers and a respect for them, and a distrust of laboratory studies as influences on practice.

Views of the Founding Figures Before Thorndike

After considering the founding figures of both the APA and educational psychology, it might be useful to review their characteristics. James, our grandfather, taught that psychology did not have the whole picture of human beings and that science probably never would. He saw activities such as mental testing and the like as reflecting only certain aspects of an individual. He saw the teacher as having a practical wisdom. Teaching, he believed, was an art that could not in any direct way be much touched by psychology, particularly its laboratory findings. Teachers, James noted, were ethical and concrete, and psychologists were abstract and analytic, thus making communication difficult between them.

In Hall and Dewey, our granduncles, we have former classroom teachers who respected teachers and the complexity of teaching more than did James. Hall's science had a common sense to it; he trusted teachers to be good observers and data collectors, and he defended passion, sentiment, and love as elements in the making of a good science of child and educational study. Although generally poorly carried out, his was a science more naturalistic than laboratory based, more clinical than experimental, and more qualitative than quantitative. Dewey held to a holistic psychology, understood the teacher as a social being, and thought that if psychology presented its findings as truths to be applied it would necessarily put teachers in a position of servitude. He saw laboratory psychology as limited and all psychological findings as tentative, as working hypotheses for teachers to test.

Despite their many personal and professional differences, these three founders of general and educational psychology had no problem agreeing that psychology had to take a major interest in education and that it was destined to be the "master science" for pedagogy. There was still a question, however, about which view of science was to dominate. This was the context for the father of our field, Edward Lee Thorndike, whose views differed from these individuals in important ways.

Edward Lee Thorndike

Much has been written about E. L. Thorndike (1874–1947), and unquestionably our discipline has prospered because of his contributions. It is difficult, therefore, to say, "Thanks, Ned, but you took too narrow a path." However, I believe that Thorndike's views resulted in a major shift in psychology, and it had serious consequences for our discipline. From a field genuinely interested in issues of schooling, psychology became disdainful of school practice. Thorndike's influence resulted in an arrogance on the part of educational psychologists, a closed-mindedness about the complexities of the life of the teacher and the power of the social and political influences on the process of schooling. It was fated, however, because Thorndike was a product of a time when an unbounded faith in what science could accomplish seemed justified. He was a product of his age as we are of ours, and we are as obligated to look differently at his contributions as he was obligated to hold the beliefs that he did.

Thorndike was a bright New England minister's son who, with his brothers, needed to get high grades to receive scholarships for college. Eventually, three Thorndikes became professors at Columbia University, attesting to the powerful values of the family.[5] We get some intimation about what was to come when Thorndike, an undergraduate at Wesleyan in 1895, wrote about the criteria for judging a novel. He commented that a proper novel was one designed to transmit information, to influence the intellect through its truth. The novel was definitely not to be judged on its ability to excite the emotions (Joncich, 1968). Permeating Thorndike's formative years, and influencing the work of his lifetime, was the belief in truth, discovered through science, as the way to perfect mankind. The mind and science, not emotion, were to be trusted. Early in his career, he wrote, "One can readily show that the emotionally indifferent attitude of the scientific observer is ethically a far higher attitude than the loving interest of the poet" (E. Thorndike, 1899, p. 61).

While at Wesleyan, Thorndike (and his fellow undergraduate Charles Judd) studied psychology from James Sully's (1889) *Outlines of Psychology*, the first edition of which was published in 1884, 6 years before James's *Principles*. Sully's book had a subtitle that is often overlooked, namely, *With Special Reference to the Theory of Education*. Sully wrote that his goal was "to establish the proposition that mental science is capable of supplying those truths which are needed for an intelligent and reflective carrying out of the educational work" (Sully, 1889, p. 1). Thorndike may have been influenced by this general and educational psychology text before he read James's *Principles*. In his autobiography, however, he noted that it was James who so interested him that he bought the two volumes of the *Principles*, the only text he purchased while an undergraduate (E. Thorndike, 1936).

After graduating from Wesleyan, Thorndike went to Harvard for two years (1895–1897), where he came under the influence of the brilliant and eclectic William James. There he took up experimental psychology, first with children and then with animals as subjects, housing his chickens in James's basement after his landlady refused to let him keep them in her house. Dissatisfied, in part, with James's increasing distance from psychology, Thorndike moved to Columbia University for a year of study with the well-respected James McKeen Cattell, a student of Wundt, Galton, and Hall. Cattell was the first person in the world to hold the title of professor of psychology and ranked second only to James as the most influential psychologist of his time (Boring, 1950; Charles, 1987). With Cattell's life devoted to the study of individual differences and mental measurement, this founder of the Psychological Corporation was cer-

---

[5]The tradition continued, as two of Thorndike's sons acquired doctorates in physics, his daughter earned a doctorate in mathematics, and son Robert L. Thorndike went on to a distinguished career as a professor in psychology and education at his father's institution, Teachers College, Columbia University. Robert L.'s son, Robert M. Thorndike, is the third generation of educational psychologists. A faculty member at Western Washington University, his scholarly work, like that of his father and grandfather, has been in the areas of educational measurement and intelligence testing.

tainly as much an educational as he was a general psychologist. Cattell allowed Thorndike to bring his chickens from James's basement to the attic of the new facilities at Columbia University. In this setting, Thorndike wrote his classic thesis, *Animal Intelligence* (1898a), and gained his first notoriety as a psychologist of considerable talent. His first job after graduation was as a professor of pedagogy and director of the practice school at Western Reserve University. Thorndike's disdain for most of what had been written about education is palpable in his claim that he read everything of use in pedagogy in the 8 weeks before the semester began.

The quality of Thorndike's teaching was not a problem, but his experience in the schools was not a happy one: "The bane of my life is the practice school they stuck me with. It takes a whole day every week and is a failure at that" (Joncich, 1968, p. 234). Instead of promoting the practice school, he tried to open an educational laboratory (Joncich, 1968, p. 163). How different from Dewey at Chicago, who saw the school as the laboratory!

A year later, in 1899, Thorndike was brought to Teachers College as an instructor in psychology, where he remained a dominant force in psychology for 43 years, writing 50 books and 400 articles, all without a typewriter or a calculator (R. L. Thorndike, 1985). Compared with the brilliant Dewey, whose students said he was at his best when he forgot to come to class (Joncich, 1968), Thorndike rated quite favorably as a teacher. But he did not handle practical concerns very well. He was not unkind when such issues arose, but when a school superintendent asked him what he might do about a particular real-world dilemma, he responded "Do? Why, I'd resign!" (Joncich, 1968, p. 217). Thorndike fought with his dean over the usefulness of real-world experience for training teachers, with Thorndike against it. In fact, by 1914, he advised his graduate students, the future leaders of our discipline, to read all they could about education in order to learn what was happening in the schools but not to bother spending their precious hours visiting the classroom (Joncich, 1968, p. 231). Arthur Gates, a student of Thorndike's at about that time, who was soon to be a nationally recognized educational psychologist on the faculty of Teachers College, had "never heard of him going into the schools" (Joncich, 1968, p. 231).

We all know of the success Thorndike had in banishing mental discipline with his transfer studies and of the success of his *Educational Psychology* textbooks, his texts on mental and social measurement, and those on general psychology. He also wrote influential books on the psychology of school subjects, such as arithmetic and reading. He gave us the first standardized achievement test (Watson, 1961) and developed intelligence tests and compiled dictionaries, as well. He was named president of the APA in 1912, early in his career. The written works and attitudes of this enormously influential teacher of educational psychology promoted and directed our field for half a century.

The Written Record

Thorndike believed that only empirical work should guide education. His faith in experimental psychological science and statistics was unshakable. In his *Introduction to Teaching* (E. Thorndike, 1906), he wrote that psychological science is to teaching as botany is to farming, mechanics is to architecture, and physiology and pathology are to the physician.

There seemed to be a mechanical model underlying Thorndike's ideas about the application of psychology to schooling. Although he often noted that schools were complex sites, he managed to ignore the difficulties inherent in applying psychological science to school problems. He didn't seem to recognize the need for the "intermediate inventive mind" that James did, nor did he feel the need to reapproximate psychological findings into the school, as Dewey did. He not only ignored the unscientific musings of educators, he ridiculed them. For example, in his introduction to his first educational psychology text, he stated,

> This book attempts to apply to a number of educational problems the methods of exact science. I have therefore paid no attention to speculative opinions and very little attention to the conclusions of students who present data in so rough and incomplete a form that accurate quantitative treatment is impossible. (E. Thorndike, 1903, p. v)

Thorndike showed this unbridled faith in science, once again, in the introduction to the brand new *Journal of Educational Psychology* (E. Thorndike, 1910):

> A complete science of psychology would tell every fact about every one's intellect and character and behavior, would tell the cause of every change in human nature, would tell the result which every educational force ... would have. It would aid us to use human beings for the worlds welfare with the same surety of the result that we now have when we use falling bodies or chemical elements. In proportion as we get such a science we shall become masters of our own souls as we now are masters of heat and light. Progress toward such a science is being made. (p. 6)

Thorndike, unlike his mentor James, did not have the courage to defend an incomplete science. It is unlikely, for example, that James could have ever thought what Thorndike (1909, reprinted in Joncich, 1962) wrote with fervor:

> Man is free only in a world whose every event he can understand and foresee. ... We are captains of our own souls only in so far as ... we can understand and foresee every response which we will make to every situation. (p. 45)

We can contrast this attitude with the one expressed by E. C. Tolman in his presidential address to the APA in 1937. There, Tolman wondered if psychology was ready to guide any kind of human behavior, because it still could not predict which way a rat would turn in a maze (Joncich, 1968). Thorndike had no such discomfort with psychology. He had absolute certainty about the potential of a rational, scientific approach to education. For example, when he applied his connectionist psychology to the learning of school subjects, as in his *Psychology of Arithmetic* (1922), he derived his practices from logic and laboratory, *not* from the teaching of arithmetic in the field. He then claimed that this new pedagogy differed from the old because

> the newer pedagogy of arithmetic ... scrutinizes every element of knowledge, every connection made in the mind of the learner, so as to choose those which provide the most instructive experiences, those which will grow together into an orderly, rational system of thinking about numbers and quantitative facts. (p. 74)

No tentativeness is shown here. Every connection is analyzable and then analyzed. Today, we would call the work commonsensical, systematic, and organized according to some reasonable principles of instruction. Today, we would probably not call the work scientific but, rather, logical. It is interesting to note and reflect on the fact that Thorndike apparently never field-tested the ideas and materials he promoted in the different subject matter areas. He was so sure of his scientific footing that field-testing his texts and educational materials in the various school subjects seemed absurd. It appears as if Thorndike had fallen into the same trap that the school administrators had fallen into when they would not accept Rice's work on spelling. The administrators with their moral philosophy and Thorndike with his science both believed strongly that they knew what was proper. Their beliefs were so powerful that empirical data were not seen as relevant (Travers, 1985).

Thorndike's surety about science carried over into his work on quantitative methods, where he wrote eloquently about the power of educational measurement (E. Thorndike, 1918):

> Whatever exists at all exists in some amount. To know it thoroughly involves knowing its quantity as well as its quality. Education is concerned with changes in human beings; a change is a difference between two conditions; each of these conditions is known to us

only by the products produced by it—things made, words spoken, acts performed, and the like. To measure any of these products means to define its amount in some way so that competent persons will know how large it is, better than they would without measurement. ... We have faith that whatever people now measure crudely ... can be measured more precisely. (p. 16)

There is more of this throughout Thorndike's writings and those of his graduate students. Psychology need not go into the classroom; it can derive its laws from the laboratory and hand them down to teachers, thus creating the very condition that Dewey in a nearby office had decried. Thorndike promoted the belief that science and only science would save education. Indeed, he believed it would save all of society. His belief was that quantitative experiments were to be preferred over qualitative, clinical, or naturalistic observation. By the time World War II was near, at many institutions these beliefs had resulted in the irrelevance of the discipline of educational psychology. It had, in general, oversold what it could deliver. For example, Frank N. Freeman wrote the conclusion to the 1938 yearbook of the National Society for the Study of Education, a publication summarizing the achievements of the scientific movement in education. Freeman (1938) remarked that what had been accomplished appeared to be superficial, addressing the husk, not the kernel, of the educational process. He speculated that the scientific movement that Thorndike headed had gone as far as it could in improving education. Hilgard (in press), reviewing the 37 chapters of that yearbook, believes they provide testimony that wrong directions were taken by the field. It was a time when members of educational psychology refused to take seriously the world of schooling and the importance of the social lives of the students, teachers, and others who spend considerable amounts of time in that setting. Disdain for practice was the prevailing attitude. Because Thorndike and his followers took too narrow a view, our field had begun to show its weaknesses.

The Nether Side of Thorndike's Influence

McDonald (1964) called that period before World War II the nadir of the profession, and this is partially true, although it was also a function of a great depression. Some enduring work of practical significance was completed during the 1930s by those whom we call educational psychologists—Gates, Brownell, Pressey, McConnell, to name just a few— but much of the work that impacted our field was being done by psychologists who were not primarily interested in education. With hindsight, however, it appears that by the time World War II began, educational psychology had gone astray. But the debacle could not be addressed properly until after the war, a time that was actually one of opportunity and progress for our discipline. Psychologists and educational psychologists found meaningful work to perform in the war, because they better than others could advise on how to take a farmer or a store clerk and 8 weeks later provide an electronics repairman or a bombardier. They tested, evaluated, and designed instruction. The theoretical debates about the status of constructs within different learning theories, which had dominated psychology in the 1930s, ended with the war and never again interested the field of psychology as they had. In part, that was because the practical concerns of education during the war made it clear that there was little hope of finding a single, all-purpose learning theory. Learning theories provided guidance for thinking about different kinds of instructional problems, but, as James long before had noted, intermediate inventive minds were needed to solve the real problems of education. The war did not require theoretical elegance from its psychologists. It required solving practical, not laboratory, problems, such as the problem of rapidly teaching masses of men to reach acceptable levels of competency in hundreds of specialty areas (see Allport, 1947; Skinner, 1961; and McKeachie, 1974 for discussions of these issues). With the help of psychologists, the task was accomplished. Some of the people who came to a better understanding of educational problems during that time period, and who later influenced our field, included Walter Borg, Lee J. Cronbach, John Flanagan, N. L. Gage, Robert Gagné, Robert Glaser, J. P. Guilford, and B. F. Skinner. The roots of some of the changes that were to come in educational psychology had their origin in World War II, but those changes were still quite slow to come.

Every few years from the end of the war on, committees were formed to deal with educational psychology's increasingly obvious problems (Grinder, 1978). A 1948 committee of APA's Division 15 (the Division of Educational Psychology), concerned with our irrelevance, noted that educational psychology had disavowed responsibility for the directions in which education would go. Educational psychologists seemed to be interested in the laws of learning, not in issues of schooling and teaching. Worse, this committee noted that educational psychologists could neither understand nor be understood by educators—the ultimate irony for a field that once accepted the homage of educators as practitioners of the "master science" (Cubberley, 1919; Grinder, 1989). Another report issued in 1954 (Grinder, 1978) pointed out that the most influential theorists were abandoning educational psychology and retreating to the field of experimental psychology. In the 1970s, yet another report noted our failures and tried to define the discipline and chart its future (Scandura et al., 1978). Each report was still burdened by the "middleman" notion, articulated well by Robert Grinder, the official Division 15 historian (1978). Grinder wrote that we should take again the middle ground once envisioned for our discipline, a position between psychology with its disciplinary rigor on the one hand and education with its messy problems on the other. But I think that it is no longer enough to advocate simply a middle position between psychology and education. That position is looked down on by psychology because it is applied and practical, and it is looked down on by teachers and teacher educators because it is scientific and irrelevant to their problems. Something a bit different than just a middle position is needed, a point I discuss shortly, after examining educational psychology at mid-century.

Educational Psychology at Mid-Century

At least one part of our problem as a field was due to the overall success of psychology in the United States. Forty years ago, A. D. Woodruff (1950) noted that educational psychology had no domain that was really its own to any greater extent than it belonged to others. The APA Divisions of Evaluation and Measurement, Childhood and Adolescence, Personality and Social, School Psychology, and Maturity and Old Age appeared to have as much claim as we did on the study of such psychological functions as learning, adjustment, individual differences, tests and measurement, statistics, and growth and development.

I believe the perception that we had no particular mission other than to apply general psychology to education is what brought us most of our trouble. Woodruff (1950) clearly understood that a problem existed. He did not see, however, that the solution was in taking seriously a slightly different mission than that of merely bringing the gifts of psychology to education, whether education wanted them or not.

With few exceptions, textbook writers in educational psychology also misperceived our mission. From Thorndike's time to the 1960s, the texts were usually rehashed versions of Thorndike's S–R associationism and general psychology, with the students required to do all the work to figure out how that material applied to education (Grinder, 1989). Although educational psychology had established itself as the "master science" in teacher education, the texts were found to be terribly wanting in studies of them conducted over many years (Hall-Quest, 1915; Remmers & Knight, 1922; Worcester, 1927; Blair, 1949). Dael Wolfle (1947), writing about psychological textbooks in 1947, gave a formula for writing textbooks in educational and child psychology. He said,

> If you wish to write an educational psychology text, start with a good average introductory text. Remove the chapters which deal with the nervous system and sense organs and write three new chapters to use up the space. These three new chapters will have such titles as Learning in the Schoolroom, Measuring Student Progress, and Social Psychology of the Schoolroom. ... While you are collecting royalties on your text in educational psychology you will

want to write a child psychology text. The rules are easy to follow. Start again with the good average elementary text ... (p. 441)

Wolfle (1947) added that if you were writing an educational psychology text you had to delete all references to *subjects* and insert the term *pupil*, whereas if you were writing a child psychology text you had to use the term *children* instead of *subjects*. His final advice to authors of educational and child psychology texts was to rearrange the order of the chapters that were found in general psychology texts. Even as late as 1968, when Ausubel (1968) wondered if there was such a thing as a discipline of educational psychology, he noted that the texts in use were

> a superficial, ill-digested, and typically disjointed and watered-down miscellany of general psychology, learning theory, developmental psychology, social psychology, psychological measurement, psychology of adjustment, mental hygiene, client-centered counseling and child-centered education. (p. 1)

In the same year in which John B. Carroll, one of our most honored educational psychologists, published his model of school learning (Carroll, 1963a), he also wrote about the discipline of educational psychology. The creator of one of our discipline's most elegant, parsimonious, and influential theories of learning, one derived from a practical problem of instruction, noted that the potential of educational psychology remained untapped because it seemed not to be concerned with genuine educational problems. Carroll said that until educational psychology provided evidence that it dealt with the real problems of schooling, "we shall continue to teach educational psychology to teachers with a mixture of pious optimism and subdued embarrassment" (Carroll, 1963b, p. 119).

Philip Jackson (1981), writing a decade ago, laid the problems of our field squarely at Thorndike's feet. He cited four ways in which the introduction to the maiden issue of the *Journal of Educational Psychology* set the stage for the difficulties that would follow. In that introduction, Thorndike first failed to distinguish between the goals of and the methods used in the physical and the social sciences. To Thorndike, people were as easy to study as stones and toads. The methods of psychology, geology, and biology were not different, and the validity of the inferences to be made were seen to be equivalent. Second, Thorndike did not pay enough attention to the social and historical contexts in which people lived and in which schools operated. Third, Thorndike had a blind faith that all of the achievements of science were desirable. He seemed to believe this even after Hiroshima and the Nazi extermination camps, events that caused many people to question their faith in science. Finally, Thorndike overlooked the aesthetic dimension of science. The art of educational psychology surfaces occasionally, as it does in every other branch of science. Ironically, although completely unaware of it, E. L. Thorndike displayed that artistic quality a number of times.

As Jackson (1981) also noted, the final blow to Thorndikian conceptions of educational science came from our own highly respected educational psychologist, Lee J. Cronbach (1975). At the APA convention in 1974, on the occasion of his receipt of one of the Distinguished Scientific Contribution Awards for 1973, Cronbach made it clear that inconsistent findings hindered certain kinds of progress in our field. Once we attend to the interactions in our data, he said, "we enter a hall of mirrors that extends to infinity" (1975, p. 119). He noted that many social science findings do not hold for long. Educational psychologists can demonstrate Decade × Treatment interactions, an occurrence almost unfathomable to most physical scientists. Thorndike would not know what to do with Cronbach's advice to social scientists, namely, to join with humanistic scholars and artists in trying to pin down the contemporary facts. For to understand individuals in their contexts, Cronbach said, is no mean aspiration. In fact, lately, our field seems to be heading that way (see Anastasi, this volume, for similar concerns about context in the area of educational and psychological measurement).

Recent Trends

As noted in the previous discussion, educational psychologists have often been functionalists. Using the functionalist approach to the history that we just covered, we should now ask what was learned that could be of use to us?

We are at the end of a century in which we psychologists first showed great *interest* in education. Eventually, although productive and busy in academic settings, we showed *disdain* for the real-world problems of schooling. And because of that we lost the special place we had in schools of education throughout the country. But educational psychology has been slowly changing, and we now, more than ever before, have come to *respect* educational practitioners and the instructional, political, and social problems they encounter. The 100-year journey from interest, to disdain, to respect has positioned our field to be more productive then ever before, although we will need to judge that productivity by different standards. We may need to abandon, for example, the heavy reliance on refereed journal articles about basic learning processes to prove our worth as scholars. We may need to also value an educational psychologist's analyses of work in demonstration projects, programs of teacher education, practitioner collaborations, curriculum development projects, and so forth. Taking seriously the work of education need not hamper productivity, but a redefinition of what it means to be productive will be needed. There are already many contemporary trends that demonstrate that a high level of productivity within scientific educational psychology can come from an increased concern for the problems of education and its practitioners. These are discussed briefly, below.

Research on Teaching

From the 1960s on, we have developed a specialty area in research on teaching (see Gage, 1963). From initial simple models of behavior using traditional psychological methodology, we have moved to more sophisticated, cognitively oriented, naturalistic, contextually sensitive, participatory studies. Many in this field have recognized the importance of knowing intimately the goals and intentions of the teachers they study, in order to make valid local inferences (see, e.g., Wittrock, 1986).

Instructional Psychology

A major area of educational psychology has been instructional psychology. Writing for the *Annual Review of Psychology* a decade ago, Lauren Resnick (1981) noted that the problems of real-world instruction were beginning to guide the development of instructional psychology:

> An interesting thing has happened to instructional psychology. It has become part of the mainstream of research on human cognition, learning and development. For about 20 years the number of psychologists devoting attention to instructionally relevant questions has been gradually increasing. In the past 5 years this increase has accelerated so that it is now difficult to draw a clear line between instructional psychology and the main body of basic research on complex cognitive processes. Instructional psychology is no longer basic psychology *applied* to education. It is fundamental research *on* the processes of instruction and learning. (p. 660)

The Psychology of School Subjects

A resurgence of interest in schooling by educational psychologists was described, appropriately enough, in the G. Stanley Hall Lecture Series by Lee Shulman (1981), over a decade ago. He and his students have once again brought to the forefront of educational psychology the study of school subjects, demonstrating a concern for practice and the problems of instruction in the real world (Shulman, 1987, in press). This time, the psychology of school subjects is not merely the commonsense psychology of Thorndike, but a cognitive psychological approach that is equally concerned about the thinking of the learner, the structure of the discipline to be learned, and the form of explanations available to the teacher (For a sampling of this contemporary literature see Leinhardt & Smith, 1985; Lampert, 1990; Wilson & Wineberg, 1988; Wineberg & Wilson, 1988).

Methodology

Our methodology increasingly has expanded to make use of (a) cases— so as to document the genuine problems faced by real people in education; (b) naturalistic studies—so that we may enhance external validity; (c) qualitative research—because many of us have decided that Thorndike was wrong and that not everything that we can describe should be measured; and (d) small samples, intensively studied—because we have seen that different but useful things are learned from studies of a few informants, in depth, rather than from studies of many subjects whose thoughts are barely known. What Thorndike took from Galton, by way of Cattell and Boas, is seen to be less useful today than it had been. It is the systemic (total environment) effects that often need to be studied. Most of the analytic techniques that we possess cannot deal with reciprocal relationships and are designed for the study of only a few variables at a time, thus simplifying the analysis of most educational situations. These techniques may not be adequate for the job (see Salomon, 1991). Ethnomethodology (e.g. Erickson, 1986), rather than biostatistics, is becoming an important source of new ideas for educational psychologists who choose to work in school settings on genuine educational problems.

Assessment

In another mainstream area of educational psychology, assessment, we see less interest in classical standardized testing of achievement, a field (like many others) that Thorndike heavily influenced. We now see more concern for (a) the assessment of portfolios—to better reflect the achievement of students in their classrooms; (b) performance tests— a venerable form of assessment brought back into the limelight because we have learned that classical forms of testing can not easily be made to tap complex aspects of human cognition; (c) informal classroom assessment by teachers—because informal assessment, conducted on the run by sensitive teachers trying to make sense out of a large group of very heterogeneous students, is how the vast majority of classroom assessments are carried out, and it is these data that are used in teachers' decisions about instruction or the need for special services for particular students; and (d) program evaluation—which now is seen as a political process, to be conducted by a whole range of social scientists and humanistic scholars, to educate decision makers for making responsible choices in a democratic nation (see Cronbach, 1980, for a synthesis of these views, as well as the writings of other distinguished evaluators such as House, Stake, or Weiss in McLaughlin & Phillips, 1991). These contemporary views of evaluation are far more Deweyan and much less Thorndikian than was true when educational psychologists began to work in program evaluation.

Other Trends

There is current work by Snow and his colleagues (Snow, Corno, & Jackson, in press; Corno, 1993) on issues of conation and volition, closely allied with James's psychology. Contemporary research on expert–novice differences in a domain of knowledge is fundamentally developmental cognition, the field developed by Hall. The current interests in socially shared cognition and the psychological work of Lev Vygotsky are closely allied with the psychology of Dewey. In every area of educational psychology, we see today more studies of psychoeducational phenomena, and more methods for the study of those phenomena, that are compatible with the ideas of our grandfathers and granduncles, William James, G. Stanley Hall, and John Dewey. The turn of the 19th century, however, was not their time to influence educational psychology; it was Thorndike's. But fashion changes. Although it is always hard to read the zeitgeist when in its midst, it does seem that as the next century dawns we have begun to pay more attention to the issues that our grandfathers and granduncles were concerned about. We have so much that is new, once again, to learn. We need only be sure not to be led astray by the currency and trendiness of methods and ideas. This we can do if we keep before us the motto of the philosopher D. C. Phillips (1987) who, when commenting on new methodology, pointed out that no matter what was said, "worry about warrant will not wane."

Redefining Educational Psychology

If we are to sustain the changes in our field that are now occurring, the definition of educational psychology will have to be modified. Many writers, particularly Wittrock (1967, 1992) and Berliner (1992), have remarked that we should not think of ourselves as a subdiscipline or merely an applied discipline, carrying psychology to education. In fact, the evidence is quite clear that the gifts to general psychology from educational psychology have been many and profound (Berliner, 1992), so that it clearly is not a one-way thoroughfare for the passing on of knowledge. I have already noted that something more than simply occupying a middleman position is needed. I think Richard Snow (1981) put it best: Our job is to psychologize about educational problems and issues and not simply to bring psychology to education, as if we were missionaries carrying out the Lord's work. The latter approach somehow breeds arrogance and disdain, characteristics that got us into trouble in colleges of education throughout the nation. The designation of our field as the "master science" by Cubberley (1919), although flattering, has not been conducive to building equality among the members of the interdisciplinary teams of social scientists and practitioners with whom we work.

I believe that to see ourselves as psychologizing about the problems and issues of education is different in important ways from simply being a middleman. The psychologizing role certainly requires that we bring our considerable talents, our rich disciplinary perspective, our concepts and methods and habits of mind to bear on the genuine problems of administrators, teachers, students, curriculum and instruction, teacher education, and so forth. But, as stated, it is the problems of the field that are the origins of our interest as psychologists. This is a subtle but crucial difference from the way educational psychology has been thought about since Thorndike conquered the field. This formulation recognizes both the importance of understanding the problems of the individuals struggling to make schooling successful *and* the importance of our disciplinary perspective. This way of defining our field lends dignity to the work of the educators, for *their work rather than our discipline becomes the basis of our inquiry*. Implicit in recognizing the primacy of the problems of practice is that we have license to explore more deeply the social, moral, political, and economic forces that impinge on the psychological processes we have a preference for exploring. To know educators as they are, in the contexts in which they work, through the eyes of psychology, is no mean achievement.

Conclusion

E. L. Thorndike is a hero of mine. I do not think we need detract from his greatness as we recognize his shortcomings. The new generation of educational psychologists would do well to read him but to recognize the limits of his views, many of which grew out of the times in which he lived. In the second century of educational psychology, our science probably needs to be more descriptive and participatory, in the style of Hall. It needs to be less strident about pronouncing, ex cathedra, its findings, a warning that was first given to us by James. Our science needs to be more tolerant of the teacher and the complexity of the social, moral, and political world of classrooms and schools, as Dewey reminded us. Educational psychology also needs to be more eclectic in its methods, for surely we have learned that science is not synonymous with measurement and experimentation. We can forget, as soon as possible, the claim of objectivity that Thorndike thought could be made. Contemporary feminist, minority, and Marxist scholars have all shown us that gender, ethnicity, and the commitments of the investigator are not to be denied in scientific investigations, but valued for their contributions to the choice of topics to be studied and the interpretations that are made of the findings. Science never was as neutral as Thorndike believed it to be, and to perpetuate that myth among the next generation is nonsensical.

For a new century, educational psychology can start again to rebuild our relationships with our partners in the educational enterprise by picking our problems to study, and designing our teacher education courses, with concern for the educational contexts in which teachers and students work. Many of us, of course, will continue to work in laboratory settings, libraries, and offices, at a distance from the problems of schools. Such preferences are always to be defended. High quality work from such approaches has been, and will continue to be, informative and admired. But many more of us in educational psychology ought to take as our starting point for psychologizing the problems that teachers and students face in the course of their work. When we come to know the people and the problems they face well, that will enrich our discipline and enhance our usefulness. We should then be able to dazzle the students in programs of teacher education, for we have the tools and the information to improve society and education, just as Thorndike thought we did. We just need to go about it differently.

Humility and tentativeness, rather than surety and arrogance, can help us build bridges to the practice community. Attempting to provide locally valid rather than broadly generalizable knowledge is probably a more reasonable goal for many of us than the one held by Thorndike (see Goldenberg & Gallimore, 1991). Educational psychology certainly has much to offer if treated more as Dewey thought it should be, as a set of working hypotheses rather than as a set of valid findings ready to be applied. We need to remember William James and the courage that it takes to be incomplete. If we attend to it, history will have taught us much that is of value as we face our second century.

Our journey from interest, to disdain, to respect for the world of practice has led us to redefine our field and its methods a number of times. But in the transformations that took place we never seemed to lose sight of our fundamental goals: to understand and improve education in our society. Those goals are likely to remain constant even as the future brings other changes to our discipline. Whatever the next century brings us in terms of new psychological theory and new educational problems,

> We shall not cease from exploration
> And the end of all our exploring
> Will be to arrive where we started
> And know the place for the first time.
> (T. S. Eliot, *Four Quartets*, 1969)

References

Adler, M. (Ed.). (1952). *The great ideas: A syntopicon of the great books of the Western world*. Chicago: Encyclopedia Britannica.

Allport, G. W. (1947). Scientific models and human morals. *Psychological Review, 54*, 182–192.

Angell, J. R. (1907). The province of functional psychology. *Psychological Review, 14*, 61–91.

Ausubel, D. P. (1968). Is there a discipline of educational psychology? *Educational Psychologist, 5*, 4, 9.

Ayres, L. P. (1912). Measuring educational processes through educational results. *School Review, 20*, 300–309.

Barzun, J. (1983). *A stroll with William James*. New York: Harper & Row.

Berliner, D. C. (1990). The place of process–product research in developing the agenda for research on teacher thinking. *Educational Psychologist, 24*, 325–344.

Berliner, D. C. (1992). Telling the stories of educational psychology. *Educational Psychologist, 27*, 143–161.

Blair, G. M. (1949). The content of educational psychology. In *Educational psychology in the education of teachers* (Reprints of the National Society of College Teachers of Education; pp. 267–274). Baltimore: Warwick & York.

Boring, E. G. (1950). *A history of experimental psychology* (2nd ed.). New York: Appleton-Century-Crofts.

Bowen, J. (1981). *A history of western education* (Vol. 3). New York: St. Martins Press.

Broudy, H. S. (1963). Historic exemplars of teaching method. In N. L. Gage (Ed.), *Handbook of research on teaching* (pp. 1–43). Chicago: Rand McNally.

Carroll, J. B. (1963a). A model of school learning. *Teachers College Record, 64*, 723–733.

Carroll, J. B. (1963b). The place of educational psychology in the study of education. In J. Walton & J. L. Kuethe (Eds.), *The discipline of education*. Madison: University of Wisconsin Press.

Charles, D. C. (1987). The emergence of educational psychology. In J. A. Glover & R. R. Ronning (Eds.), *Historical foundations of educational psychology*. New York: Plenum Press.

Comenius, J. A. (1657). *Didacta magna*. Amsterdam: D. Laurentii de Geer.

Corno, L. (1993). The best-laid plans: Modern conceptions of volition and educational research. *Educational Researcher, 22*, 14–22.

Cronbach, L. J. (1975). Beyond the two disciplines of scientific psychology. *American Psychologist, 30,* 116–127.

Cronbach, L. J. (1980). *Towards reform of program evaluation: Aims, methods, and institutional arrangements.* San Francisco: Jossey-Bass.

Cronbach, L. J., & Snow, R. E. (1977). *Aptitudes and instructional methods: A Handbook on interactions.* New York: Irvington.

Cubberley, E. P. (1919). *Public education in the United States.* Boston: Houghton Mifflin.

Davidson, E. S., & Benjamin, L. T. Jr. (1987). A history of the child study movement in America. In J. A. Glover & R. R. Ronning (Eds.), *Historical foundations of educational psychology* (pp. 41–60). New York: Plenum Press.

Dewey, J. (1886). *Psychology.* New York: Harper.

Dewey, J. (1894). The psychology of infant language. *Psychological Review, 1,* 63–66.

Dewey, J. (1895). Interest as related to will. In C. A. McMurray (Ed.), *Second supplement to the Yearbook of the National Herbart Society for the Scientific Study of Education* (pp. 5–34). Chicago: University of Chicago Press.

Dewey, J. (1896). The reflex arc concept in psychology. *Psychological Review, 3,* 357–370.

Dewey, J. (1900). Psychology and social practice. *Psychological Review, 7,* 105–124.

Dewey, J. (1910). *How we think.* Lexington, MA: Heath.

Diehl, L. A. (1986). The paradox of G. Stanley Hall: Foe of coeducation and educator of woman. *American Psychologist, 41,* 868–878.

Eliot, T. S. (1969). *The complete poems and plays of T. S. Eliot.* London: Faber & Faber.

Erickson, F. (1986). Qualitative methods in research on teaching. In M. C. Wittrock (Ed.), *Handbook of research on teaching* (3rd ed., pp. 119–161). New York: Macmillan.

Freeman, F. N. (Ed.). (1938). *The scientific movement in education* (Thirty-seventh Yearbook of the National Society for the Study of Education, Part 2). Bloomington, IL: Public School Publishing Co.

Gage, N. L. (Ed.). (1963). *Handbook of research on teaching.* Chicago: Rand McNally.

Goldenberg, C., & Gallimore, R. (1991). Local knowledge, research knowledge, and educational change: A case study of early Spanish reading improvement. *Educational Researcher, 20(8),* 2–14.

Grinder, R. E. (1978). What 200 years tells us about professional priorities in educational psychology. *Educational Psychologist, 12,* 284–289.

Grinder, R. E. (1989). Educational psychology: The master science. In M. C. Wittrock & F. Farley (Eds.), *The future of educational psychology* (pp. 3–18). Hillsdale, NJ: Erlbaum.

Hall, G. S. (1897). A study of fears. *American Journal of Psychology, 8,* 147–249.

Hall, G. S. (1923). *Life and confessions of a psychologist.* New York: Appleton-Century-Crofts.

Hall-Quest, A. L. (1915). Present tendencies in educational psychology. *Journal of Educational Psychology, 6,* 601–614.

Harris, W. T. (1897). The relation of school discipline to moral education. In C. A. McMurray (Ed.), *The Third Yearbook of the National Herbart Society for the Scientific Study of Education* (pp. 58–72). Chicago: University of Chicago Press.

Hilgard, E. R. (in press). History of educational psychology. In D. C. Berliner & Robert C. Calfee (Eds.), *Handbook of educational psychology*. New York: Macmillan.

Hothersall, D. (1984). *History of psychology*. Philadelphia: Temple University Press.

Jackson, P. W. (1981). The promise of educational psychology. In F. H. Farley & N. J. Gordon (Eds.), *Psychology and education: The state of the union*. Berkeley, CA: McCutchan.

James, H. (Ed.). (1920). *The letters of William James* (Vol. 1). Boston: Atlantic Monthly Press.

James, W. (1890). *Principles of psychology* (2 Vols.). New York: Holt.

James, W. (1892). *Psychology: The briefer course*. New York: Holt.

James, W. (1983). *Talks to teachers on psychology and to students on some of life's ideals*. Cambridge, MA: Harvard University Press. (Original work published 1899)

Joncich, G. (Ed.). (1962). *Psychology and the science of education. Selected writings of Edward L. Thorndike*. New York: Teachers College Press.

Joncich, G. (1968). *The sane positivist: A biography of Edward L. Thorndike*. Middletown, CT: Wesleyan University Press.

Judd, C. H. (1925). The curriculum: A paramount issue. In *Addresses and proceedings* (pp. 806–807). Washington, DC: National Education Association.

Kramer, J. J. (1987). School psychology. In J. A. Glover & R. R. Ronning (Eds.), *Historical foundations of educational psychology* (pp. 121–130). New York: Plenum Press.

Lampert, M. (1990). When the problem is not the question and the solution is not the answer: Mathematical knowing and teaching. *American Educational Research Journal, 27*, 29–63.

Leinhardt, G., & Smith, D. (1985). Expertise in mathematics instruction: Subject matter knowledge. *Journal of Educational Psychology, 77*, 247–271.

McDonald, F. J. (1964). The influence of learning theories on education (1900–1950). In E. R. Hilgard (Ed.), *Theories of learning and instruction* (Sixty-third Yearbook of the National Society for the Study of Education, Part 1, pp. 1–26). Chicago: University of Chicago Press.

McKeachie, W. J. (1974). The decline and fall of the laws of learning. *Educational Researcher, 3(3)*, 7–11.

McLaughlin, M. W., & Phillips, D. C. (Eds.). (1991). *Evaluation and education: At quarter century* (Ninetieth Yearbook of the National Society for the Study of Education, Part 2). Chicago: University of Chicago Press.

Monroe, W. S. (1952). *Teaching–learning theory and teacher education, 1890 to 1950*. Urbana, IL: University of Illinois Press.

Münsterberg, H. (1898a). The danger from experimental psychology. *Atlantic Monthly, 81*, 159–167.

Münsterberg, H. (1898b). Psychology and education. *Education Review, 16*, 105–132.

Phillips, D. C. (1987). Validity in qualitative research: Why worry about the warrant will not wane. *Education and Urban Society, 20(1)*, 9–24.

Quintilian, F. B. (1953). *Institutio oratoria* (4 Vols.; H. E. Butler, Trans.). Cambridge, MA: Harvard University Press.

Quintilian, F. B. (1966). *Quintilian on education* (W. M. Smail, Trans.). New York: Teachers College Press.

Remmers, H. H., & Knight, F. B. (1922). The teaching of educational psychology in the United States. *Journal of Educational Psychology, 13,* 399–407.

Resnick, L. B. (1981). Instructional psychology. In M. R. Rosenzweig & L. W. Porter (Eds.), *Annual review of psychology* (Vol. 32, pp. 659–704). Palo Alto, CA: Annual Reviews.

Rice, J. M. (1912). *Scientific management in education.* New York: Hinds, Noble, & Eldredge.

Ross, D. (1972). *G. Stanley Hall: The psychologist as prophet.* Chicago: University of Chicago Press.

Salomon, G. (1991). Transcending the qualitative–quantitative debate: The analytic and systemic approaches to educational research. *Educational Researcher, 20(6),* 10–18.

Scandura, J. M., Frase, L. T., Gagne, R. M., Stolurow, K., Stolurow, L. T., & Gruen, G. (1978). Current status and future directions of educational psychology as a discipline. *Educational Psychologist, 13,* 43–56.

Shulman, L. S. (1981). Educational psychology returns to school. In A. G. Kraut (Ed.), *G. Stanley Hall Lecture Series* (Vol. 2). Washington, DC: American Psychological Association.

Shulman, L. S. (1987). Knowledge and teaching: Foundations of the new reform. *Harvard Educational Review, 57,* 1–22.

Shulman, L. S. (in press). The psychology of school subjects. In D. C. Berliner & R. Calfee (Eds.), *The handbook of educational psychology.* New York: Macmillan.

Siegel, A. W., & White, S. H. (1982). The child study movement: Early growth and development of the symbolized child. In H. W. Reeses (Ed.), *Advances in child development and behavior* (Vol. 17, pp. 233–285). San Diego, CA: Academic Press.

Skinner, B. F. (1961). The flight from the laboratory. In *Current trends in psychological theory* (pp. 50–69). Pittsburgh: University of Pittsburgh Press.

Snow, R. E. (1981). On the future of educational psychology. *Newsletter for Educational Psychologists* (Division 15, American Psychological Association), *5(1),* 1.

Snow, R. E., Corno, L., & Jackson, D. (in press). Conative and affective functions in educational psychology. In D. C. Berliner & R. C. Calfee (Eds.), *Handbook of educational psychology.* New York: Macmillan.

Sully, J. (1889). *Outlines of psychology with special reference to the theory of education: A textbook for colleges.* New York: Appleton.

Thorndike, E. L. (1898a). Animal intelligence. *Psychological Review,* Monograph Supplement II, No. 2, Whole No. 8.

Thorndike, E. L. (1898b). What is a psychical fact? *Psychological Review, 5,* 645–650.

Thorndike, E. L. (1899). Sentimentality in science teaching. *Educational Review, 17,* 56–64.

Thorndike, E. L. (1903). *Educational psychology.* New York: Science Press.

Thorndike, E. L. (1906). *The principles of teaching based on psychology.* New York: A. G. Seiler.

Thorndike, E. L. (1909). Darwin's contribution to psychology. *University of California Chronicle, 12,* 65–80.

Thorndike, E. L. (1910). The contribution of psychology to education. *Journal of Educational Psychology, 1*, 5–12.

Thorndike, E. L. (1918). The nature, purposes, and general methods of measurements of educational products. In *The measurement of educational products* (Seventeenth Yearbook of the National Society for the Study of Education, Part 2, pp. 16–24). Bloomington, IL: Public School Publishing Company.

Thorndike, E. L. (1922). *The psychology of arithmetic.* New York: Macmillan.

Thorndike, E. L. (1936). Edward L. Thorndike. In C. Murchison (Ed.), *History of psychology in autobiography* (Vol. 3, pp. 263–270). Worcester, MA: Clark University Press.

Thorndike, R. L. (1985, April). *E. L. Thorndike—A personal and professional appreciation.* Paper given at the meeting of the American Educational Research Association, Chicago, IL.

Travers, R. M. W. (1985, April). *Thorndike's scientific empiricism and the pragmatic approach.* Paper presented at the meeting of the American Educational Research Association, Chicago, IL.

Tyack, D., & Hansot, E. (1982). *Managers of virtue: Public school leadership in America, 1820–1980.* New York: Basic books.

Vives, J. L. (1913). De tradendis disciplinis. In *Vives on education* (F. Watson, Trans.). Cambridge, England: Cambridge University Press. (Original work published 1531)

Watson, R. I. (1961). A brief history of educational psychology. *Psychological Record, 11*, 209–242.

Wilds, E. H., & Lottich, K. V. (1964). *The foundations of modern education.* New York: Holt, Rinehart & Winston.

Wilson, S. M., & Wineberg, S. S. (1988). Peering at history through different lenses: The role of disciplinary perspectives in teaching history. *Teachers College Record, 89*, 525–539.

Wineberg, S. S., & Wilson, S. M. (1989). Subject matter knowledge in the teaching of history. In J. E. Brophy (Ed.), *Advances in research on teaching.* Greenwich, CT: JAI Press.

Wittrock, M. C. (1967). Focus on educational psychology. *Educational Psychologist, 4*, 7–20.

Wittrock, M. C. (Ed.). (1986). *Handbook of research on teaching* (3rd ed.). New York: Macmillan.

Wittrock, M. C. (1992). An empowering conception of educational psychology. *Educational Psychologist, 27*, 129–141.

Wolfle, D. (1947). The sensible organization of courses in psychology. *American Psychologist, 2*, 437–445.

Woodruff, A. D. (1950, February). Functional structure needed. *Newsletter of Division 15*, American Psychological Association, p. 5.

Worcester, D. A. (1927). The wide diversities of practice in first-courses in educational psychology. *Journal of Educational Psychology, 18*, 11–17.

FRANK J. LANDY

EARLY INFLUENCES ON THE DEVELOPMENT OF INDUSTRIAL/ ORGANIZATIONAL PSYCHOLOGY

F rank Landy is a professor of psychology at The Pennsylvania State University and the director of the Center for Applied Behavioral Sciences. Landy received his PhD in industrial and organizational psychology from Bowling Green State University in 1969 and has been at Penn State since that time. In 1976 and 1979, he was a Fulbright scholar at the University of Stockholm. In 1983, he received an IREX grant to lecture and conduct research in Romania, and in 1986 he received a Fulbright grant to lecture and conduct research in Yugoslavia.

Landy has published on a wide variety of topics including personnel selection, the philosophy of science, psychosomatic disorders, job satisfaction, work motivation, and most recently, stress in the workplace. Landy has conducted substantial research and review of the process and substance of performance evaluation and, with James Farr, has published a widely cited review of rating techniques that eventually was expanded to book length. As an expert in personnel testing, he has written several theoretical articles on construct validity and testing methods. He has recently published several works on the concept of time urgency and has integrated that work into the broader fabric of healthy work and stress at the workplace. He has been involved in the planning and execution of the first and second joint APA/NIOSH conferences on stress in the workplace. He has been conducting historical research for the past 5 years and has published several articles on the early years of the subdiscipline as well as presented numerous lectures on the topic.

Landy is the author of eight books, including introductory psychology texts and survey texts in industrial and organizational psychology. He has also coauthored two texts in performance measurement. He has published over 40 articles, 15 book chapters and monographs, and numerous technical reports.

Landy has received numerous grants to support his research, including grants from the Law Enforcement Assistance Administration to study police performance, the Office of Naval Research to study work motivation, the Nuclear Regulatory Commission to study safety in nuclear power plants, the U.S. Department of Agriculture to examine government hiring practices, and the Equal Employment Opportunity Commission to research aging and human abilities. He is a fellow of four divisions of the American Psychological Association (Divisions 5, 14, 21, and 47) and has served as a council representative and president for Division 14. In addition, Landy is active in the American College of Sports Medicine.

FRANK J. LANDY

EARLY INFLUENCES ON THE DEVELOPMENT OF INDUSTRIAL/ ORGANIZATIONAL PSYCHOLOGY

T he history of industrial/organizational (I/O) psychology is unique in some respects, as compared with other areas of psychology. The early years of both experimental psychology and clinical psychology were characterized by battles between competing theories and paradigms. In experimental psychology, the structuralists disagreed with the functionalists, the functionalists were at odds with the gestalt movement, and the behaviorists annoyed everyone. Similarly, in personality theory and psychopathology, the ego theorists disagreed with the orthodox Freudians, who were at odds with Jung and Adler.

In comparison, I/O psychology, at least in its early years, was remarkably catholic, and there were relatively few theoretical disagreements. It might be fair to say that during the period from 1893 to 1930, there were only three figures and one paradigm. The figures were Hugo Münsterberg, Walter Dill Scott, and Walter Van Dyke Bingham, and they simply succeeded rather than replaced one another. Münsterberg reigned

Earlier versions of this chapter were reviewed by Stacey Kohler, Rick Jacobs, and Cathy Cline. Laura Shankster, Patricia Kelley, Paula Caligiuri, Kat Ringenbach, and Paul Tesluk assisted in the literature search. In addition, the graphics work was done by Joe Hinish and Steph DiCamillo, and the transcribing by Joy Struble. Various libraries such as Carnegie Mellon, Northwestern, and the Boston Public Library were also helpful. Finally, Michael Sokal has been extremely helpful with both encouragement and information.

from 1893 until his death in 1916. Although his influence was dampened by his overbearing personality and his allegiance to Germany as World War I approached (Landy, 1992), Münsterberg was widely recognized as the voice, if not the heart and soul, of the emerging area of I/O psychology. His death in 1916 transformed what might have been a battle for prominence and influence into a natural succession. Walter Dill Scott was then emerging as a conceptual leader in the application of psychological principles to the problems of business. He had begun these applications 10 years earlier, as a young assistant professor of experimental psychology at Northwestern University. He had started by applying the principles of attention to the challenges of advertising. Now, 10 years later, Scott was the intellectual engine in a research unit at Carnegie Institute that was devoted to the application of psychology to business. His books on the psychology of advertising (1903, 1908) had provided him with the visibility necessary to assume a leadership role, just as his degree with Wundt had provided him with the necessary scientific credentials to be accepted by his colleagues as a "voice."

Thus, with the death of Münsterberg, it was no surprise to see the mantle passed to Scott. It was his time. Given his visibility, credentials, and enthusiasm for application (Ferguson, 1965), it would have been reasonable to assume that his leadership would stretch over a considerable period. This was not the case. The intellectual, organizational, and interpersonal skills that allowed him to emerge as a leader of the discipline also made him attractive as an administrator, and in 1920, he became president of Northwestern University, a position he was to hold for over 30 years. When he assumed that position, he largely abandoned the field of psychology and devoted himself to administration. The only exception to this shift of emphasis occurred during World War II, when he volunteered his services to the Department of Defense as a reprise of his World War I contribution to the placement of enlisted men and commissioned officers. So his reign was brief, lasting from 1916 until 1920.

Thus, once again, in 1920, the throne was vacant through natural causes. This was to be the time of Walter Van Dyke Bingham. His interests in applied and industrial psychology were ignited by a period at Harvard University with Münsterberg at a time when Münsterberg was obsessed with the potential applications of psychology. Bingham received a degree at the University of Chicago in 1907 and went to Columbia University to work with Cattell and Thorndike. Like Scott's, Bingham's talents and credentials were quickly recognized, and he assumed a leadership role at Dartmouth College as the head of their newly developed psychological laboratory. In 1915, he was recruited by the new Carnegie Institute of Technology to head a multidisciplinary research and application unit, the first of its kind in the United States. The unit was to formalize the application of psychological principles to the world of business, both through the training of students and through direct application supported by grants and contracts from business organizations. This unit was an example of being in the right place at the right time. Bingham had assembled a very strong staff for his research team and was able to simply divert the activities of these professionals from business to military needs as World War I approached. Thus, although Scott received considerably more attention during the war years than did Bingham, they worked very closely with each other, and Bingham acquired great respect for Scott's vision, organizational skills, and interpersonal effectiveness. When Scott assumed his new role as president of Northwestern, all eyes turned toward Bingham, and he accepted the role of leader and spokesperson for I/O psychology, a role he occupied for the next 20 years.

If the leadership sociogram was simple, the prevailing paradigm was even simpler. I/O psychology, in its earliest stages, could be characterized as field based, quantitative, and atheoretical, driven more by an interest in individual variability than in general laws or individual similarity.

Given the uniformity of the early prevailing paradigm, it should be possible to appreciate the history of the subdiscipline by tracing the careers of the three leaders, and this is the approach that I take. For a complete understanding of those early developmental years, it is only necessary to add one more name—James McKeen Cattell. Cattell was obsessed with application (Sokal, 1984a), and although he had little personal success in applying psychological principles to the solution of the everyday problems of the business world, his many technological and theoretical insights (e.g., rating scales and individual differences measurements) influenced several generations of applied psychologists. In addition, he was the architect of one of the most substantial and enduring organizations dedicated to application—the Psychological Corporation. For these reasons, it is also useful to explore his role in the development of I/O psychology.

This chapter focuses on the early development of I/O psychology by examining the careers and contributions of the above-mentioned four individuals. Three of them (Münsterberg, Scott, and Bingham) would each qualify in some important way as a "father" of I/O psychology. Cattell played a supporting, but nevertheless important, developmental role.

There is one final introductory comment that should be made. It will become quickly apparent that this chapter focuses on the personnel aspect of I/O psychology (i.e., issues largely related to selection and placement). This might seem somewhat narrow because there are other areas of I/O psychology that might be considered from a historical perspective, namely, human factors and organizational/social. But I plan to cover the years from 1890 to 1930,[1] and that period can be characterized almost exclusively by the selection/placement paradigm. Human factors pursuits did not really appear in any formal sense until World War II, with the new demanding technology and armaments. And organizational/social concepts were ushered in by the Hawthorne studies and the new human relations movement resulting from those studies. Morris Viteles did not write his classic book on motivation in industry until 1953 because there was little or no applied motivational research to write about prior to that point.

Hugo Münsterberg (1863–1916)

Hugo Münsterberg[2] was born in Danzig in 1863, the son of a well-to-do shipping agent. His mother died when he was quite young, but for the

Figure 1. Hugo Münsterberg (1863–1916). (Courtesy of John A. Popplestone, the Archives of the History of American Psychology.)

---

[1]A recent article by Katzell and Austin (1992) covers much of the development of I/O psychology during the period after 1930.

[2]Much of the Münsterberg material has been synthesized from my recent biography of Münsterberg [Landy, 1992].

most part, his childhood and adolescence were relatively tranquil. He was an accomplished poet and cellist, and entered the University at Leipzig in 1882, intending to pursue studies in both philosophy and medicine. It was at Leipzig that he first encountered the new science of psychology while attending the lectures of Wilhelm Wundt. By 1884, Münsterberg had nearly completed the requirements for his medical degree and needed only a medical thesis to get it. Simultaneously, he sought his PhD in Wundt's laboratory and completed a dissertation intended to earn him that degree. Wundt canceled the dissertation because he did not agree with the line of research that Münsterberg was pursuing. It challenged Wundt's propositions about the "will" (Keller, 1979). Undaunted, Münsterberg completed a second dissertation that was accepted, and he received his PhD in 1885. He next moved to Heidelberg University where he completed a medical thesis and received his MD in 1887. He then published the dissertation that Wundt had disapproved, thereby announcing his independence from the master.

Münsterberg's first job was as a privatdocent at Freiburg University. A privatdocent was an individual who was paid by the students for lecturing. He was quickly promoted to the position of extraordinary professor, which was the equivalent of an advanced assistant professor or associate professor in today's scheme (Hale, 1980). He began publishing the results of his previous research with Wundt almost immediately and set up laboratories in his home to conduct experimental research. It was this experimental work that brought him to the attention of William James.

William James was an enigma at Harvard. He was an MD who taught physiology courses, philosophy courses, and eventually psychology courses. He was housed in the philosophy department but had begun his own psychological experimentation in his home in 1875. By 1892, James was nervous because G. Stanley Hall and his colleagues at Clark University were proclaiming preeminence in the new field of psychology (Ross, 1972). Unless Harvard was able to capture a first-class experimental psychologist, the department was likely to lose prestige as Clark and other universities began to develop their behavioral laboratories. Labs were up and running at the University of Wisconsin, Yale University, the University of Pennsylvania, and Johns Hopkins University, to mention just a few of the two dozen or so active facilities. The problem was that James could not tolerate the reductionism of the "modern" psychology laboratory of the 1890s. And although he wanted Harvard to have a great laboratory, he did not want to be responsible for its supervision.

James traveled frequently to Europe and read German quite well. As a result, he was familiar both with Münsterberg's work and with his reluctance to follow the orthodox structuralism of Wundt. This heightened Münsterberg's appeal, because James was no great fan of the structuralist school or of Wundt. James favored pragmatism and functionalism. He had met Münsterberg at a conference in Paris in 1889, and in

1892 he invited Münsterberg to come to America for 3 years and run the laboratory at Harvard. Münsterberg agreed and came with his family in the fall of 1892. With the exception of a 2-year hiatus in Germany from 1895 to 1897 and a sabbatical in 1910, Münsterberg was to remain at Harvard until he died in 1916. During that period, he was *the* laboratory director, controlling most research and publications that came out of the laboratory. He represented Harvard in the psychological community of the time. He was also chosen as the chairman of the philosophy department in 1900 and managed to effect an amicable split between philosophy and psychology that provided psychology a base of operation (and a building) independent of philosophy.

Until 1900, it was common for philosophy and psychology to exist side by side in philosophy departments. Münsterberg was one of the new breed of psychologists who were uncomfortable with that co-habitation. At the time, psychology was often referred to as mental philosophy. It was not that Münsterberg was uneasy with philosophy. On the contrary, he wrote extensively in philosophy journals and was widely respected for those writings. In fact, he was elected president of the American Philosophical Association in 1908, 9 years after he had been elected president of the American Psychological Association (APA). He simply believed that the disciplines were very different and that psychology needed to strike out on its own.

By the turn of the century, Münsterberg was very well known. He had been invited to join in the founding of the APA in 1892 and was on the editorial boards of most of the prestigious journals of the time.

Because Harvard had the premier philosophy department at the turn of the century and Münsterberg was so closely associated with that department, anyone who aspired to prominence in the new science of psychology would likely pass through Münsterberg's laboratory at one time or another, either as a student or as a visiting colleague. Because many universities did not have top-notch philosophy departments, it was common for graduate students to take up residence at Harvard for 6 months or a year to study with James, Münsterberg, George Santayana, Josiah Royce, or other members of the illustrious department.

But Münsterberg had a strong personality and was often involved in disputes with colleagues both at Harvard and at other institutions. As a result, he was the academic that people loved to hate. He was frequently ridiculed publicly in the press and privately by his colleagues. Nevertheless, he was considered nothing short of a genius by most of the students who came in contact with him. Although all agreed that he was weak on experimental design and statistics, he was able to engender great enthusiasm for research among students

In his years at Harvard, Münsterberg had much to say about the application of psychology to everyday life. He made pronouncements on education, the law, clinical psychology, job design, employee selection, spiritualists, and so on, but resisted actually doing research on these topics for some time. He also discouraged the application of psychological principles in these areas by nonpsychologists.

From Münsterberg's perspective, 1907 was a confusing year (Landy, 1992). He had been at Harvard for 15 years at the time, with a brief sabbatical in Germany in 1895. He was considered a philosopher and a "new age" experimental psychologist. (I describe as *new age* those psychologists who took the functionalist perspective and recognized the importance of individual differences.) But Münsterberg had not yet fully embraced applied psychology. As recently as 1905, he was still publicly criticizing colleagues who stooped to suggest such applications. He had also taken quite a beating from his colleagues in 1905. William James had rebuked him for taking too much credit for the development of psychology at Harvard (Münsterberg Papers). He had actually resigned as department head as a result of that incident (although he reconsidered 18 hours later and reassumed his duties). What had hurt him most in that exchange was that he had been labeled an outsider and a German–American, and thus a second-class citizen. This was tough for Münsterberg to take. He had a Copernican view of his world and saw himself as the center of the psychological universe. No matter that he had refused to become an American citizen and kept all of his financial investments, which were considerable, in Germany.

By 1907, a transformation in Münsterberg had begun. He was beginning to realize the potential applicability of what had been confined to laboratories up to this point. He had announced the development of a "lie detector" (the first modern polygraph) and had agreed to use this and other techniques for an article in a popular magazine that was to be a "scientific" analysis of the truthfulness of several individuals involved in a spectacular murder trial in Idaho. (This was the infamous "Harry Orchard" trial.) Shortly after this episode, Münsterberg seemed to shift his interest from the laboratory and talked of nothing else except the new "psychotechnology" that would save civilization.

Münsterberg's transformation to application was most likely the result of several influences. William Stern, a leading German psychologist, had published a book on psychology and the law several years earlier, in 1903. This would have annoyed Münsterberg. Walter Dill Scott had also published two books on the psychology of advertising (1903, 1908). This would have also been seen as a challenge to Münsterberg's status. Finally, Münsterberg was far from being "accepted" by his Harvard colleagues and thus had little to lose by changing direction. Santayana was beginning to mock him openly by now (Cory, 1955), and Edwin Holt was beginning to question Münsterberg's professional ethics (Hale, 1980).

One thing Münsterberg knew for sure: Any foray into the application of psychology would guarantee newspaper and magazine coverage. And he liked that. It was likely that Münsterberg saw this period as a window of opportunity, so he changed his views. He now embraced applied psychology, which he called *psychotechnology*, and claimed it for his own. And regardless of how or why he came to this position, he was good at promoting it. By 1910, he had written his first books in industrial psychology (in German), in legal psychology (Münsterberg, 1908), and in clinical psychology (Münsterberg, 1909b). Furthermore, he was beginning to use the popular press as an avenue for proselytizing about the potential of psychology for bettering the lot of the common man. He wrote articles that appeared regularly in *Harper's Weekly*, the *New York Times, McClure's Magazine*, and many other popular publications.

He was a strong advocate of selection testing and worked out the details of a testing program for the Boston Automated Railway, who were attempting to reduce accidents involving trolley cars and pedestrians. These tests were intended to be high-fidelity simulations and, today, we would call them *work samples*. These were very different from the basic tests of sensation, reaction time, and mental ability being constructed by Cattell. Münsterberg's testing interest was of long standing. In 1893, he and Joseph Jastrow presented examples of psychological tests at the World's Fair in Chicago (Hale, 1980), and he corresponded frequently with Cattell about the testing program that Cattell was constructing at Columbia. The difference was that Münsterberg was less interested in students and more interested in workers. He eventually developed tests for hiring sales representatives, telephone operators, ship captains, production workers, and drivers and motormen. He was clever enough to realize that at some point one needed to see if the tests were doing any good, so he regularly conducted validity studies by having current workers take the tests and comparing these test scores to performance indicators. We would recognize this today as the concurrent method of criterion-related validation. Unlike Cattell, whose validity calculations demonstrated the uselessness of basic reaction time tests for predicting college grades, Münsterberg was able to show that his tests of complex mental abilities and work samples could predict the efficiency of industrial workers. This was an early indication of the probable value of tests of complex mental ability (such as those being developed by Binet and Terman) compared with the simpler mental tests of the 19th century.

It is ironic that Münsterberg died in December of 1916 while lecturing at Radcliffe University, where he had presented his first English lecture in 1894. Thus, his first and last lectures were given at the same location. Somehow, this symmetry seemed fitting given that the only constituency to remain devoted to him was the student constituency.

Münsterberg's Legacy

More than anything else, Münsterberg can be credited with raising the consciousness of the American public with regard to applied psychology.

He was a promoter of the first order, and it was precisely because of his efforts that the Carnegie Institute was willing to fund a Division of Applied Psychology and other universities were willing to hire this new breed of applied or industrial psychologist. Münsterberg was also responsible for instilling in several generations of new PhDs a confidence that psychology had something to offer to business and industry leaders.

If he had a professional flaw, it was that he failed to realize the importance of keeping his feet planted in both camps—the applied and the theoretical. He abandoned the latter for the former, and it took its toll on his academic credibility. Ultimately, however, it was more his personal flaws than his professional flaws that diminished his perceived impact.

The Transition

Münsterberg's death received extensive coverage nationally and internationally. Over 200 domestic newspapers and at least that many foreign newspapers reported the smallest details of his last hours. The comments about his past were muted. Although people talked about him as a "controversial" figure, for the most part they emphasized his accomplishments and honors, which were substantial. He thus achieved the respectability in death that he had hungered for throughout his life.

For applied psychology, however, the loss bordered on the catastrophic. Few had been able to get the attention of the public and policy makers as Münsterberg had done. Few were as capable of galvanizing a colleague or student with respect to research or application. Few had the vision that Münsterberg had and presented with such ease. Applied psychology was poised to do something big, but someone would need to pick up the banner that had fallen with Münsterberg. Who would that be?

Cattell wanted the notoriety that Münsterberg had achieved, but no matter how many letters he wrote to the *Times*, no one seemed to notice his scientific efforts. He was known instead as the village scold, always criticizing one person or another (Sokal, 1984b). Bingham had just begun to develop an entire unit at the Carnegie Institute that would be devoted to applied psychology, but he was counting on Münsterberg to provide the conceptual framework *and* the horsepower in the form of new PhDs (Landy, 1992; Münsterberg Papers). Moreover, Bingham had not yet achieved the visibility necessary to "lead" a field. Scott had been working with Bingham for a year but was a reluctant public figure. He seemed to shun the spotlight and had actively hidden his applied interests for many years (Kuna, 1974). Thorndike was a possibility, but he had become more interested in educational psychology and statistics and had been urging students to pursue applied measurement activities. So, he was more a passive than an active proponent of the field. There were some new people working in the area, such as Hollingworth, Poffenberger, Strong, and Paterson, but they were hardly household names and had barely completed their doctoral studies. Viteles was still in high school. By reputation, training, and aspiration, the most likely candidate was Cattell.

James McKeen Cattell (1860–1944)

James McKeen Cattell[3] was born in 1860 in Easton, Pennsylvania. His father was president of Lafayette College, and as a result, the younger Cattell never received formal schooling. Instead, he was tutored by the faculty of the college until he was 14, at which point he entered Lafayette to begin his college education (Ross, 1973).

While at Lafayette, Cattell was greatly influenced by the philologist Francis March (Ross, 1973). March was an admirer of the philosopher Francis Bacon. Although Bacon had much to say about theory building on the basis of induction, March only saw the empiricism of the Baconian system. This view of Bacon's system glorified the collection of data without any regard to hypotheses or theories. This philosophy has also been labeled *vulgar utilitarianism* (Sokal, 1982). It is interesting to note that during the period following World War II, this same tendency to lionize data and statistical analysis at the expense of theory and logic became known as *dust bowl empiricism*, but the concept was identical to that of vulgar utilitarianism and, as such, has at least some (misguided) precedent in the Baconian framework.

After graduating from Lafayette in 1881, Cattell traveled to Germany to study philosophy with Hermann Lotze at Göttingen, but Lotze died shortly after Cattell's arrival. So, Cattell transferred to Leipzig and attended the lectures of Wilhelm Wundt for the rest of that academic year. In 1882, Cattell returned to a fellowship at Johns Hopkins with G. Stanley Hall, fully intending to complete his graduate training and receive an American PhD. However, he changed his mind, returned to Leipzig, and completed his education there, receiving his PhD with Wundt in 1886.

One of the characteristics that set Cattell apart from other American students in Wundt's laboratory was the fact that he worked hard at his German and did not abandon his studies with Wundt. He stuck with the program for 3 years and by 1886 was perhaps the single most knowledgeable English-speaking psychologist in the world with respect to Wundt and his research (Blumenthal, 1975). This provided Cattell with instant status in the research community

---

[3]Much of the material describing Cattell was taken from various works by Sokal (1981a, 1981b, 1982, 1984a, 1984b, 1990).

When Cattell left Wundt's laboratory, he moved rapidly away from the sterile laboratory methods for probing mental life. He also abandoned introspection. For Cattell, the future was in objective measurement, quantification, and statistical analysis. Following the completion of his dissertation, Cattell traveled to Cambridge University and came to know and admire the work of Sir Francis Galton, the cousin of Charles Darwin.

Biological variation (or what psychologists would later call *individual differences*) was an important part of the theory of natural selection developed by Darwin. Galton pursued this principle in his study of the genetic transmission and inheritance of various physical and psychological traits. To pursue this research line, Galton opened a laboratory in Kensington in which he could gather the necessary individual differences data. Although he had a good handle on physical characteristics and variations, he was less sophisticated about variations of a "psychological" variety, but nonetheless he was intrigued by them. As a result, Galton contacted Cattell when the latter arrived in Cambridge. Galton was a renaissance scientist and was familiar with the work of Wundt and Ebbinghaus, and by extension, the work of their students, such as Cattell. Thus began a series of discussions with Cattell about the parameters of mental life that might be measured, particularly reaction time—an area in which Cattell had published his research findings from Wundt's laboratory (Cattell, 1886).

Galton's approach perfectly suited the empiricist tendencies that Cattell had learned at Lafayette from Francis March. Cattell could gather data without the excess baggage of a theory or hypotheses about mental life. Galton had accepted his cousin Darwin's theory, and it did not distinguish between mental and physical life. All traits were thought to be transmitted similarly.

Cattell gradually developed an appreciation of the potential importance of differential measurement from his discussions with Galton. Although his reaction-time experiments at Leipzig had involved such measurement, he had not placed any great emphasis on the phenomenon. This would have been in keeping with Wundt's generally negative attitude toward the topic.

While Cattell was pursuing his medical studies at Cambridge, his father had managed to secure a lectureship in psychology for him at the University of Pennsylvania. So, in 1888, Cattell left medicine, Cambridge, and Galton and returned to Philadelphia to teach at both the University of Pennsylvania and Bryn Mawr College. In 1889, he was appointed professor of psychology at Pennsylvania. In the next few years, Cattell began giving guest lectures at Columbia University, commuting by train from Philadelphia. He was the first to introduce the term *mental testing*, which he did in 1890 in an article published in the British journal, *Mind* (Cattell, 1890). In that article, he suggested tests including the following: sight, hearing, taste, touch, smell, temperature, time estimation, and memory. Although he was interested in getting a testing program like Galton's started with the students at the University of Pennsylvania, he was unsuccessful.

In 1892, barely 6 years after receiving his PhD, Cattell was asked by G. Stanley Hall to join with 23 of his fellow psychologists in forming the APA, and Cattell agreed. In 1893, he was offered and accepted a full-time position at Columbia, a position he would hold until he was fired in 1917. His salary at the University of Pennsylvania had been $1,250. Columbia doubled that salary. In 1894, Cattell and James Mark Baldwin, a developmental psychologist, pooled their money and formed the Psychological Review Company. The publications of this company included *Psychological Review, Psychological Monographs, Psychological Index* (an early version of *Psychological Abstracts*), and eventually *Psychological Bulletin*.

When Cattell arrived at Columbia in 1893, he immediately began a campaign to test all incoming students with a battery of tests patterned after those he had developed with Galton (Cattell & Farrand, 1896). When the president of Columbia asked him what tests would be used for what purposes, Cattell was at a loss to answer. He simply asserted that it would be obvious after the data had been gathered what data could be used to what end (Sokal, 1982). The general assumption was that these data would permit the more accurate placement of students in fields of study. A secondary advantage would be the adaptation of curricula to meet the capacities of students. Nevertheless, following March's version of Baconian training, Cattell saw no need for a complex theory of mental life to undergird these assumptions.

During the period from 1893 to 1900, Cattell was permitted to gather these data on all incoming students. Many students were retested in subsequent years as well. During this 7-year period, Cattell proclaimed the value of mental testing to anyone who would listen and published widely describing his testing program. As president of the APA in 1895, he formed a committee to consider the issue of testing on a national scale. The object was to develop a unified testing protocol for all college students.

Although there was general enthusiasm for a testing program, there was some disagreement about the content of the tests (Sokal, 1982). Cattell pushed for simple tests of reaction time and sensory ability. Others, such as Jastrow and Baldwin, were more inclined to tests of "higher mental abilities," such as those being pursued by the French testers Binet and Simon (and eventually by Münsterberg, Scott, and Bingham, as well). This debate would continue for many years, but Cattell remained firm in his belief in the simple tests. In fact, in 1921, when he began the Psychological Corporation, Cattell was still the champion of these simple laboratory tests (Hilgard, 1987). He believed that there was more to be gained by collecting measurements on objective, standardized, and easily measured parameters. His critics likened this

Figure 2. James McKeen Cattell (1860–1944). (Courtesy of the National Library of Medicine.)

approach to that of a person who loses money on a dark street but goes to the next street to look for the money because there is a street lamp there. Philosophical differences notwithstanding, the results of Cattell's extensive testing program were eagerly awaited by the psychological community.

In 1900, after 7 years of testing, Cattell felt it was time to analyze the mass of data that resulted from his mental testing program at Columbia. Much to Cattell's horror, there were no significant correlations *among* the tests and no significant correlations *between* the tests and academic accomplishments. This meant that his unitary theory of mental mechanics was down the drain as well as his utilitarian view of the role of testing in the academic environment. For 7 years, Cattell had been telling anyone who would listen that the intercorrelations among the tests would reveal the structure of intelligence and that this structure would represent a tool for predicting academic success and for placing students. This resounding lack of significance of the correlation coef-

ficients meant that both Cattell's "theory" of intelligence and his prediction about the utility of mental testing were bankrupt. At this point,
Cattell became an embarrassment to the fledgling mental testing community, and the whole American testing movement went into a period
of decline that lasted almost a decade.

In retrospect, one can see that the testing movement was thrown
into disarray by the absence of theory more than by these disappointing
correlations. The distorted Baconian paradigm of March had failed, and
nothing had emerged from the calculations. However, this lesson was
lost on many psychometrists who would follow Cattell 40 years later.
During the 1940s and 1950s, many tests were developed for industrial
use. These tests were to be "supported" not by theory or logic but by
correlation coefficients, now called *validity coefficients*. As in the time
of Cattell, this approach led to failure. With no guiding theory, the validity
landscape was confusing, and testing, once again, went into a period of
decline, culminating in critical social commentary on the value of testing
in industry (Gross, 1962). It was primarily through the passage of legislation (i.e., Title VII of the Civil Rights Act of 1964) that the hard work
of building tests that were based on theory began.

The period from 1910 to 1917 was one of great social activism for
Cattell. He was at odds with the administration at Columbia and was
dismissed by the University in 1917 (Gruber, 1972). He had also taken
an antiwar stance that made it difficult if not impossible to join with
other applied psychologists who were developing group tests of mental
ability for soldiers and officers.

The Psychological Corporation

Cattell had always been an advocate of applied psychology, although
he had never successfully done anything applied himself. In fact, Sokal
(1990) has characterized Cattell as the advocate of *applicable* psychology rather than *applied* psychology. The Psychological Corporation[4] was
to be his opportunity to make the leap from applicable to applied. In
addition, he saw it as an opportunity to regain a position of scientific
prominence among working scientists—a position that he had not held
since he abandoned his research program in 1900. He identified mental
testing as his entrée into the applied arena. World War I had provided
an opportunity for psychology to enter the public awareness, but without
Cattell. Yerkes and Scott had done a magnificent job of using the testing
program for promotion of psychology. As a result, after the war, there
appeared to be a great demand for testing services. During the war,

---

[4]A detailed history of the development of the Psychological Corporation is presented
by Sokal (1981b).

Cattell had kept a low profile and devoted himself to his journal work. But with the war at an end, it was time to come out of hibernation.

Cattell decided to provide a mechanism by which psychological research could be funded without dependence on massive institutions such as universities or federal agencies. He would provide psychological consulting for a fee directly to users. The funds received for these services were to be split between the psychologists and the Corporation, with the corporate revenue being split further into operating costs and research funds that were at the disposal of individual psychologists. In 1919, he began discussions that would launch the Psychological Corporation. These discussions included Scott, Bingham, Yerkes, Strong, Watson, and Thorndike. In 1921, he began the corporation by selling shares at $10 per share to members of the APA. More than half of the 400 members of the APA bought one or more shares, so he must have been persuasive (Sokal, 1981b). Cattell, of course, bought the largest block of shares so that he could control the Corporation. There were to be branches throughout the country, with branch directors and associates. Although the plans looked and sounded good, the Psychological Corporation was a dismal failure under Cattell's leadership. This was in spite of a blue-ribbon board of directors including people such as Walter Van Dyke Bingham, William McDougall, G. Stanley Hall, Walter Dill Scott, Carl Seashore, Lewis Terman, E. L. Thorndike, Edward Titchener, J. B. Watson, R. Woodworth, and R. Yerkes (Cattell, 1923).

The first several years of operation were chaotic, with little direction or even communication from Cattell. Representatives of the Corporation at various universities around the country threatened to revolt and disown the organization unless Cattell showed more effective leadership. These representatives (or branch executive officers) included George Arps, Harold Burtt, Knight Dunlap, Guy Whipple, and many members of the Corporation's board of directors. It was a veritable "who's who" of American applied psychology. But Cattell's ideas for application remained rooted in his 19th-century model of anthropometric testing that had failed miserably 20 years earlier. While Scott and his colleagues had been advocating work-sample testing, Cattell continued to advocate simple sensory and reaction-time tests and continued to oppose tests of "higher mental processes" such as those measured by the Army Alpha and the Stanford–Binet.

During the first 2 years of the Corporation's existence, the total income amounted to $215 (with profits of $51), and Cattell was forced to lend money to the Corporation to pay most of the expenses. He eventually provided over $5,000 (which was never repaid). He was forced to resign as president in 1926 and was replaced by Bingham; Cattell's handpicked secretary was replaced by Paul Achilles, although even these replacements had only minimal impact on the efficacy of the Corporation. In 1929, the Corporation's *gross* income had risen to a modest $1,642! But by this time, the Depression era was beginning, and business did not improve until the late 1930s. George K. Bennett (of Mechanical Comprehension Test fame) became the director just before World War II, and things improved noticeably after that. In 1969, the Psychological Corporation reported $5 million in sales and was sold to Harcourt Brace Jovanovich. In 1979, this publisher reported $30 million in revenues for tests and testing services. (Harcourt Brace Jovanovich was bought by the General Cinema Corporation in 1991.) Thus, we might conclude that the Psychological Corporation eventually became successful, but it seems clear that this success was in spite of Cattell rather than because of him.

Immediately after the Psychological Corporation debacle, Cattell experienced one more flurry of visibility. In 1924, he was elected president of the American Association for the Advancement of Science (AAAS), and in 1929, he was chosen to chair the Ninth International Congress of Psychology. This was the first international congress to be held on American soil, so his selection was no small honor. In spite of a career full of personal difficulties and professional failures, he was still considered preeminent in the scientific community. By 1930, however, his heavy-handed use of his journals for social commentary and his radical disposition led many scientists to distrust him and submissions to *Science* began to wane (Sokal, 1990). Similarly, the AAAS began to lose influence because of Cattell's stranglehold on the organization as secretary of the executive committee. He was eventually forced out of that position (one he had held for 20 years) in 1940 (Sokal, 1990).

Cattell's Legacy

It is interesting to note that one of the most prestigious awards given by the Division of Industrial and Organizational Psychology of the APA has been named the James McKeen Cattell Award, and it is awarded yearly for excellence in research design. So, it is clear that I/O psychology identifies with Cattell. What can be recognized as the enduring contributions of Cattell to the research and practice of I/O psychology? Some influences are clear and positive. He was committed to quantification. He was also a pioneer in recognizing the importance of individual differences. These two tendencies led inevitably to a heavy dependence on psychological testing for purposes of prediction. I/O is certainly characterized by this testing zeitgeist and has been since Cattell's time.

He was also an advocate for the application of psychology to the problems of business and industry. The Psychological Corporation is clear testimony to that philosophy. No matter that it failed under his leadership—the concept was a good one. He also tried to maintain a scholarly tone to this applied work through his journals and the scholarly and academically oriented board of directors. He clearly recognized the need for maintaining a credible scientific base.

But there is a dark side to his contributions as well. He must be seen as at least partially responsible for the lack of enthusiasm for theory building and testing. His brand of empiricism is apparent in a great deal of the psychometric research up to and including the validity research of the 1950s.

In summary, it would appear that Cattell had a good view of what it would take to develop the discipline but that his downfall was execution. Like Münsterberg's, his personal attributes could be considered both his greatest strengths and his most tragic shortcomings.

Walter Van Dyke Bingham (1880–1952)

Walter Van Dyke Bingham[5] was born in 1880 in Swan Lake, Iowa. He chose the University of Kansas to begin his undergraduate education but eventually transferred to Beloit College in Wisconsin to finish his undergraduate career. While at Beloit, he took philosophy courses from Guy Tawney, who had received a degree in Wundt's laboratory in 1897 (Bingham, 1952). In 1901, with an undergraduate degree, he headed off to teach mathematics and the natural sciences to high school students, a job he held for 4 years. But he was restless and returned for a graduate education in psychology at the University of Chicago in 1905 (Bingham, 1952). It was exactly at this time that the Chicago school of functionalism was developing under John Dewey, melding with the pragmatism of William James and his Harvard colleagues and the functionalism of Thorndike, Cattell, and other luminaries at Columbia. For the functionalists, when considering a mental activity, the questions were always "What does this process do?" "What is it for?" "What good is it?" and "How does it help the individual to adjust to his or her environment?" Bingham was quite comfortable with that approach, as were many American psychologists of the time.

As mentioned earlier, it was not uncommon for students in the new American programs to travel to other universities and study under well-known philosophers and psychologists for brief periods. This was largely due to the fact that most programs were young and were not "full service" programs. Thus, there were holes in the coverage. It was in this spirit that Bingham left Chicago and traveled to Harvard in 1907. Bingham was minoring in philosophy and had identified Harvard as the philosophical center of the universe at that time. He was correct. In addition to Josiah Royce, George Santayana, and George Herbert Palmer, the

---

[5]Much of the detail regarding Bingham, Scott, and the Division of Applied Psychology can be found in the series published by Ferguson (1965) as well as his autobiography in the Murchison series (Bingham, 1952).

philosophy department at Harvard included the philosopher/psychologists Hugo Münsterberg and William James. Münsterberg had already agreed to allow Bingham to use the Harvard laboratory facilities to continue collecting his dissertation data on the perception of tones (Kuna, 1974). The nice thing about the fact that all laboratories were patterned after Wundt's was that no matter where you went, you would find the same equipment and the same environment (Blumenthal, 1975).

At Harvard, William James became Bingham's advisor and role model. This was not a relationship peculiar to Bingham. James fulfilled that role for almost all of his students. Bingham and other students would gather at James's home in front of his fireplace to discuss psychology and philosophy. In many biographies of early Harvard PhDs, you can find comments about the nights by the fireplace of William James. But Bingham was galvanized by Münsterberg and began thinking seriously about the possibility of applied psychology when he left Harvard and returned to Chicago.

In 1908, Bingham received his degree at the University of Chicago, with a dissertation related to the perception of melodies. His was the ninth PhD to be conferred by the psychology department (Ferguson, 1965). His advisor was James Angell, one of the leading functionalists of the time. In fact, in the year when Bingham began his study with Angell at Chicago, Angell was elected president of the APA. In addition, he was exposed to the research and teaching of John B. Watson, a new assistant professor at Chicago who had received his PhD, the *first* PhD in psychology at Chicago, 2 years earlier. John Dewey, another well-known member of the faculty at Chicago, had just left to join Cattell and Thorndike on the faculty at Columbia. Bingham noted that Watson was not initially a behaviorist or even a functionalist. Instead, he taught a strict form of structuralism, using Titchener's four-volume series, but he had a very difficult time introspecting and was quite frustrated by this inability. Bingham later speculated that this inability was probably a driving force in the eventual development of behaviorism by Watson (Bingham, 1952), a system that required no facility in introspection.

Bingham's first appointment after receiving his degree was at Columbia Teacher's College, assisting E. L. Thorndike (Kuna, 1974). At Columbia, Bingham continued to pursue his research in the psychology of music, but because of the influence of Thorndike and Cattell, he now added investigations in educational psychology and mental testing. He collaborated with Thorndike in gathering data that would refute Spearman's g theory. He agreed with Thorndike that there were at least three process parameters to intelligence—speed, difficulty, and range. He describes with great enthusiasm the joy of having his desk next to Thorndike's and the two of them calculating correlation coefficients at all hours of the day and night (Bingham, 1952).

In 1910, Bingham accepted a position in the department of psychology at Dartmouth College. He supervised the experimental laboratory there and instituted a student testing program patterned after the program that Cattell had envisioned at Columbia. In 1914, while attending the APA meetings in Philadelphia, he was approached by the president of the relatively new Carnegie Institute of Technology. He asked if Bingham would please come for a site visit and advise him with respect to what psychology could do for the new Institute. Bingham accepted the challenge and visited Carnegie. After some observation and interviewing, he suggested that psychology could help the students to understand and influence people. He further suggested that psychology could help the students make reasonable career choices (much as his research program was attempting at Dartmouth). Finally, he suggested that psychology could help to identify who should be a student in the first place (Bingham, 1952).

After submitting his report, Bingham was offered the job of establishing and directing a division of Carnegie that would accomplish these objectives, and he was given a free hand to staff that division and hire consultants. It was to be called the Division of Applied Psychology and would include the following units: the Bureau of Mental Tests, the Department for Training Teachers, and the Department of Psychology and Education. The bureaus that actually evolved were somewhat different than originally anticipated, but they all dealt with applied psychology in one way or another. The major difference was that the original concept directed most of the Division's efforts inward, toward students. What actually came to pass was more clearly directed outward, toward businesses and government agencies.

Bingham's first hires were Guy Whipple, Raymond Dodge, L. L. Thurstone, and J. B. Miner. At the time, Thurstone had an engineering degree and had worked with Thomas Edison in his laboratory in Menlo Park, New Jersey. Shortly after starting up the Division, Bingham was approached by a group of businessmen who asked if he could help in the training of sales personnel. He agreed to undertake such a project but felt that he needed to know more about sales before beginning to train sales personnel. He began the Bureau of Salesmanship Research and was promised $500 from each of 30 companies each year for a total of 5 years. In today's dollars, that $75,000 is the equivalent of a grant for $750,000. Not bad for an applied subdiscipline that had only been in existence for 3 to 5 years. As soon as the Bureau was formed, Bingham persuaded Northwestern University to loan Carnegie the services of Walter Dill Scott, and Scott was named the first professor of applied psychology in the country. Bingham was particularly interested in Scott because he was familiar with Scott's early work in advertising and his more recent spin-off research in the selection of sales personnel.

Not long after the Bureau of Salesmanship Research was formed, another group of businessmen approached Bingham to begin a companion bureau for retail training. As before, they supplied a substantial grant to support this new bureau. In fact, during the 9-year period when the Division of Applied Psychology at Carnegie flourished, Bingham had hardly enough time to count the money that flowed in for support. Over the time that the Division of Applied Psychology was in operation, many famous I/O psychologists were on the employment roster. In addition to those already mentioned, the list included Marion Bills, Max Freyd, Beardsley Ruml, Richard Uhrbrock, and Clarence Yoakum.

Bingham and Scott at War

When war[6] was declared, Bingham, Scott, and virtually everyone else in the Division of Applied Psychology offered their services to the U.S. Army for the duration of the war. Yerkes was the president of the APA and saw the war as an opportunity for psychology to secure a foothold with the federal government. In that spirit, he immediately mobilized the APA Council and leading figures in applied psychology to develop a testing program (Ferguson, 1965).

Scott attended the first meeting of the group but stormed out after several hours of heated discussion. Scott's position was that psychologists should do whatever they could to help the United States win the war and should forget about trying to use the war to the advantage of the profession. Another point of contention was that Yerkes made it clear that his plan was to test every recruit individually using a test he had developed for the "feeble minded" in psychiatric hospitals. Scott was more realistic and knew that only a group test would work. He suggested the revision of the Binet test that was currently being prepared by Terman and his colleagues in California. A final area of disagreement related to the branch of the service that would be the home for this psychological effort. Yerkes was closer to medicine and biology, and he wanted to be in the Surgeon General's office. Scott was opposed to this. He felt that psychology would become subordinate to medicine if they reported to the Surgeon General (Ferguson, 1965). He was more inclined toward The Adjutant General's office. The Adjutant General controlled administration, including personnel.

Even though Bingham was very close to Scott personally and professionally, he stayed at the meeting and continued to work with Yerkes throughout the war. Scott set off to carve out his own niche in the war effort. Yerkes got his wish and reported to the Surgeon General's office. Scott got his wish and was placed in The Adjutant General's office, concerning himself with placement rather than selection or classification. Scott had a harder time of securing his position than Yerkes, however. Over a period of 3 months, Scott traveled to various army camps

---

[6]Yerkes (1921) has provided voluminous detail regarding the actual activities of the mental testers during World War I.

doing dog and pony shows to convince camp commanders to permit him to take part in the placement activities. After several false starts and disastrous encounters with military commanders, he prevailed. By August 1917, both Scott and Yerkes had set up shop and were beginning to assemble staffs. Bingham remained a confidant of both men, often acting as an intermediary between them. Yerkes and Scott were very careful to carve out nonoverlapping areas, and in all communications they were civil and supportive of the other's effort. Each encouraged the army to pay close attention to the work of the other person. They took pains to point out the complementary nature of their efforts. But, at a personal level, they seldom communicated and each thoroughly disliked the other.

The work of Yerkes's group was to perform a type of personnel placement. They were to separate recruits into four classes: those who could be assigned to combat, those who could be assigned only to labor battalions, those who could be assigned to a "developmental" unit in which additional training was provided before assignment to a combat unit, and those who could not be used in any capacity and were to be discharged. Scott's efforts were devoted to the placement of individuals who "passed" Yerkes's tests. In addition, Scott was concerned with identifying talent that could be used in creating noncommissioned officers as well as with assessing the future potential of commissioned officers for higher ranks. From a personnel perspective, this bifurcation of effort made good sense, but that was accidental to the development of these dual efforts. They worked separately because they could not agree, either philosophically or operationally. In this case, the incompatibility probably resulted in greater overall progress.

Bingham's Postwar Years

Bingham left the army with the rank of lieutenant colonel and returned to Carnegie Institute. But, by 1924, the Carnegie dynasty had ended, and he moved to New York City to become head of the Personnel Research Federation (Hilgard, 1987), and in 1926, the head of the Psychological Corporation. Like Münsterberg and Cattell, Bingham felt strongly that the public needed to be exposed to as much psychology as they could handle. One social commentator of the time wryly noted that the country was experiencing an "outbreak of psychology" (Kuna, 1974, p. 78). If that was true, people such as Bingham, Scott, Münsterberg, Cattell, Yerkes, and Thorndike were the carriers of the disease. In that spirit, in 1930, Bingham launched a radio series titled "Psychology Today" that consisted of Saturday morning broadcasts for CBS on topics associated with the application of psychology. The program ran for almost 20 years and included talks by James Angell, Walter Miles, Gardner Murphy, Arnold Gesell, Leta Hollingworth, John B. Watson, Floyd Allport, E. L. Thorndike,

Carl Seashore, Elton Mayo, and Morris Viteles, among others. Bingham appeared on the show often. A home-study guide in the form of a book accompanied these radio programs (Bingham, 1932).

After the war ended, Scott left Carnegie to form the Scott Company, the first psychological consulting firm to appear. Although Bingham was affiliated with the Scott Company, he returned to Carnegie on a part-time basis. The rest of his time was devoted to chairing the new psychology section of the National Research Council, a section that Yerkes had initiated several years before. During the next 2 years, Bingham commuted frequently between Washington, DC, and Pittsburgh.

From 1926 to 1940, Bingham devoted his efforts toward achieving recognition and respectability for I/O psychology. He did this through speeches, journal articles, popular press and magazine articles, and radio interviews. During this period, he was *the* spokesperson for the field. This is how it looked at the end of that period. Münsterberg was dead, Scott was devoting his efforts to university administration, Cattell had largely withdrawn to journal editing duties, Yerkes was back with his animals, and the second generation of applied psychologists such as Viteles and Kornhauser had not yet achieved national prominence.

In 1940, shortly before the United States entered the war against the Axis powers, the National Research Council was asked to create a committee to advise The Adjutant General of the U.S. Army on the classi-

Figure 3. Walter Van Dyke Bingham (1880–1952). (Courtesy of the Carnegie Mellon University Archives.)

fication of personnel. Bingham was appointed chairman of that committee. Other committee members included C. Shartle, C. Brigham (of World War I notoriety), H. Garrett, and L. L. Thurstone.

By August, Bingham had accepted a full-time position in the war department and had the title of Chief Psychologist. There was quite a difference between the two wars. In World War I, the applied psychologists practically begged to be permitted to join in the war effort. In World War II, they were sought out immediately, and over 1,300 psychologists were involved in the effort and tested over 10,000,000 recruits and officers. Bingham remained Chief Psychologist for 7 years and then became an advisor and consultant to The Adjutant General and the general staff of the war department. Bingham died at the age of 71 on July 7, 1952.

Bingham's Legacy

Bingham's contributions to the development of I/O psychology are in the areas of application and promotion. It would seem that the most impressive programmatic effort toward the application of psychological principles to the problems of business and industry is represented by the Division of Applied Psychology at Carnegie. This unit was almost exclusively the brainchild of Bingham. It was through the early efforts of Bingham in forming that unit and developing its charter and procedures that Scott was able to add coherence to his many practical exercises and applications. The success of this unit before the war, plus the practice gained in classifying soldiers, laid the groundwork for a renewed interest in psychology and testing after the war.

From 1925 until his death, Bingham was a major spokesperson for I/O psychology. He had credibility by virtue of both training and experience, and he was centrally concerned with public policy as it could be affected by the practice of I/O psychology. In that respect, he was similar to both Münsterberg and Cattell. Where he differed from those two individuals, however, was in terms of impact on students. Because of the structure and charter of the Carnegie Institute and the Division of Applied Psychology, there was little or no formal instruction nor was there a legitimate degree program. As a result, there is no clear family tree of psychologists that has Bingham at its base. This makes his reputation and accomplishments all the more impressive as there were no students to carry his message.

Walter Dill Scott (1869–1955)

Walter Dill Scott was born in Cooksville, Indiana, in 1869. When he graduated from Northwestern in 1895, he hoped to become a missionary

Figure 4. Walter Dill Scott (1869–1955). (Courtesy of the Northwestern University Archives.)

and receive a call to go to the Far East (Jacobson, 1951). After 3 years of training at McCormick's Theological Seminary, a Presbyterian training facility, he awaited a call for a station in China. The call never came. Greatly disappointed, he traveled to Leipzig to study psychology with Wilhelm Wundt and received his PhD in 1900 (Benjamin, Durkin, Link, Vestal, & Accord, 1992). His dissertation was one of the few nonexperimental dissertations to be completed under Wundt. It was essentially a philosophy dissertation titled "The Psychology of Impulses—Historically and Critically Considered." Scott was always interested in motivation. At Leipzig, he became involved in the study of suggestion and persuasion. It was this work that would form the foundation for his later application in advertising and consumer psychology.

After receiving his degree, Scott stopped at Cornell University to get some instruction from Titchener on how to establish a psychological laboratory. He stayed with Titchener for a year and then returned to Chicago and assumed a position at Northwestern as an assistant professor of psychology and pedagogy. Titchener eventually repudiated Scott for applying psychological principles in industry.

It was in this initial period of adjustment at Northwestern that Scott became interested in applied psychology. A group of Chicago businessmen had failed to get either Hugo Münsterberg or E. L. Thorndike interested in applying psychological principles to advertising. The businessmen finally turned to their own backyard and asked Scott for help. At first, Scott was reluctant. Like Münsterberg, he was afraid that his career would suffer from any association with application and, at the time, this was a reasonable fear. But Scott did see this as an excellent opportunity to pursue his interest in attention, suggestion, and persuasion, so he agreed to their proposition but told none of his academic colleagues about the activity (Kuna, 1974).

His entry into the psychology of advertising was modest. He agreed to give a speech at the Agate Club, a businessman's club in Chicago composed primarily of those in publishing. Scott's speech was well accepted and an offer was made to begin a magazine to highlight his thoughts (Kuna, 1976). He agreed to prepare a column each month for the magazine on the topic of psychology and advertising. He was paid $250 for the project. The magazine was called *Mahin's Magazine*, named after the publisher, John Lee Mahin. Scott published 33 different popular articles on the topic of advertising over a period of 8 years.

As a result of his concern for his scholarly reputation, Scott led a double life for some period. He was both a traditional academic psychologist and a pioneer in the field of advertising psychology. As an academic, he taught the usual courses in experimental psychology and pedagogy. One of his students was Edwin G. Booz, who was to later found the general management consulting company of Booz, Allen and Hamilton. From 1901 to 1910, Scott's name was prominent in the business community as a result of his contributions to advertising. His success in the more traditional academic arena was somewhat more modest, although he did regularly write a type of annual review chapter on the topic of "suggestion" for the *Psychological Review* from 1906 to 1910.

The columns that appeared in *Mahin's Magazine* were so well received that Scott collected 14 of them into book form. This book, titled *The Theory of Advertising*, appeared in 1903 and may have been the first book dedicated to the application of psychological principles to business activities. In 1908, he published a second book titled *The Psychology of Advertising*, which included an additional 19 articles. By the time this second book appeared, his first book had sold over 10,000 copies. The publication of essays as bound volumes was common at this time. Münsterberg's first several books, including one of his most famous, *On the Witness Stand* (1980), were similarly constructed.

It was in 1908 that Scott accepted a consulting contract with the American Tobacco Company to select salesmen. This foray into applied psychology predated Münsterberg's work in personnel selection by at least 4 years. By 1910, the application of psychological principles to real-world problems was respectable, and articles in advertising were published by Robert Yerkes and E. K. Strong. By now, Scott had begun to turn to other problems of business, much as Münsterberg was doing on his sabbatical in Germany that year. Simultaneously, Scott and Münsterberg published basic texts in industrial psychology, Scott's in English and Münsterberg's in German. Münsterberg's would not be translated until 1913, under the title *Psychology and Industrial Efficiency*. Scott's book was called *Increasing Human Efficiency in Business* (1910) and was, as before, a collection of essaylike articles that had already appeared in a popular business magazine called *Systems*. The two books were very different in structure. Münsterberg began his book with a recitation of what had been discovered about sensation, perception, and learning in the laboratory. It represented a primer in psychology. Having accomplished this basic education, Münsterberg then invited the reader to consider the application of these principles. Scott's book presented none of this basic psychology but focused immediately on application. It is not hard to see which would have appealed more to business leaders.

Scott's book consisted of a series of aphorisms or inspirational exhortations that were based on his interviews of successful business leaders. It was strong on stories and vignettes but weak on theory or research. Scott also tended to idealize high achievers. He was particularly impressed with a 70-year-old man named Edward Payson Weston who claimed to have walked from New York to San Francisco in 104 days, without halt or rest (Scott, 1910, p. 13). Scott concluded that most workers were capable of much more than they realized. Like Bingham, Cattell, and Münsterberg, Scott was most interested in the upper end of the talent register.

Scott also introduced the notion of incentive and piece-rate pay as a motivating influence. This was based on combining the work of Thorndike on the law of effect with the emerging notions of John B. Watson on behaviorist models of action. Scott was also convinced that the climate or culture of an organization was central to efficiency and motivation. He called it an "atmosphere of efficiency" (Scott, 1910). As a motivation theorist, Scott believed firmly in instincts and suggested that incentive pay could be used to satisfy the instincts of self-preservation, social distinction, and hoarding (Scott, 1910). Scott was in good company with respect to instincts. Ordway Tead, Henry Tipper, E. L. Thorndike, and other notables of the period were firmly in the instinct camp. Scott's interest in instincts could have been easily predicted from his dissertation topic in the area of "impulses" (Scott, 1900). He also wrote extensively on the role of worker attitudes on productivity, a good 20 years before Elton Mayo made similar suggestions on the basis of the Hawthorne experiments. Consider the following proposition from his 1910 book: "Success or failure in business is caused more by mental attitude even than by mental capacities" (p. 134).

Scott often blended his interest in application with a principle derived from laboratory research to make a concrete suggestion. Consider the following suggestion that ties rewards, punishments, and feedback to the principle of conditioning or association:

If for any reason, a member of the organization deserves or requires the executive's personal attention, his birthday may be chosen as the date of the interview. Then whether the man merits an advance for extra good work or needs help to correct a temporary slump in efficiency, the reward or appeal takes on added meaning because it coincides with a turning point in his life. (1910, pp. 146–147)

Finally, consider Scott's primitive approach to job enrichment. In speaking of the development of loyalty in an employee Scott observes: "Few things so stimulate a boy as the feeling that he is responsible for a certain task, that he is expressing himself in it, and that he is creating something worthwhile" (1910, p. 193).

Note that Scott is saying this at a time when scientific management is sweeping the domestic and international scenes. The scientific management systems of Taylor (1911) left little room for expression or creation or responsibility. The worker was to follow the instructions of the supervisor without question or modification. Although Scott did not directly oppose scientific management, he could not have been very enthusiastic about its principles because they flew in the face of his beliefs about the effects of attitudes, instincts, climate, and motivation.

In 1909, Scott was appointed a professor of advertising in the School of Commerce at Northwestern. In 1912, he received a joint appointment of professor of psychology in both the College of Liberal Arts and the School of Commerce.

In 1916, he was given leave by Northwestern to direct the Bureau for Salesmanship Research at Carnegie Institute under Walter Van Dyke Bingham and was appointed a professor of applied psychology—the first appointment of that title to be made anywhere. At this point, Scott and Bingham were the two most prominent industrial psychologists in the country. In the early part of the year, Münsterberg was keeping a low profile because of the war in Europe. By the end of the year, Münsterberg was dead.

Scott's interest in industrial psychology was a natural progression from his work in advertising, and it all related to his early interest in attention, persuasion, and suggestion. He began by studying advertising and how ads influence buying behavior. He then moved on to the study of persuasion by sales personnel. He was interested in how they influence potential customers. From there, it was a simple step to considering the characteristics of successful sales personnel and finally to directing the Bureau of Salesmanship Research. Finally, he became interested in selection in the broadest sense, regardless of the particular occupation in question.

In the short period between his arrival at Carnegie in 1916 and his departure for the army testing project in 1917, Scott developed the following devices to be used in the selection of sales personnel: a model application blank; a standardized letter to former employers; a set of interviewer's guides and record blanks; and a series of tests to measure an applicant's "intelligence, alertness, carefulness, imagination, resourcefulness, and verbal facility." It was clear where Scott stood with respect to the construct of intelligence. He believed it to be multidimensional, as did Thorndike, and he favored the higher mental processes over the simple measures of Cattell. As indicated in the discussion of Bingham, the next 3 years of Scott's life were eventful and completely consumed by the testing of army recruits.

Postwar Years

In 1919, Scott was elected President of the APA. He had received considerable visibility from his work with the armed forces. In the same year, the Scott Company, a consulting firm devoted to the application of psychology to industry, was formed and located in Philadelphia. It was quite successful, receiving many contracts from large and small organizations, and had a stellar list of associates, including Walter Van Dyke Bingham, James Angell, John B. Watson, E. L. Thorndike, and, as surprising as it might seem, even Robert Yerkes. The Company had an interesting and somewhat unusual philosophy. It was determined to transfer technology to the client. Company associates believed that it was inappropriate, over the long term, to have outside consultants do the personnel work of an organization. There was another interesting aspect to the Scott associates. They were well respected by both management and labor and were often called on to mediate labor disputes.

Scott's association with the consulting company was short lived, however. In 1920, he agreed to become president of Northwestern University. He remained in that position until his retirement in 1939. Virtually all of his activity henceforth was administrative. He excelled in representing the University to the outside world and was one of the best fund-raisers that Northwestern had ever known.

As World War II approached, Scott once again offered to assist the U.S. Army in the selection and classification of men. But this time, and in contrast to the army's response to Bingham, Scott received a polite refusal. Perhaps it was an issue of timing. Scott recognized the likely need for classification in 1938, 3 years before the United States entered the war, and made his offer then. But Bingham was called on in 1940, immediately before the declaration of war. Scott did little else of importance to I/O psychology after 1940, with the exception of several additional revisions of his famous text in personnel psychology, written with Clothier (Scott & Clothier, 1923; Scott, Clothier, & Mathewson, 1931; Scott, Clothier, Mathewson, & Spriegel, 1941). Scott died in 1955 at the age of 86.

Scott's Legacy

Like Bingham, Scott had no students to sing his praises. Furthermore, he left the discipline for a career in administration in 1920, thus his contribution is somewhat truncated. Nevertheless, his early work in advertising is widely recognized as the first programmatic attempt to apply psychology to the problems of business and industry. His work at Carnegie in 1916 and during the war, from 1917 to 1919, was both prolific and insightful. He was the first to develop many of the types of instruments that are used today, including interview formats, standardized tests, application blanks, and performance rating forms. And, unlike Cattell, he strongly favored the development of field-based measures of complex mental abilities. Where Münsterberg and Cattell dealt in ideas and possibilities, Scott traded in realities.

Links Among the Founders

As I have indicated in the earlier sections of this chapter, there were substantial interactions among the figures who have been considered. The strongest links were between Scott and Bingham. They were contemporaries despite having been trained in very different environments—Scott in the German tradition with Wundt and Bingham in the new American system with Angell. They collaborated on virtually everything from 1916 until 1920. And they conceptualized the problems of industry virtually identically, both before they met and after they parted.

Cattell had links to everyone by virtue of his formal positions in the scientific community, but he was close to no one (with the possible exception of Thorndike). Cattell traded lecture visits with Münsterberg frequently, and each gave lecture programs at the other's university once each year or so. In addition, they corresponded regularly, and each sought the other's advice on personal and professional issues. Cattell worked with Bingham briefly when Bingham was at Columbia before his departure for Dartmouth. Cattell's interactions with Scott were more limited and dealt with APA and university business.

Bingham had spent a year with Münsterberg (and James) and was greatly influenced by that visit. Nevertheless, his relationship with Münsterberg was formal rather than friendly. They corresponded occasionally. Bingham sought the opinion of Münsterberg, but that was not reciprocal. The relationship between Scott and Münsterberg was almost the reverse. Münsterberg contacted Scott frequently by mail and offered (unsolicited) advice. Scott was polite but distant in his responses.

It is interesting to note that although it was common to ridicule Münsterberg in the years before his death, he was never treated that way by any of the three other figures considered in this chapter. They were uniformly respectful and sympathetic. Even Scott was deferential (although detached) in his dealings with Münsterberg. In fact, little can be found that would indicate any strong enmities among them. Each seemed to recognize and value the positive attributes of the others without being unduly distracted by any of their negative characteristics.

It might be illuminating to consider the commonalities among these figures. First, all but Münsterberg valued quantification, measurement, and statistical analysis. In addition, they were all utilitarian, pragmatic, and functional in their orientation. They all believed fervently in psychology and in its application. They were all tireless promoters and, with the exception of Cattell, had the social skills necessary to capture the opportunities to present their wares. All, including Münsterberg, abandoned research relatively quickly and expended their efforts in proselytizing and promotion. They all maintained ties with various national scientific and professional organizations, most notably the APA, the AAAS, and the National Research Council.

Some might claim that they all allowed their confidence in psychology as an applicable science to outrun their accomplishments. As a result, they all seemed to promise more than they could deliver. It is arguable whether this helped or hurt the field. I am inclined to think it hurt—at least internally, with respect to other subdisciplines. All four demonstrated a greater interest in the standard deviation of a distribution of scores than the mean of that distribution.

On the personal level, they all held strong convictions, often perhaps wrong, but nevertheless strongly held. They were all capable of both intrigue and revolution, although Bingham was more likely to accept conflict only as a last resort. They also shared the characteristic of resilience. Each experienced major setbacks but overcame them.

All had an involvement with organized labor. Bingham and Scott were known as mediators during the brief life of the Scott Company. Cattell communicated with Gompers frequently about the possibilities of mental testing to help the worker. Münsterberg actually collaborated with Gompers in 1912 on a job satisfaction questionnaire.

Finally, each would be characterized as "dynastic" in orientation. They had an eye on history and fully expected to be identified as a driving force in the area of applied psychology. In that sense, they saw themselves as competing with each other for a place in history. It was most likely that sense of competition that propelled the discipline to the point at which Viteles discovered and codified it in his 1932 book.

It is interesting to speculate what might have occurred had Münsterberg lived. Certainly, none of the other three were his equal in political intrigue, self-advancement, or scientific promotion. He would have remained firmly in control of the field. It is also likely that, in this leadership role, Münsterberg would have managed to get subcabinet status for industrial psychology. He would have used a combination of the behavioral wing of the National Research Council, firmly under the control of Yerkes, and the Departments of the Army and Labor to accomplish that. He would have controlled the *Journal of Applied Psychology* from behind the scenes, and he would have been a driving force at the Psychological Corporation. By 1930, however, his star would have declined once again. The Depression would have robbed him of his platform—testing. His appreciation of motivation was undeveloped and simplistic. Furthermore, as Germany rearmed, he would have again protested that the German people were peace loving and simply protecting their borders. By 1936, he would have been in disrepute once again.

The fact is that industrial psychology did not develop as it might have. There was little of the theoretical or philosophical that emerged after the field's hour in the sunlight. The legacy was one of social and biological Darwinism, a glorification of the upper end of the talent distribution, a triumph of administrative and operational procedures, and a grab bag of atheoretical devices. This legacy lasted well into the 1960s and haunts us today.

Although there are others who were active from 1900 to 1920 and deserve attention as well—Paterson, Poffenberger, Hollingworth, Strong— they were dwarfs compared with the giants considered here. Along with Viteles, Kornhauser, Thurstone, and others, they were to lead the discipline into the pre-World War II period. Their roles and influences must be left for another time and another chapter.

Discussion

History does not need justification. It is enough to educate, illuminate, or clarify past events. Nevertheless, the reader often expects more. Are there lessons that could be learned? Are there mistakes that need not be repeated? Are there fruitful avenues that, having been introduced, were overlooked? In the present case, there are some current issues that might bear such examination. There are three issues, in particular, that I will consider: (a) the glorification of "talent," (b) the overstatement of value, and (c) the battle between science and practice.

Glorification of Talent

I/O psychologists have been portrayed as the "servants of power" (Baritz, 1960). The charge is that because management (or the interests of management) most often supplies the capital for practice or research by I/O psychologists, these psychologists are concerned only with issues that are of interest to management. Münsterberg was an unabashed servant of power. He was interested in selection for the purpose of improving efficiency. Cattell was interested in selecting the "best" students for Columbia. His major focus from 1900 to 1930 was in identifying "eminent" scientists. Bingham and Scott were devoted to winning the war and finding the best soldiers and officers to accomplish that goal. The point is that all of these central figures were concentrating on the "talented" end of the ability continuum. From their work, we learned little about the development of talent, about the design of work for the less talented, or even about the limits to talent—namely, those instances when talent might be counterproductive. They were empiricists and Darwinists (and Cattell and Yerkes were eugenicists). Bingham was content to leave the less talented or ill-adjusted to the social workers (M. T. Bingham, 1953).

There are two critical elements to modern Darwinism—random variation and natural selection. Personnel testing is directed toward illuminating "relevant" aspects of random variation (among applicants). Employers tend to control the natural selection mechanism by specifying work conditions, job duties, and so on. It is not at all clear that our founders gave that much thought. Beginning with Münsterberg, they accepted on faith the right of management to govern and determine those conditions. Although this might have been great for General Motors, it was not necessarily conducive to a complete statement of a psychology of work.

For almost 30 years, critics of psychological testing have argued that the standardized psychological test may do more harm than good by stigmatizing the less-than-talented test taker. Today's employers, like the employers 50 years ago, want the best possible employee. The assumption is made that the best possible employee is the person scoring the highest. It is fair to say that in many instances this is a correct assumption. Nevertheless, as psychologists, we need to know more about the 95% of the applicants who are not hired, the trainees below the 75th percentile, and the individuals who don't fit a management-defined environment.

In the past 30 years, I/O psychology has been bullied into considering the rest of the talent continuum. In particular, legislation such as the Civil Rights Act, the Age Discrimination in Employment Act, and more recently, the Americans With Disabilities Act, have forced us to demonstrate the relevance of talent. Many applied psychologists have resisted this pressure, citing orthodoxies rooted in the psychometric models of Cattell, Thurstone, Spearman, and similar practitioners of differential psychology. It might be wise to look at the efforts of those early psychometricians as attempts to establish a paradigm to fill a void. It may be time for a paradigm shift. It may be time to consider more than the top 5% of the talent continuum.

Overstatement of Value

It is common to look at the testing movement as a linear progression of thought and practice. Many psychometricians take comfort in the myth that the testing movement, begun with the first halting steps of Cattell, has increased in breadth and depth from its earliest days. This is certainly not the case. Testing went into a deep depression after the failure of Cattell's Columbia initiative. This depression was likely the result of the fact that Cattell oversold the value of the process. Like Münsterberg, he proclaimed that testing would be the salvation of 20th-century society. Then, he failed to do what he promised, and the public noticed.

It was not until Yerkes seized the moment in 1917 that testing was taken seriously again. Although well over 1 million recruits and officers were tested, the testing effort was trivial in terms of the conduct of the war. It came too late and produced too little of value. In spite of that, Yerkes was able to put the appropriate "spin" on the war effort, and industry was once again ready to follow the piper. And again, there was little of substance delivered by the testers. Granted, the environment was wrong because the economy was faltering after the war and layoffs began to exceed hires. But also, there was no convincing demonstration of the value of testing. In fact, some movements, such as scientific management and neonatal behaviorism, thumbed their noses at differential psychology and demonstrated the value of environmental control. For whatever reasons, testing went into decline again.

This cycle was repeated during and after World War II. Testing was introduced for placement, and new tests were developed. The testing momentum was carried into the postwar economy, promises were made, and promises were broken. In the early 1960s, social critics (followed by legislators) put the brakes on testing again. We have seen at least three periods of the growth and decline of testing. Each of the declines has been preceded by a substantial overstatement of the contribution of testing to the economic welfare of the country, in general, and individual employers, in particular. In the past decade, utility theory has purported to show, once again, the substantial contribution of differential psychology to industrial efficiency. Once again, we may be overselling the product. It appears that in the past, the consumer has cooled to the value of testing because promises could not be kept. A lesson we might learn from this would be to try to be more realistic about potential gains from testing, or better yet, undersell rather than oversell the product.

Science Versus Practice

In many areas of psychology, there has been a widening gap between the scientist and the practitioner. The gap is apparent in clinical psychology and is becoming more apparent in I/O psychology. The founders of I/O psychology understood the value of research and the academy. In fact, it is likely that they were able to have the impact that they did by virtue of maintaining their connections with basic research. It was the second generation of I/O psychologists (Viteles, Kornhauser, etc.) who might have driven the first wedge between science and practice. Viteles and his colleagues made no distinction between "theory" and "armchair theory." There was good reason for this because most of what passed for early theory was nothing more than common sense or magical thinking. One reason for this was the dearth of empirical and objective data. Remember that the discipline had been formed by the structuralists with their dependence on introspection. Thus, in 1930, there were few reasonable theories of work of any kind.

This was the legacy of the second-generation I/O psychologist—a dust bowl empiricist's view of the world. Fortunately, that has changed. I/O psychologists are now providing conceptual and theoretical leadership in research areas such as stress, motivation, skill acquisition, and environmental design. Nevertheless, it is important to remember that the connection between science and practice is critical. Without it, we are at the mercy of data sets of unknown properties. For the first generation of I/O psychologists, there was neither data nor theory, and they provided data. The second generation accepted data collection and analysis as the paradigm. Later generations, however, have recognized the practicality of good theory. For continued growth of the subdiscipline, this link must be maintained and enhanced. This is an area in which we are well advised to depart from our founding fathers.

References

Baritz, L. (1960). *The servants of power*. Middletown, CT: Wesleyan University Press.

Benjamin, L., Durkin, M., Link, M., Vestal, M., & Accord, J. (1992). Wundt's American doctoral students. *American Psychologist, 47*, 123–131.

Bingham, M. T. (1953). *Tribute to Walter Van Dyke Bingham*. Portland, ME: National Audubon Society.

Bingham, W. V. (1932). *Psychology today: Lectures and study manual*. Chicago: University of Chicago Press.

Bingham, W. V. (1952). In C. Murchison (Ed.), *Psychology in autobiography* (p. 1–26). Worcester, MA: Clark University Press.

Blumenthal, A. L. (1975). A re-appraisal of Wilhelm Wundt. *American Psychologist, 30*, 1081–1088.

Cattell, J. M. (1886). The time taken up by cerebral operations. *Mind 2*, 220–242.

Cattell, J. M. (1890). Mental tests and measurements. *Mind, 15*, 373–381.

Cattell, J. M. (1923). The Psychological Corporation. In C. King (Ed.), *Psychology and business: The annals* (Vol. CX, pp. 165–171). New York: New York Academy of Sciences.

Cattell, J. M., & Farrand, L. (1896). Physical and mental measurement of the students of Columbia University. *Psychological Review, 3*, 618–648.
Cory, D. (1955). *The letters of George Santayana.* New York: Scribner.
Ferguson, L. (1965). *The heritage of industrial psychology.* Hartford, CT: Finlay Press.
Gross, M. L. (1962). *The brain watchers.* New York: Random House.
Gruber, C. (1972). Academic freedom at Columbia University, 1917–1918: The case of James McKeen Cattell. *AAUP Bulletin, 58*, 297–305.
Hale, M. (1980). *Human science and social order.* Philadelphia: Temple University Press.
Hilgard, E. R. (1987). *Psychology in America: A historical survey.* New York: Harcourt Brace Jovanovich.
Jacobson, J. Z. (1951). *Scott of Northwestern.* Chicago: Louis Mariano.
Katzell, R. A., & Austin, J. T. (1992). From then to now: The development of industrial and organizational psychology in the United States. *Journal of Applied Psychology, 7*, 803–835.
Keller, P. (1979). *States of belonging: German–American intellectuals and the first world war.* Cambridge, MA: Harvard University Press.
Kuna, D. P. (1974). *The psychology of advertising.* Unpublished doctoral dissertation, University of New Hampshire, Durham.
Kuna, D. P. (1976). *The psychology of advertising: 1896–1916.* Ann Arbor, MI: Xerox University Microfilms.
Landy, F. J. (1992). Hugo Münsterberg: Victim or visionary? *Journal of Applied Psychology, 77*, 787–802.
Münsterberg, H. (1908). *On the witness stand.* New York: Doubleday and Page.
Münsterberg, H. (1909a). *Eternal values.* Boston: Houghton Mifflin.
Münsterberg, H. (1909b). *Psychotherapy.* New York: Moffat, Yard.
Münsterberg, H. (1913). *Psychology and industrial efficiency.* Boston: Houghton Mifflin.
Münsterberg Papers. Boston: Boston Public Library, Rare Books Room.
Ross, D. (1972). *G. Stanley Hall: The psychologist as prophet.* Chicago: University of Chicago Press.
Ross, D. (1973). James McKeen Cattell. In E. T. James (Ed.), *Dictionary of American biography* (Supplement 3, pp. 1941–1945). New York: Scribner.
Scott, W. D. (1900). *Die psychologie der triebe.* Unpublished doctoral dissertation, University of Leipzig, Germany.
Scott, W. D. (1903). *The theory of advertising.* Boston: Small, Maynard.
Scott, W. D. (1908). *The psychology of advertising.* Boston: Small, Maynard.
Scott, W. D. (1910). *Increasing human efficiency in business.* Chicago: The System Company.
Scott, W. D., & Clothier, R. C. (1923). *Personnel management.* New York: A. W. Shaw.
Scott, W. D., Clothier, R. C., & Mathewson, S. B. (1931). *Personnel management.* New York: McGraw-Hill.
Scott, W. D., Clothier, R. C., Mathewson, S. B., & Spriegel, W. R. (1941). *Personnel management.* New York: McGraw-Hill.
Sokal, M. M. (Ed.). (1981a). *An education in psychology: James McKeen Cattell's journal and letters from Germany and England, 1880–1888.* Cambridge, MA: MIT Press.

Sokal, M. M. (1981b). The origins of the Psychological Corporation. *Journal of the History of the Behavioral Sciences, 17*, 54–67.

Sokal, M. M. (1982). James McKeen Cattell and the failure of anthropometric mental testing: 1890–1901. In Woodward & Ash (Eds.), *The problematic science: Psychology in nineteenth century thought*. New York: Praeger.

Sokal, M. M. (1984a). James McKeen Cattell and American psychology in the 1920s. In J. Brozek (Ed.), *Explorations in the history of psychology in the United States*. Lewisburg, PA: Bucknell University Press.

Sokal, M. M. (Ed.). (1984b). *Psychological testing and American society*. New Brunswick, NJ: Rutgers University Press.

Sokal, M. M. (1990). Lifespan developmental psychology and the history of science. In M. M. Sokal (Ed.), *Beyond history of science: Essays in honor of Robert E. Schofield*. Bethlehem, PA: Lehigh University Press.

Taylor, F. W. (1911). *Principles of scientific management*. New York: Harper & Row.

Viteles, M. S. (1932). *Industrial psychology*. New York: Norton.

Yerkes, R. M. (Ed.). (1921). *Memoirs of the National Academy of Sciences* (Vol. XV). Washington, DC: U. S. Government Printing Office.

KURT SALZINGER

THE EXPERIMENTAL APPROACH TO PSYCHOPATHOLOGY

K urt Salzinger received his PhD in experimental psychology from Columbia University in 1954. He is currently professor of psychology and director of the Graduate Program in Clinical and School Psychology at Hofstra University. He was principal research scientist at the New York State Psychiatric Institute until 1991 and professor of psychology at the Polytechnic University until this year. During two summers, he worked as a visiting investigator at the Jackson Laboratories in Bar Harbor, Maine; he also served as a program officer at the National Science Foundation from 1979 to 1981, setting up a program in applied experimental psychology.

He has been active in a number of professional organizations, having served as president of the New York Academy of Sciences, president of the Division for the Experimental Analysis of Behavior in the American Psychological Association (APA), and chair of the board of the Cambridge Center for Behavioral Studies. He is a fellow of four divisions of the APA, the American Association for the Advancement of Science, the American Psychopathological Association, the New York Academy of Sciences, and the American Psychological Society; he is a clinical fellow of the Behavior Therapy and Research Society. He is presently serving as a member of the APA Board of Directors.

He has written or edited 9 books, 31 chapters in books, and 68 journal articles. He has served or is serving on 11 editorial boards and has served as consulting editor on more than a dozen other journals.

His work has ranged from the conditioning of goldfish, dogs, and rats to the study of social networks of people. He has promulgated a theory of schizophrenia, conditioned the verbal behavior of schizophrenic patients, conditioned the speech of children who had none, trained the parents of brain-injured children and the caregivers of Alzheimer's patients in the application of operant conditioning to improve their behavior; he has studied the comprehensibility of speech in schizophrenic patients and in Alzheimer's patients; and he has examined the verbal transactions of pilots and control tower operators. More recently, he has been investigating the goldfish as an early warning system for pollutants and has studied the effect of electromagnetic fields on the behavior of rats exposed in utero. He has also been studying the applicability of behavior analysis to the study of human error. In all cases, he has always answered questions of substance by experimentation.

KURT SALZINGER

THE EXPERIMENTAL APPROACH TO PSYCHOPATHOLOGY

D espite the fact that psychologists used the experimental approach to abnormal psychology before the clinical one and despite the fact that experimentation in this field has continued throughout the history of modern-day psychology, much of it has remained separate from (if not equal to) the clinical work of the practicing psychologist of today. The object of this chapter is to trace enough of this history to show the continuity of experimentation in psychopathology and to describe enough of the present work to convince the current practitioner to read the literature, learn from it, and eventually contribute to it.

I begin by discussing the general role of experimentation in science and then its role in psychopathology. That role is explored by describing some experiments with animals; reviewing some historical precedents; emphasizing the importance of single-subject design; viewing psychotherapy as an experiment; and, finally, briefly listing the most frequently used techniques in the experiments. In the next section, I take up some of the problems confronting typical experimenters when applying their work to psychopathology. The next section provides examples of experiments, categorizing them according to their reason for being. The first reason is to improve the tools available to the student of psychopathology; the second is to better describe the nature of the various disorders; the third establishes models of abnormality using human beings, computers, or animals as subjects; the final reasons for doing experiments are to determine the effectiveness of various forms of therapy as well as to determine the various specific effects, including side effects. The last section of the chapter presents my conclusions.

The Role of Experimentation in Science

Heinz Pagels (1982) tells of a dispute among medieval physiologists; it seems that they set themselves the task of explaining how elephants copulate. It is unclear why they conceived of this—so to speak—as a problem, but dispute it they did. Their explanations were not spoiled by any empirical knowledge such as observations of the event of interest. They knew that elephants were large and heavy and therefore devised many solutions to explain the "copulation problem." One physiological savant suggested that the animals back up into one another; another maintained that they copulate underwater where their weights are less than on solid ground; a third proposed that the male elephant digs a large hole and fits the female into it. My feminist colleagues will have no problem recognizing a male view of things here. The important point is that actual observation of the behavior of the elephants, who clearly manage quite well by simpler and more graceful means than those suggested by the medieval scientists, posed no obstacles to these speculations.

The moral of this little story is that we in psychology also have our elephants and our theories to explain their behavior. I consider it my job to convince you of the usefulness of observation under the controlled conditions of experimentation. I expect to persuade you that experimentation adds to our knowledge in many ways: It systematizes our thinking and clarifies our procedures, whether we seek to analyze the behavior in question or to change it; whether we simulate the malady we are trying to explain and understand or we analyze the processes of intervention; whether we learn about the nature of various disorders or we acquire knowledge about behavior in general. We must add here Claude Bernard's (1957) recommendation to physicians that they use therapies not

> according to authority and with a confidence akin to superstition, [but that] they will administer them with philosophic doubt which is appropriate to true experimenters; they will verify the results in animals, and by comparative observations on man, so as to determine rigorously the relative influence of nature and of medicine in curing disease. In case it is proved that the remedy does not cure, and all the more if it's shown to be harmful, experimenters should

renounce it, and, like the Hippocratists, should await events. (Bernard, 1957, p. 211)

The experimental approach clarifies. Used well, it sifts out those extraneous statements that add no meaning to the understanding of a particular phenomenon; also, because experimentation converts verbal behavior into activities engaged in by the experimenter, it removes ambiguity. One cannot behave in contradictory ways, although one can talk in that manner. In one sense, experimentation does not differ from the deductive method; indeed, it refines that method by forcing one to be more precise. If one conducts an experiment, then one must specify, in concrete terms, what is meant by each variable and each manipulation.

The Role of Experimentation in Psychopathology

Animal Experiments

Clarification of variables is in one sense most effective in animal experiments. The hand waving and vague verbal instructions some experimenters use to address human subjects cannot move animals. As a result, what is often viewed as a deficit in animal models of psychopathology—inability to use language—becomes an asset. Computer models have similar advantages except that specification of the variables can still remain abstract, with values of the measures unaffected by measurement operations in the real world; the results are also less likely to be surprising, although not inevitably so, than those produced by animal models. Achieving surprising results should not be the sole reason for experimentation; on the other hand, limiting experiments to verification of obvious inferences is unproductive. Unlike human subjects who assent to understanding what they do not, neither animals nor computers will engage in lawful behavior when instructions or reinforcement contingencies remain unspecified. Human beings, on the other hand, tend to make up their own instructions as to what to do, thus erroneously leading poor experimenters to think that the subjects have in fact listened to their instructions.

Many reviews of animal experiments in psychopathology have appeared in the literature (Keehn, 1986; Koob, Ehlers, & Kupfer, 1989; Maser & Seligman, 1977; McKinney, 1988; Mineka & Zinbarg, 1991). Let us examine the major reasons for such research. In addition to the elucidation produced through exposing animals to well-specified variables, research on animals has, through mere accretion of knowledge, informed us about the acquisition, maintenance, reduction, and elimination of behavior in human beings. Many principles discovered in the animal laboratory have themselves proved applicable to human behavior. These principles have given rise to behavior therapy and biofeedback techniques in psychopathology and medicine, to programmed instruction in education, to teaching language to children who had none and to brain-injured adults who lost it, to child-rearing practices that are based on bonding in nonhuman primates, and so on. I return to this discussion of animals in the section on models of abnormal behavior.

Historical Precedents

Despite their number, experiments in psychopathology have affected psychological testing only slightly. Brems, Thevenin, and Routh (1991) suggested that the establishment of the Wundt laboratory, the traditional start of experimental psychology, had no obvious clinical influence. On the other hand, Emil Kraepelin (1896), Wundt's student, emphasized what he called the *psychological experiment in psychopathology* and inspired much research using techniques originated in Wundt's laboratory. Had it not been for the lack of a position in psychology, Kraepelin might have remained a psychologist instead of becoming the psychiatrist who produced a diagnostic system whose offspring haunts us to this day. Psychological tests have unfortunately remained separate from experimental psychopathology, although some inroads by cognitive experiments are being made.

Hugo Münsterberg (Roback, 1952) was another early psychologist interested in psychopathology. Like Kraepelin, he was attracted to medicine, but when he heard a lecture by Wundt, he decided to work in the latter's laboratory. He subsequently received his PhD under Wundt, but his interaction with him was decidedly unpleasant. Two years after getting his PhD, Münsterberg went to Heidelberg to get an MD degree. Although Wundt continued to criticize Münsterberg, the latter much impressed William James, resulting in an invitation to take charge of the Harvard Psychology Laboratory. Münsterberg worked in many areas of applied psychology, publishing a book on psychotherapy in 1909. Although he eventually gave up psychotherapy, which he did for free, after a patient threatened him with a gun, he continued to do experimental research in abnormal behavior. Interested in hysterical patients, he tried to elicit a second personality from normal individuals by having them divide their attention in a process that ultimately consisted of having subjects write one word but pay attention to the words they had written earlier. Among his celebrated subjects and students was Gertrude Stein, who published a paper on the subject with Solomons in 1968 (more about this is in the section on human models of abnormal behavior).

Another milestone in the experimental study of abnormal behavior was reached in 1938, by Henry Murray, in his classical *Explorations in Personality*. "All we workers," he said, "were bound by a common compulsion: to inquire into the nature of man; and by a common faith: that experiment would prove fruitful" (Murray, 1938, pp. vii–viii).

I found Murray's emphasis on the study of individual subjects particularly interesting. Not that group data and group statistical analysis fail to provide us with information; but there is inherent in the study of psychopathology the assumption (one that we often forget as we race from one complex statistical method addressed at group differences to another) that human beings differ from one another, and it is that difference that engages our interest. When we do therapy, we do not concern ourselves with the average amount of improvement in a group of patients; our interest is naturally drawn to the amount of improvement that we manage to produce in each person. Although data on the average tells a lot about the success of a particular intervention, ignoring *which* people improve deprives us of the opportunity of administering the most appropriate therapy to each person and exposes patients to the danger of receiving a service that may even be harmful. Murray (1938) stated, attributing the phrase to Whitehead, "Averages obliterate the individual characters of individual organisms" (p. viii). He continued, "The objects of study are individual organisms, not aggregates of organisms" (p. 38). He then added, "Since, at every moment, an organism is within an environment which largely determines its behaviour, and since the environment changes—sometimes with radical abruptness—the conduct of an individual cannot be formulated without a characterization of each confronting situation, physical and social" (p. 39). It should, therefore, not surprise us that Murray, whose achievement was the Thematic Apperception Test (TAT) has obscured his other contributions, recognized the importance of the environment and, therefore, the importance of experimentation. His book describes experiments with some 50 subjects, all normal, because as he said, without knowing how normal individuals behave, one cannot understand personality in its totality. The experiments included questionnaires, the TAT, the galvanic skin response, a tremor response directed at detecting emotional reactions, a memory task, aesthetic appreciation, an abilities test, and reaction to frustration. Some of the experiments have become tests that are still in use today; Murray's so-called Diagnostic Council combined his coworkers' observations of the same person under a variety of circumstances, that is, in reaction to many experimentally controlled conditions, thus providing the kind of information that one needs to arrive at a behavioral description of a person that is general.

What is perhaps most interesting about this brief historical review is that single-subject design is not only old but rather well practiced and deliberately so. In our embrace of the "new," we tend to forget the valuable old. Also, the diagnostic approach is centered on individuals, without giving up any objectivity in measurement. Indeed, Murray's approach makes much more use of objective measurement than the current-day diagnostic procedures such as *DSM–III–R* or *DSM–IV* (*Diagnostic and Statistical Manual of Mental Disorders*; 3rd ed., rev. and 4th ed., respectively). There is a lesson to be learned here in the inclusion of experimental techniques in describing individual persons.

Single-Subject Experimental Design

Others also have chosen the single-subject design approach, as we now call it (Barlow & Hersen, 1984). Ebbinghaus's (1885/1964) classic work made use of the experimental technique in a tour de force still cited, although not sufficiently well understood to exert the influence that it should. He maintained by exhortation and by example that the way to discover which variable affects behavior is to change it and to measure its effect; to that he added what has become rare in psychology— replication, that is, repeating experiments, even though he was the only one on whom each experiment was repeated. Ebbinghaus established another critical aspect of experimentation: When it is well done, not only does one subject suffice, but that one subject can be the experimenter him- or herself. Few experimental results have withstood the ravages of replication as well as have Ebbinghaus's. More recently, other psychologists have embraced single-subject design, notably behavior analysts (Sidman, 1960). The obvious problem, which Sidman (1952) pointed out some 40 years ago, is that average group functions may not reflect individual behavior but instead the frequency of animals, or human beings, with various scores. In psychopathology, as already shown in Murray's work, it is the individual's behavior which is of interest.

Let us look next at the single-case experiments Galton (1908) conducted with himself as subject. One approach to experimentation in psychopathology is the induction of abnormal behavior. Galton worked on generating paranoia in himself. He did so, as he said, by investing "everything I met, whether human, animal, or inanimate, with the imaginary attributes of a spy" (p. 276), while on his usual walk. After covering a mile and a half, he reported that "every horse on the stand seemed watching me, either with pricked ears or disguising its espionage" (p. 276). Hours passed before the paranoia wore off, and he felt that he could easily reestablish it.

More recently, M. B. Shapiro (Inglis, 1966) approached the single case by constructing what were essentially form-fitting personality questionnaires appropriate to the particular symptoms of each patient; then he invoked an independent variable. In the case of a paranoid person, that variable consisted of producing rational arguments against the paranoid ideas; he measured any changes with his individually constructed scales. In one study, he found a statistically significant reduction on the paranoid scale but no concomitant change on the guilt scale. I do not present this study to suggest a new technique for treating paranoia but rather as an example of an experiment specific to each patient's difficulties. In this example, it is also of interest to note that we have an application of the experimental technique to psychotherapy.

Psychotherapy as Experiment

This brings us to the experiment that all practitioners perform, namely, psychotherapy. I use the term *psychotherapy* to include all forms of nondrug therapy, specifically including behavior and cognitive therapies of various kinds. To be sure, therapy procedures are often so loosely specified that one cannot measure the effect on a dependent variable as precisely as in a typical experiment. Nevertheless, application of the experimental approach to therapy would do much to improve both the information obtained and the effectiveness of the therapy. Barlow, Hayes, and Nelson (1984) argued for such a scientific approach to clinical practice. More recently, Sanderson and Barlow (1991) separated the case study from the single-case experimental design, maintaining that only the latter permits us to isolate cause and effect. I believe that it is, however, important to encourage private practitioners to use even approximations to single-case experimental designs. Eventually, as private practitioners work in this way, the whole field will improve, because psychotherapy as experiment allows one to evaluate the effectiveness of the techniques both for a particular case and in a more general sense. Single-case experimental design enables one to use subjects as their own control—a natural marriage between experimentation and psychotherapy.

The big difference between psychotherapy as usual and the attempt at an experimental approach is keeping track of when one engages in one technique or another and keeping records of the effects. This does not imply using the latest measurement techniques, although that would obviously be most effective. It implies, as a start, simply keeping an anecdotal record so as initially to instruct oneself on which techniques work most frequently and eventually to let others know, informing them on the anecdotal nature of the record, what the effects are. I should also mention that the use of the experimental approach does not imply the use of new techniques; it simply means keeping a record of any variation in what the psychotherapist does from time to time. Old techniques also must be evaluated and reevaluated and related whenever possible to specific problems.

Content of Experiments

Milberg, Whitman, and Maher (1983) and Whitman, Milberg, and Maher (1983) came up with a short list of frequently used experimental techniques for describing the nature of a disorder or measuring the effects of interventions: reaction time; memory tasks; various forms of attribution theory; physiological measures consisting essentially of the application of sensing devices to various parts of the human anatomy, including GSR (galvanic skin response); electrical activity of the brain (especially event-related responses); cardiovascular responses; and, in an attempt to measure the lateralization of the nervous system, the dichotic listening procedure.

Experimentation in psychopathology has taken many routes, as we have seen. It has been applied to the study of animals; it has been done for many years; it has often used a single-subject design, despite the more recent embrace of group statistics; and it lends itself very naturally to the study of psychotherapy, indeed to the conduct of therapy. Finally, even the most frequently used experimental techniques show themselves to be quite varied, that is, to range from social to psychophysical and physiological techniques.

Problems in the Application of Experiments to Psychopathology

There are basic, some say insurmountable, problems in applying experimental techniques to abnormal psychology. Why? Because the identification of the people we are trying to study is so vague or ambiguous as to make the subsequent precision seem both inappropriate and futile. Who is to be called "abnormal," or worse, "schizophrenic"? How are we going to elucidate schizophrenia if we cannot agree on who is suffering from it? A partial answer is to use the experimental method itself to build a better system. What, however, if we want to make use of the classification already in existence? One approach is a bootstrap operation in which we use what Sutton (1973) referred to as the *iterative method*, in which we start by selecting a group of people according to the best categorization available (on the basis of a structured interview). Then, we test them by experiment, yielding subgroupings that we can subsequently characterize by reexamining the parts of the interview that yielded a grouping similar to that supplied by the experiment. This procedure is replicated by having the relevant part of the interview select a new group of patients and then examining them by the objective technique to see if we get the same results. I have suggested a more radical solution to the diagnosis problem, pointing out the many other ways that lend themselves to the classification of behavior (Salzinger, 1986). A problem exists, however, before diagnosis, namely, the original identification of the "abnormal" individual for experimentation before any professional diagnostic procedure is superimposed. How does that early identification of the abnormal person happen? Clearly, this calls for more study, but it is too far off the current topic for discussion here.

One final point in this section: As we struggle to make better and more meaningful diagnoses, it is noteworthy that in a recent survey (Rabinowitz, Sechzer, Denmark, & Wilkins, 1992) of studies of depression, a full 44% failed to specify the gender of the subjects.

Some Examples of Experiments in Psychopathology

Experiments to Investigate and Improve Methodology

I will use one of my own experiments to demonstrate the advantages of the experimental process. I began by assuming what is still true, namely, that the most important clinician's tool is the interview. No matter how precise the tools that follow, whether they be PET (positron emission tomography) or CAT (computerized axial tomography) or evoked potentials, the selection of the patient is determined by the interview. I tried, therefore, to gain a better understanding of the interview process. Starting with the behavior analytic approach (see Figure 1), I looked for the stimuli that precede and those that follow the patient's responses. In other words, I used the reinforcement contingency. Questions asked by the interviewer are clearly among the discriminative stimuli that produce patient talk.

Clinicians ask many questions of patients and, recently, the structured interview has been increasingly used to improve the comparability of interviews and therefore the diagnosis of patients; the structured interview assures one that the same topics have been broached. In addition, we also knew that every conversation, including the interview, contains within it encouraging remarks, that is, statements of agreement or at least understanding. Such comments are reinforcers in behavior analysis. We decided, therefore, to determine whether they have a significant role to play in the interview. It remained for us to find an important response class in our patients.

We chose to examine the effect of reinforcement on schizophrenic patients (Salzinger & Pisoni, 1958). A factor critical in the diagnosis of schizophrenia is flatness of affect. We therefore identified statements of affect. Using an ABA format, we conducted the interview by asking general questions of the person, beginning with "Why are you here in the hospital?" and then asking about how the patient spent his or her time at home, on the job, and with the family—all intended to get the patients to talk without necessarily eliciting affect. The first 10 minutes consisted of questions only, that is, without any interviewer responses. The interviewer waited about 2 seconds after each reply and then asked an-

VARIABLE SETS

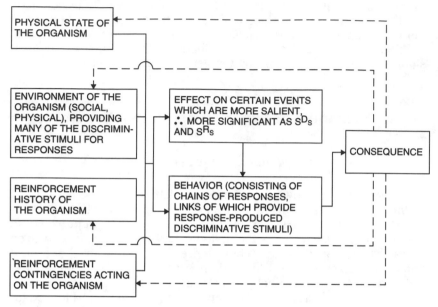

THE BEHAVIORAL MECHANISM

Figure 1. The behavioral mechanism explains the various ways in which behavior is controlled by variables that precede or follow it. (From "The Behavioral Mechanism to Explain Abnormal Behavior" by K. Salzinger, 1980, *Annals of the New York Academy of Sciences, 340*, p. 68. Copyright by New York Academy of Sciences. Reprinted by permission.)

other question to elicit more talk; in the second 10 minutes of the interview, the interviewer asked questions as before whenever the patient stopped talking for more than 2 seconds but also reinforced every self-referred affect statement by saying "yeah," "yes," "mm-hum," "I see," or "I can understand that." During the last 10 minutes, the interviewer continued to ask the same kinds of questions as before, administering no further reinforcers.

The results were clear. The largest number of self-referred affect statements occurred during the conditioning period (Figure 2). We also found that the larger the number of reinforcers administered, the larger the number of affect statements during extinction, thus providing more evidence for the applicability of the behavior analytic model (Figures 3 and 4). Our conclusion: Interviewers influence the results of their observations by the process of measurement. Heisenberg is as right in psychology as he was in physics. The implications are that the lack of reliability of the findings that are based on interview data might well

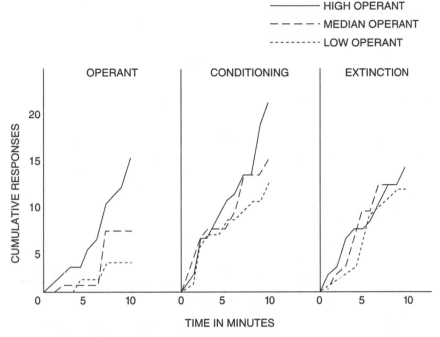

Figure 2. Individual cumulative response curves for three patients who showed the conditioning effect. (From "Reinforcement of Affect Responses of Schizophrenics During the Clinical Interview" by K. Salzinger and S. Pisoni, 1958, *Journal of Abnormal and Social Psychology, 57*, p. 87.)

result from different interviewers reinforcing different response classes and, therefore, deriving their varying conclusions on the basis of discordant sets of data.

We followed this study up with a number of variations in procedure. We placed the reinforcement period during the first 10 minutes; we conducted interviews without any reinforcement; and we (Salzinger & Pisoni, 1961) still found an effect that was due to reinforcement. Further experimentation allowed us to discover that the effect was specific to the particular response class reinforced and was unaffected by the questions or the face-to-face situation of the interview. We (Salzinger, Portnoy, & Feldman, 1964a) found that by using a monologue procedure in which the patients could not see the experimenter, the experimenter asked no questions, and the reinforcer was a red light (with the instruction given that it signified the patients were speaking of important things that would make them feel better), the effect of reinforcement was clear: It influenced the response class on which it was contingent (Figures 5 and 6). In addition, some natural shaping took place, with speech in general increasing first, then self-referred statements, and finally self-

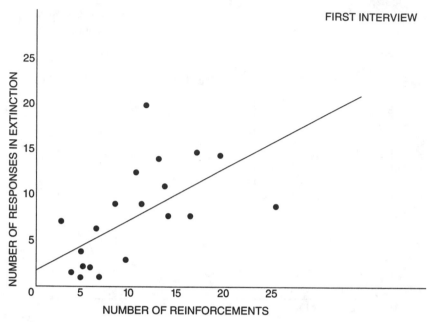

Figure 3. Number of affect responses during extinction as a function of number of reinforcements in the first interview. (From "Reinforcement of Affect Responses of Schizophrenics During the Clinical Interview" by K. Salzinger and S. Pisoni, 1958, *Journal of Abnormal and Social Psychology*, 57, p. 87.)

referred affect statements. This showed that one can get a patient to speak more by reinforcing speech in general and thus can obtain more material to evaluate, but that one could bias the results of one's interview by making reinforcement contingent on a particular response class. These experiments demonstrated that one must monitor, if not control, the interviewer's reinforcing behavior to be certain that the responses obtained are not biased.

Baughman (1954) evaluated another basic clinical tool, the Rorschach, by experiment. It is well known that after patients say what they "see" in each card, they are asked to identify what made them "see" the particular "clown" or what not. Exner (1990, p. 27) explains: "The words of the subject are the data from which coding decisions evolve." He supplies examples from which one is to conclude what determined the response, such as, "It's colored like they are" or "The different shades here give that impression." From this kind of response psychologists have deduced such concepts as color shock or shading shock, which have in various ways been associated with different diagnoses. Given this background, it is surprising that it should have taken as long as it did for someone such as Baughman to examine the Rorschach in the

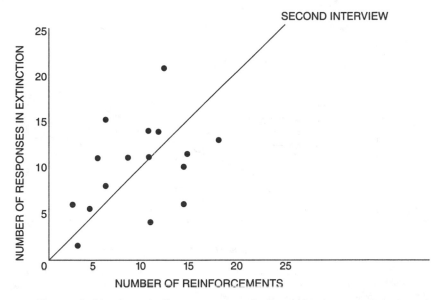

Figure 4. Number of affect responses during extinction as a function of number of reinforcements in the second interview. (From "Reinforcement of Affect Responses of Schizophrenics During the Clinical Interview" by K. Salzinger and S. Pisoni, 1958, *Journal of Abnormal and Social Psychology*, 57, p. 87.)

only way one can uncover the stimulus that determines responses to the Rorschach cards. Would psychophysicists ask subjects what determines their response when presenting an array of stimuli or would they do so by varying the array of stimuli? Is it not obvious that if you wish to find out what constitutes the stimulus, you must vary it, present it in one magnitude, then in another, and so on, and have a condition in which the suspected stimulus is entirely absent? This has not been the case for the Rorschach; it has been viewed as one instrument to be used just as it is. Baughman did the unthinkable by altering the cards in a systematic fashion, achieving the following versions: the peripheral form obtained by tracing the outline of each blot; the silhouette that was the same as the peripheral except that it was filled in solid black areas; the internal form series that added to the peripheral series the internal forms differentially indicated by shading or color in the original cards; and, last, an achromatic series that were black-and-white photographs of the regular Rorschach cards.

The study first asked, What role did the suspected stimulus characteristics of the cards play in determining the patients' responses; and then asked, What is the value of the inquiry in which patients are asked to tell what part of a card determines their responses? Comparable

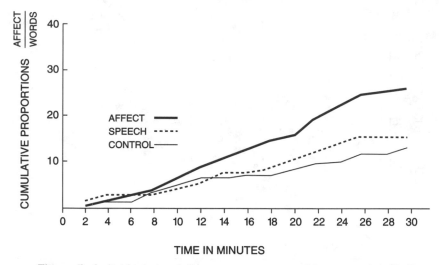

Figure 5. Individual cumulative response curves of the proportion of affect to words for three subjects selected at the median of each of the three groups. (Adapted from "Experimental Manipulation of Continuous Speech in Schizophrenic Patients" by K. Salzinger, S. Portnoy, and R. S. Feldman, 1964a, *Journal of Abnormal and Social Psychology, 68,* p. 512. Copyright 1964 by the American Psychological Association.)

groups of neurotic patients responded to the Rorschach in the various forms described, and then experienced Rorschach interpreters judged whether the response and time patterns indicated color shock, gray–black shock, or both. Out of 60 possible comparisons among the different versions of the Rorschach cards, only two statistically significant differences were observed, with one judge finding more color-shock patterns for the peripheral than for the chromatic or achromatic forms. Thus, the answer to the first question is that Rorschach interpreters do not know what stimulus in each card determines the responses, and the suspected stimuli play minimal roles in determining the so-called perceptual responses. As for the answer to the second question, the inquiry is not helpful because the patients, like the Rorschach interpreters, do not know what stimulus determined their verbal responses.

Zubin, Eron, and Schumer (1965, p. 251), in a book unfortunately too much ignored by practitioners, said, "The current popularity of the Rorschach technique has focused attention on the paradox it presents. No other technique has captured the attention of so many on such little evidence. This in itself warrants sociological investigation into the problem of social acceptance of unestablished measuring devices." The point here is that the experimental technique holds out much hope for the

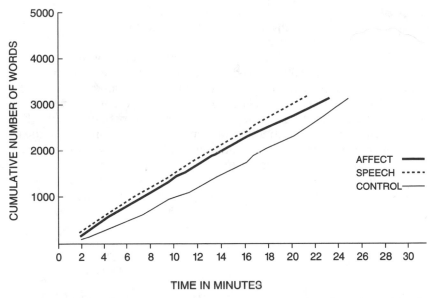

Figure 6. Individual cumulative response curves of total number of words for three subjects selected at the median of each of the three groups. (From "Experimental Manipulation of Continuous Speech in Schizophrenic Patients" by K. Salzinger, S. Portnoy, and R. S. Feldman, 1964a, *Journal of Abnormal and Social Psychology*, *68*, p. 513. Copyright 1964 by the American Psychological Association.)

improvement of assessment techniques, and we should take advantage of it.

Experiments to Describe the Nature of the Disorder

Returning to my experiments on the interview, it may be recalled that those studies showed that the interviewer could increase the frequency of self-referred affect statements by verbal reinforcement. Having demonstrated that schizophrenic patients show a sensitivity to reinforcement in the course of the interview, it seemed to us that this unobtrusive experiment—patients had no way of knowing that they were part of an experiment—might help us to check on the hypothesized characteristic of flatness of affect in schizophrenia. We therefore did the equivalent interview with physically ill patients (Salzinger & Pisoni, 1960). When we inspected the operant level, that is, the period when no reinforcement was administered, we found that normal, physically ill patients in a hospital did not differ in the number of self-referred affect statements from schizophrenic patients. On the other hand, when we compared the rates of extinction, we found that schizophrenic patients extinguished more rapidly than the physically ill individuals (Figure 7).

This suggests that it may not be affect that differentiates schizophrenic patients from normal individuals, but the schizophrenic patient's rate of extinction of self-referred affect statements. Affect is almost always measured in terms of reactivity to another person and thus might account for the flatness of affect phenomenon so often reported. More recently, I was able to examine the schizophrenic patient's diminished responsiveness during extinction in terms of my immediacy hypothesis (Salzinger, 1984), which states that schizophrenic patients tend to respond predominantly to those stimuli closest in time. Failure to continue to respond during extinction shows that the absence of the reinforcers was sooner felt by the schizophrenic patients than by the normal individuals.

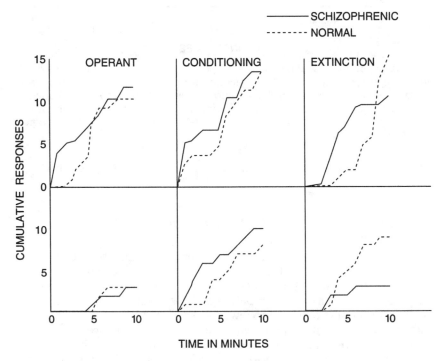

Figure 7. Individual cumulative self-referred affect response curves for two pairs of matched schizophrenic and normal subjects. (The top pair shows two subjects with high operant levels; the bottom pair shows two subjects with low operant levels. From "Reinforcement of Verbal Affect Responses of Normal Subjects During the Interview" by K. Salzinger and S. Pisoni, 1960, *Journal of Abnormal and Social Psychology, 60*, p. 129.)

We used the interview data in another way as well (Salzinger & Portnoy, 1964). Following up on 58 schizophrenic patients, we asked whether those who were out of the psychiatric hospital at 180 days differed in the rate of self-referred affect statements during the operant level (when no reinforcement was given) from those still hospitalized, and we found no significant difference. No difference arose for rates either during the conditioning or during the extinction periods. On the other hand, when we examined the individual increase from operant level to conditioning and the decrease to extinction, we found that those who showed such changes had left the hospital by 180 days, whereas those not showing sensitivity to reinforcement had not. We also scrutinized those patients whom we had administered no reinforcement and found that the three 10-minute periods (corresponding to the periods of operant level, conditioning, and extinction) did not differ from one another nor did they relate to outcome, thus showing that it is the change due to conditioning that differentiates the two groups of schizophrenic patients. Although the literature reports that low affect means poor prognosis, our findings suggest that it is the sensitivity of affect to reinforcement that separates patients with a good and a poor prognosis. Note that our experiment yielded interesting results when comparing the same patient under different conditions. In other words, the patients in or out of the hospital differ from each other in the manner in which they differ from themselves. Again, we are talking about the single-subject approach to research.

Let us look next at another way of using an experiment. The literature on schizophrenia emphasizes the patients' inability to communicate; indeed, thought disorder is a mainstay of this diagnosis. An interesting question is how to quantify such a complex process. The usual response to this kind of problem in clinical psychology, and psychiatry for that matter, is the all-purpose rating scale. You want to quantify? Construct a rating scale. What we forget in this approach is that the specification of the measurement operation of "rating" is simply never supplied. Our joy at having arrived at a number is such that we run with it, applying the world's most sophisticated statistical techniques to arrive at our questionable conclusions. Maybe we cannot give up the ubiquitous rating scale, but I think we must find ways of specifying what determines the various ratings of 1 or 2 or 100. Without going off on too much of a tangent, let me remind you of the evidence from the experimental literature that people are unable to make more discriminations than seven (Miller, 1956). Despite that fact, there exists at least one much-used rating scale calling for 100 discriminations.

But to return to the question at hand, how do you retain the essence of communication while quantifying the concept? Some years ago, we came across a technique originated by Taylor (1953); he had used it to measure the comprehensibility of the writings of various authors. The technique, which he named the *cloze procedure*, consisted of deleting every fifth word of a given text and then asking subjects to guess what each deleted word was. The larger the number of correct guesses, the more comprehensible the text is assumed to be. The beauty of the technique is that it provides an objective score of a complex social process, namely, comprehensibility or communicability, as we prefer to call it. We (Salzinger, Portnoy, & Feldman, 1964b, 1966, 1978) decided to apply this technique to the schizophrenic monologues that we had collected.

The critical experiment in this case took place after we had obtained the behavior of interest from the patient. We learned that with the proper instructions, schizophrenic patients can deliver a monologue as easily as normal individuals (Salzinger et al., 1964a). As already described, we essentially promised them reinforcement but did not deliver it until after we had obtained samples of sufficient size for the experiment. That size, incidentally, was some 200-odd words of monologue.

The basic experiment varied the supposed communicability of speech by contrasting schizophrenic with normal mutilated speech as the stimulus material. The results were that normal speech was more effectively restored than schizophrenic speech; the second 100 words of schizophrenic speech were harder to restore than the first 100 words, that is, as the schizophrenic patient continued to talk, his or her speech became less comprehensible. We also found that the greater the number of correct guesses for a particular patient's speech, the briefer his or her stay in the hospital. I interpreted the results as being congruent with the immediacy hypothesis, saying that the greater difficulty in restoring the mutilated transcripts was due to the fact that the response-produced stimuli of other words in the speech sample were largely confined to the immediate ones.

We tested that hypothesis directly (Salzinger, Portnoy, Pisoni, & Feldman, 1970) by matching the blanks of schizophrenic and normal speech samples in terms of a number of variables, including the number of people who guessed the missing word in the cloze procedure. We then presented each blank with varying context (numbers of words of original text surrounding it, i.e., 2, 4, 8, 16, and 28 words) to normal subjects. Both the schizophrenic and the normal speech samples elicited an increasing number of correct responses with increasing amounts of context; however, the schizophrenic speech increased more slowly than the normal speech in correct matches with increasing context, finally reaching a lower level of correct guesses (Figure 8). This demonstrated that the closer words, but not the more remote ones, in the speech of the schizophrenic patients acted as discriminative stimuli. The lack of communicability of schizophrenic speech can thus be explained by the shorter spans of connected words or ideas instead of by what is usually said about schizophrenic speech, namely, its lack of connectedness. In terms of the usefulness of experimentation, note that the patient's verbal

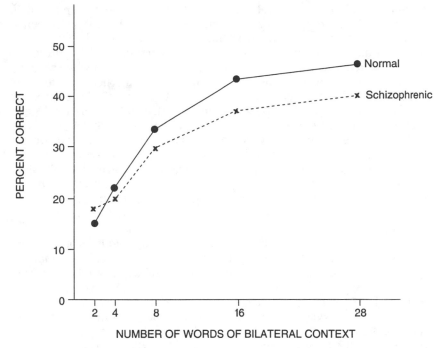

Figure 8. Percent of correct words guessed to schizophrenic and normal speech segments as a function of the number of words of bilateral context. (From "Communicability Deficit in Schizophrenics Resulting From a More General Deficit" by K. Salzinger, S. Portnoy, and R. S. Feldman. In S. Schwartz [Ed.], 1978, *Language and Cognition in Schizophrenia*, p. 47, Hillsdale, NJ: Erlbaum. Copyright 1978 by Erlbaum. Reprinted by permission.)

behavior is the stimulus material for an experiment with normal subjects to shed light on schizophrenia.

Models of Abnormal Behavior

Human Models

One way to understand a particular disorder is to produce a model for it. An early, interesting model of abnormal behavior was produced in a study by Gertrude Stein (Solomons & Stein, 1896). The basic idea was to study the extent to which automatic behavior can be generated and to shed some light on the concept of multiple personality. The authors produced such automatic behavior by having the subject keep a pencil moving while reading a story; the subject reported sometimes being conscious of having written a word but not conscious that he was about to do so and sometimes being wholly unconscious of the writing. In another procedure, they had the subject listen to dictation while reading a book; after some hours of practice the subject learned to attend to the book while writing the dictated words quite automatically, ultimately not being aware of having written the word. Finally, Gertrude Stein herself apparently served as the subject for an automatic writing experiment; here, the method was looking back some three to four words before, while writing new words, and this procedure resulted in disappearance of consciousness of what she was writing even though what she was writing was described by the authors as "stuff that sounds all right" (p. 506). It also gave rise to repetition, a result that led B. F. Skinner (1934) to suggest that Stein had used this method for some of her writing.

Models or theories of schizophrenia have been quite prominent in the literature of psychopathology (e.g., Spaulding & Cole, 1984). Indeed, some have suggested that we ought to take a holiday from theories and spend the time collecting data. Nevertheless, theory underlying the collection of data is important. Allow me to return to my immediacy theory (Salzinger, 1984), which begins with the immediacy hypothesis that states that the behavior of schizophrenic individuals is controlled primarily by stimuli immediate in their environment. Immediacy theory takes into account the interaction of this control with environmental conditions producing the behavior symptomatic of schizophrenia. Finally, that interaction is governed by the laws of behavior theory. The advantage of the immediacy theory is that it is, in the words of Herbert Spohn (1984), "eminently operationalizable" (p. 354). Experiments can be constructed allowing one to compare schizophrenic patients with other diagnostic categories or with normals by examining differences in responses to stimuli varying in their temporal distance from the required response.

Immediacy theory has another advantage, namely, its extension to the kind of clinical behavior observable during interviews, on the ward, or in other aspects of the patient's life. By way of contrast, the experiments and resulting genetic theory by Holzman (1991), ingenious as they are, do not even try to show the behavioral mechanism through which the posited deficit in eye movements relates to the symptomatic behavior (cf. Salzinger, 1992).

Computer Models

In 1968, J. C. Loehlin wrote a book on computer models of personality. He showed with a simple example of a program how complex an interaction can become. Using the variables of "frustration" and "anger" and assigning quantitative values to each as well as to their interrelation, he could, by assigning different values, have the computer "blow its top" or not. Frustration is the input value, or stimulus, to anger; the value of frustration when it occurs is added to anger and if the sum is larger than a preset value, the computer blows its top; if not, then the frustration value is reduced by half and added to the anger, while waiting for the next frustrating event and its value. Eventually and depending on the spacing of the frustrating events, the computer blows its top again, unless the frustrating events allow for the dissipation of the anger because the input frustration is too small. Everybody, especially the computer expert, admits this is a simple model, but the usefulness of specific assignment of values to the two variables and to their interaction shows how much one can gain by first specifying these values and then embarking on an experiment. A more recent description of computer models of personality by Cranton (1976) discusses other models but concludes that although fascinating and potentially useful, the area has been neglected. Nevertheless, I believe it is worthwhile to explore this area further, particularly by following the model with an experiment.

Animal Models

The first animal experiment in psychopathology occurred by accident. In a classical conditioning experiment known to every undergraduate in psychology, a student of Pavlov, Shenger-Krestovnikova (Pavlov, 1927), pressed a dog to make successively finer discriminations between a circle and an ellipse that increasingly resembled the circle. Food was the unconditional stimulus; the circle was the positive and the ellipse was the negative conditional stimulus. The object was to determine the limits of the dog's sensory system; the dog stopped making an effective discriminative response when the semiaxes of the ellipse were in a ratio of 9 to 8. Pavlov spoke of an "experimental neurosis" because when the discrimination broke down, the formerly placid dog struggled against the restraint that had uneventfully bound him to the apparatus for many weeks before, became violent, and, even when brought back to the compartment after a rest from the apparently traumatic event, displayed difficulty with the easy discriminations. Pavlov interpreted the phenomenon as a clash between excitation and inhibition in the dog's nervous system.

Pavlov's invention of the label *experimental neurosis* was less important than his idea of studying psychopathology by experiment. If one can produce a particular form of psychopathology, as for example, by making a discrimination too difficult, then one can hypothesize that the natural malady develops in a similar way. It also follows that if one knows how to produce a malady, one should be able to eliminate it. The fact that this important result happened without having been planned is a tribute to serendipity and more important to the study of behavior for its own sake. Eventually, newly garnered knowledge will be relevant to behavior under other conditions or in related forms. I am arguing for experimentation because it supplies us with new information.

It is worthwhile to ponder the label given to the aberrant behavior of the dog. Nowadays we call such a label *diagnosis*. The question arises as to how soon after the discovery of a phenomenon such as this one should one try to find the counterpart in human problems. Could the label have been restricted to a description, such as a reaction to too difficult a discrimination?

Pavlov did not restrain himself from labeling. He not only labeled the aberration he had induced experimental neurosis, he also used a personality classification related to different nervous systems. The first category was *sanguine*, a category that he took from Hippocrates, who classified behavior in terms of physical disease even back then. Pavlov described sanguine dogs as follows: "Under quick changes of stimuli they are energetic and highly reactive, but with the slightest monotony of the environment they become dull, drowsy and inactive" (Pavlov, 1927, p. 286). Here the excitatory process predominates. The other extreme, in which the inhibitory process predominates, he called *melancholic*. These dogs are quiet and restrained, whereas the first type is lively, active, and often aggressive. Pavlov admitted to some types between these two extremes but maintained that the same task produced different effects in dogs of different temperament.

In another experiment (Pavlov, 1927) from Pavlov's laboratory, Erofeeva paired an electric shock as a conditional stimulus with food as the unconditional stimulus. She conditioned an alimentary reflex of salivation to an electric shock stimulus that ordinarily elicits the defense reaction of withdrawing from the shock. She accomplished this by first presenting the dog with a very weak shock as the conditional stimulus and then gradually increasing its magnitude until, in Pavlov's words, "it was extremely powerful" (p. 289). The salivary reflex remained stable for many months, until the experimenter shocked areas of the dog far from the original site. At that point, each of three dogs eventually manifested a violent defense reaction without producing the salivary response. The alimentary reflex to the shock could not be restored in two dogs and took many months to be reinstated in the remaining one. Pavlov interpreted this to mean that the dog was in a chronic pathological state. As for the experimental neurosis experiment, Pavlov accounted for what happened in terms of the clash of excitation and inhibition in the nervous system. When the electric shock was the conditional stimulus, the dog had to inhibit the excitation of the defense reaction; in the case of the circle and ellipse experiment, the dog had to inhibit the excitation of the salivary response to the ellipse.

Pavlov (1927) continued to investigate abnormal reactions using his reflex paradigm by selecting dogs of different temperaments. He used the method of the delayed reflex, in which the interval between the conditional stimulus and the unconditional stimulus gradually grows longer from trial to trial. First, the dog receives food, the unconditional stimulus, 5 seconds after the conditional stimulus; the next day, after 10 seconds, then after 15 seconds, and so on, until eventually the dog receives the food 3 minutes after the conditional stimulus. Under these circumstances, the dog learns to inhibit his salivation (according to Pavlov) during the delay interval. Pavlov conditioned six different reflexes in this way. Dogs with a tendency to inhibition had no difficulty learning this delayed conditioning task; on the other hand, dogs with a tendency to become excited began to enter a general state of excitation, becoming "quite crazy, unceasingly and violently moving all parts of its body, howling, barking and squealing intolerably" (p. 294). We thus have an early example of the interaction of diagnosis and reaction to a particular procedure in eliciting abnormal behavior. The diagnosis was not complicated; indeed, one might say that it was a description of a baseline tendency to behave in a particular way; nevertheless, it turned out to be very important.

Pavlov's research contrasts interestingly with the work of Seligman and Maier (1967) and Overmier and Seligman (1967). When they first reported the phenomenon that Seligman eventually called a paradigm for depression, they simply described it with such phrases as a "failure to escape traumatic shock." Such noninterpretive description may be accounted for by the experimental journal in which they published the article. It is also of interest that Seligman (1975) now speaks of a learned-helplessness type of depression to protect himself and his model (that was originally based on animal work but was eventually validated with human subjects) from the charge that it does not explain all depressions or for that matter any of the recognized subcategories of depression. My own belief is that experiments, whether with animals or with human beings, should be used to construct a classification system of abnormal behavior that is independent of existing systems, unless the behaviors naturally fall into an existing system. If the experiments produce the same categories as those that govern a current diagnostic system, then we have additional evidence for its validity; if on the other hand, they produce a different way of slicing the behavioral pie, then we should follow the new lead.

There are those who will ask why we need another diagnostic system when we already have a serviceable one (e.g., *DSM–III–R*). The answer has to be that the *DSM*s are all less than perfect and that we also know quite a bit about behavior and its determinants that is not taken into account by this diagnostic system. A system that is primarily topographic in describing behavior, that is, one that fails to pay enough attention to the functional relationships of behavior to its controlling variables, is bound to be inadequate for categorizing behavior. The experimental approach, on the other hand, is perfectly set up to lay bare those functional relationships that relate to behavior, whether normal or abnormal.

Mineka and Zinbarg (1991) described how pharmaceutical companies used animals exposed to the learned helplessness paradigm to screen antidepressant drugs. The authors pointed out that exposure to uncontrollable events (the essence of the model) produced higher levels of fear and anxiety as well as of depression. A similar discovery in clinical cases has led to the recent comorbidity fashion in diagnosis, a trend that seems to me like still another excuse for the basic problem of inadequacies of diagnosis. But to return to the learned helplessness model, it has recently been changed by consideration of what people exposed to uncontrollable events say to themselves, or to use the cognitive jargon of the day, to what they attribute their problem. Application of this model to human behavior has thus led to the hypothesis that hopelessness is the global attribution producing depression. A question is whether one needs to remain faithful to the original animal model when explaining the disorder in human beings or whether the animal model ought merely to inspire us to think systematically about the malady in question.

Animal experiments can also be used to test an existing theory. Harlow and Suomi (see McKinney, 1988) have examined the effect of maternal separation on nonhuman primates to determine the effect of these early bonds on depression as well as on the neurobiology of the animals.

Animal models of schizophrenia might seem quite hopeless at first glance; how do you model paranoid ideas, for example, or hallucinations for that matter? The approach to animal models can, however, take a different route. Remembering that behavior is multiply determined, we must, nevertheless, look for a central cause that differentiates schizophrenic patients from normal individuals to account for many aberrant behaviors. One such hypothesized cause of schizophrenia is chronic arousal, a state that makes it hard to filter out irrelevant stimuli.

Taking their cue from the continuous performance test, Kornetsky and Markowitz (1975) constructed an analogue method of testing animals. Their basic hypothesis was that schizophrenic patients suffered from a dysfunction in the subcortical parts of the brain. They stimulated those sections of the brain while the rat was working on a task that resembled the continuous performance test in human subjects. Stimulation of that section of the brain produced a decline in performance, whereas administration of chlorpromazine (a drug effective with some schizophrenic patients) reversed the decline. Such an animal model can be used to test other therapeutic agents in schizophrenia. Reasoning in such models is tight, and assumptions are explicit. At the same time, although it is difficult if not impossible to reproduce all the symptoms of schizophrenia, what is more important is the model's ability to posit an underlying cause. I should mention other methods of generating symptoms of schizophrenia, namely, the administration of such substances as amphetamines and LSD.

Another approach to extrapolating from animals to human beings examines the learning and conditioning literature. Various undistinguished, that is, common, behavioral paradigms exist that generate behaviors giving the appearance of abnormality. This approach uses a theory of behavior capable of describing normal behavior. Then it asks, Is there a way to generate aberrant behavior by the same means that produce normal behavior, and if so, what known abnormal behavior does this behavior resemble? Reasoning here is straightforward. If one can generate abnormal behavior in the laboratory, then perhaps nature uses the same pathways.

I (Salzinger, 1975) reviewed a series of such paradigms from the animal literature, showing how behavior, seemingly anomalous or at least inefficient, could be generated relatively easily by a particular management of reinforcement contingencies that by themselves are not particularly exceptional. To take but one example, my review described an experiment by Miller (1960), who showed that animals trained to run down an alley to food continue to run even while a slowly increasing electric shock accompanies the ingestion of food and reaches a high value; in contrast, when that high value of shock is given for the first time, after the animal has run down that alley many times without having received punishment for that response, it stops running altogether. This shows first that punishment, or for that matter any aversive stimulus, must be defined functionally instead of topographically to be understood. Second, it provides us with a paradigm for masochistic behavior, because the previously conditioned animal continues to endure the punishment that the so-called normal rat (the one that did not undergo the special conditioning procedure) avoids.

The point is that the conditioning procedures used are undistinguished: Punishment paired with a positive reinforcer follows an operant response. We generate abnormal behavior through the systematic application of the principles of behavior analysis. The history of the pairing of stimuli makes the difference in the effect of any stimulus on the rats' response. The results suggest that (contrary to similar experiments described by Pavlov in classical conditioning) one can convert a stimulus that ordinarily evokes an escape response into a discriminative stimulus or even a conditioned reinforcer. An interesting question is why Pavlov's dogs went berserk whereas Miller's rats became masochistic. A study of the different conditions under which the organisms acquired these responses might well be productive.

Sechzer (1977) presented an example of an animal model for minimal brain dysfunction. Using the split-brain operation on kittens in which the corpus callosum is cut, thus severing connections between the two hemispheres of the brain, she reported that the split-brain kittens (like hyperactive children) who became overly active within a few days after surgery showed a decreased span of attention by flitting from place to place, unlike the normal kittens. The split-brain kittens also showed learning and memory deficits and the so-called paradoxical response to amphetamine found in hyperactive children. Although the experiment does not imply that hyperactive children have severed callosal connections, Sechzer pointed to a similarity in the functional reduction of neuronal processes to explain both the behavior of the kittens and that of the hyperactive children.

Testing the Effectiveness of Various Modes of Therapy

One form of therapy stemming directly from laboratory experiments is behavior modification. Success in training animals up and down the phylogenetic scale inspired behavior analysts to deal with the behavior of people whose deficits were such that nobody else would work with them. One example was chronic schizophrenic patients. The token economy (which allows patients to earn tokens that they can exchange for various goods and services in a hospital, such as cigarettes, better located beds, a chance to speak to the social worker) resulted directly from the conditioning approach (Ayllon & Azrin, 1968). Applying an alternation of contingent reinforcement and noncontingent reinforcement, they showed that these so-called back-ward patients were capable of emitting adaptive behavior. Many behavior analysts have challenged conventional thinking in various areas of psychopathology; most important have been the challenges to treatment of deficiencies of the mentally retarded, autistic children, the physically handicapped, and chronic psychotic patients.

A good 30 years ago, my colleagues and I (Salzinger, Feldman, Cowan, & Salzinger, 1965) were challenged by a medical student to show the effectiveness of behavior analysis on a mute child in the hospital where we were working. Ferster and DeMyer (1961, 1962) had applied operant conditioning to the nonverbal responses of autistic children, and Isaacs, Thomas, and Goldiamond (1960) had reinstated speech in two acute schizophrenic patients. But, at the time, no one had applied behavior-analytic techniques to the verbal behavior of mute children. Using candy, we increased rates of vocalization, with some occasionally understandable words not under strict discriminative control, in one boy, and eventually effected substantial language production and understanding in a second boy. We worked with the first child for some 9 months and had not finished working with him when he was removed to another institution. With the second boy, we were more successful in using reinforcers to produce appropriate speech. These boys had been given a whole series of diagnoses, including hyperactivity, minimal brain injury, and autism, all suggesting that they would not be responsive to social stimuli. They responded to conditioning in ways that other techniques did not evoke. Our procedure of pairing candy with verbal praise, as well as with hugging and smiling, allowed us to test the effectiveness of verbal reinforcers in the following experiment.

The experimenter waited until the boy, who had toys he could play with, uttered the first word, and the experimenter repeated that word immediately after that, making his utterance as long as the boy's utterance. This procedure was alternated with the experimenter talking in a noncontingent way, that is, his speech was unrelated to the boy's speech. The data showed that the experimenter's utterances acted as reinforcers because more speech was produced by the contingent than by the noncontingent procedures. Thus, we were able to establish verbal behavior as a reinforcer merely by pairing it with the candy. The important point was that although we used candy as a reinforcer in this experiment, we always accompanied the candy with verbal behavior of praise and the like; furthermore, the experimenters talked to the boys when teaching them to name objects in the room, when it was time to take them to the bathroom, and generally whenever changes in situation took place. Because the experimenters established themselves as sources of positive reinforcement, what they said, and their verbal behavior in general, became positively reinforcing for children one of whose primary problems was paying too little attention to social situations.

A more recent experiment done by Harris, Handleman, and Alessandri (1990) taught autistic children an interesting social response, that is, to offer help to a person who said he or she could not complete a task. The purpose of this experiment was not only to see whether a particular technique could be used as a therapeutic procedure but also to determine the degree to which one could modify a child's behavior that the child is, according to the diagnostic criteria of autism, unable to do. Early studies of operant conditioning were often focused on easily measurable but not clinically significant response classes. More recent studies have shown that one can use the experimental approach for complex behavior in the same manner as for simple behavior.

Three autistic adolescents were first put into a situation in which another person asked for help in putting a key in a lock, buttoning a jacket, putting a letter in an envelope, and so on. Unlike normal adolescents, none of the subjects made a response to such a discriminative stimulus. Using a multiple baseline approach across the three subjects, the experimenters measured different lengths of baselines and trained each subject on a different task by prompting each to offer help, which was then accepted by the confederate and for which subjects were thanked. The study found that the situation in which each subject was trained was the one that showed the change; although there was no spontaneous generalization to other situations, conditioning the offer to help was much faster for the second and the third situation. Furthermore, some subjects eventually generalized to other people and other locations, but generalization for others was not perfect from the training area to the mother in her home (something that also sounds altogether too normal for those of us who are parents). More seriously, this shows us an experiment evaluating a form of therapy while telling us something about a particular diagnostic category that we did not know before.

Examining the Nature of the Effects and Side Effects of Therapy

Pavlov (1927) reported what appears to be the first application of drugs to abnormal behavior generated by conditioning, which was combined with his classification of his dogs into two types, excitable and phlegmatic. The dogs were required to salivate in a delayed conditioning procedure. The phlegmatic dog showed a weakening of excitation, whereas the excitable one showed a weakening of inhibition. The experimenter then gave the dogs 100cc of a 2% solution of potassium bromide. The drug reestablished the dogs' earlier efficient performance, that is, although the inhibition that had been weakened was restored, the drug did not affect the positive reflex at all. The bromide did not act as a general sedative but influenced the inhibitory process only. Eleven days of administration of this drug cured the excitable dog, but the phlegmatic dog did not profit from the same therapy. Pavlov left this dog alone for what he called "a very long time," and it eventually recovered.

Much research and controversy have arisen with respect to the most effective and the most ethical form of treatment of children who suffer from self-injurious behavior. Such children sometimes injure themselves irremediably and therefore must be stopped for their own good. Nonetheless, punishment, which has been successful with these children, has been rejected on "ethical" grounds, namely, that therapists should inflict no punishment on their patients. Cowdery, Iwata, and Pace (1990), using a single-subject design, both evaluated the effectiveness of two different schedules of DRO (differential reinforcement of "other" behavior) and looked for any untoward side effects from these procedures. Although reinforcing "other" behavior materially reduced the rate of self-injurious behavior and allowed the child for the first time in years to return home, a low rate of that behavior continued nonetheless after a period of some 4 months of intervention. This study also showed that although token reinforcement procedures were effective—the child could exchange tokens for primary reinforcers such as food—social reinforcers were ineffective in controlling self-injurious behavior. In addition, it found that positive reinforcement procedures of "other" behavior engendered emotional behavior during those early periods of conditioning when the child received no reinforcement and thus underwent an extinction procedure. It is important to note this because it is simply assumed that only punishment procedures elicit emotional behavior such as crying.

Conclusions

The road to experimentation is not an easy one. Experimentation calls for patience and for both regimented thinking and planning when carrying out the experiment and loose, creative activity when designing it. It calls for the courage to interfere with or divide a process thought to be indivisible, the courage to question received dogma, and the courage to change the design when the data show that the systematically derived design is inadequate. Experimentation requires a belief in data over theory, in new theory over old theory, and often even in hunch or common sense over theory. Experimentation requires a trust in rules of procedure and trust in ignoring those rules; it requires that you remain flexible in thinking up things to do while standing firm against sloppy procedure. It requires a willingness to give up your favorite theory, your most loved method or statistical procedure; it requires that you trust your statistically significant correlations but are willing to dismiss them when they are contradicted by your replicated experiments.

Only in psychology do we give equal weight to theory and data instead of using data to challenge and change theory. Often, this is most true in abnormal psychology. Joe Zubin (1975) reported how as a graduate student in the early 1930s he and his colleagues tried to test a part of Freud's theory, namely, the preference for the parent of the opposite sex. He used such test items as, "Suppose you were out in a canoe with both (parents) and could save only one, whom would you save?" According to Zubin, Freud was proved right; until about age 6, the children preferred the parent of the opposite sex, but after that age—what with the latency period beginning—even the girls preferred the mother. When he sent these results including statistical tables to Freud, he received an answer after a long while: "Ganz amerikanisch [quite American], but I do not quite see what you can prove with your statistics" (Zubin, 1975, p. x).

Disdain for experimentation or at least for empirical results continues to be with us. When Noam Chomsky gave a talk at the New York State Psychiatric Institute shortly after his generative grammar had become the talk of psychology and the inspiration for many ingenious experiments by George Miller to test that theory, I asked him about some experiments that found his notion that native speakers can discriminate the difference between grammatical and nongrammatical sentences to be untenable. His response was clear and immediate. I don't have his exact words but the message was, That's all right; it is just a matter of doing another experiment that will prove my theory right. I believe we must have the courage to reject that kind of thinking.

References

Ayllon, T., & Azrin, N. H. (1968). *The token economy: A motivational system for therapy and rehabilitation.* New York: Appleton-Century-Crofts.

Barlow, D. H., Hayes, S. C., & Nelson, R. O. (1984). *The scientist practitioner: Research and accountability in clinical and educational settings.* Elmsford, NY: Pergamon Press.

Barlow, D. H., & Hersen, M. (1984). *Single-case experimental designs.* Elmsford, NY: Pergamon Press.

Baughman, E. E. (1954). A comparative analysis of Rorschach forms with altered stimulus characteristics. *Journal of Projective Techniques, 18,* 151–164.

Bernard, C. (1957). *An introduction to the study of experimental medicine* (H. C. Green, Trans.). New York: Dover.

Brems, C., Thevenin, D. M., & Routh, D. K. (1991). The history of clinical psychology. In C. E. Walker (Ed.), *Clinical psychology: Historical and research foundations* (pp. 3–35). New York: Plenum Press.

Cowdery, G. E., Iwata, B. A., & Pace, G. M. (1990). Effects and side effects of DRO as treatment for self-injurious behavior. *Journal of Applied Behavior Analysis, 23,* 497–506.

Cranton, P. A. (1976). Computer models of personality: Implications for measurement. *Journal of Personality Assessment, 40,* 454–463.

Ebbinghaus, H. (1964). *Memory: A contribution to experimental psychology* (H. A. Ruger & C. E. Bussenius, Trans.). New York: Dover. (Original work published 1885)

Exner, J. E., Jr. (1990). *A Rorschach workbook for the comprehensive system.* Asheville, NC: Rorschach Workshops.

Ferster, C. B., & DeMyer, M. K. (1961). The development of performances in autistic children in an automatically controlled environment. *Journal of Chronic Disabilities, 13,* 312–345.

Ferster, C. B., & DeMyer, M. K. (1962). A method for the experimental analysis of the behavior of autistic children. *American Journal of Orthopsychiatry, 32,* 89–98.

Galton, F. (1908). *Memories of my life.* London: Methuen.

Harris, S. L., Handleman, J. S., & Alessandri, M. (1990). Teaching youths with autism to offer assistance. *Journal of Applied Behavior Analysis, 23,* 297–305.

Holzman, P. S. (1991). Eye movement dysfunctions in schizophrenia. In S. R. Steinhauer, J. H. Gruzelier, & J. Zubin (Eds.), *Handbook of schizophrenia: Neuropsychology, psychophysiology and information processing* (pp. 129–145). New York: Elsevier.

Inglis, J. (1966). *The scientific study of abnormal behavior.* Chicago: Aldine.

Isaacs, W., Thomas, J., & Goldiamond, I. (1960). Application of operant conditioning to reinstate verbal behavior in psychotics. *Journal of Speech and Hearing Disorders, 25,* 8–12.

Keehn, J. D. (1986). *Animal models for psychiatry.* Boston: Routledge & Kegan Paul.

Koob, G. F., Ehlers, C. L., & Kupfer, D. J. (Eds.). (1989). *Animal models of depression.* Boston: Birkhauser.

Kornetsky, C., & Markowitz, R. (1975). Animal models and schizophrenia. In D. Ingle & H. Schein (Eds.), *Model systems in biological psychiatry.* Cambridge, MA: MIT Press.

Kraepelin, E. (1896). Der psychologische Versuch in der Psychiatrie [The psychological experiment in psychiatry]. *Psychologische Arbeiten, 1,* 1–91.

Loehlin, J. C. (1968). *Computer models of personality.* New York: Random House.

Maser, J. D., & Seligman, M. E. P. (Eds.). (1977). *Psychopathology: Experimental models*. New York: Freeman.

McKinney, W. T. (1988). *Model of mental disorders: A new comparative psychiatry*. New York: Plenum Press.

Milberg, W. P., Whitman, R. D., & Maher, B. A. (1983). Experimental psychology for the clinical psychologist. In C. E. Walker (Ed.), *The handbook of clinical psychology* (Vol. 1, pp. 31–55). Homewood, IL: Dow Jones–Irwin.

Miller, G. A. (1956). The magical number seven, plus or minus two: Some limits on our capacity for processing information. *Psychological Review, 63*, 81–97.

Miller, N. E. (1960). Learning resistance to pain and fear: Effects of overlearning, exposure, and rewarded exposure in context. *Journal of Experimental Psychology, 60*, 137–145.

Mineka, S., & Zinbarg, R. (1991). Animal models of psychopathology. In C. E. Walker (Ed.), *Clinical psychology: Historical and research foundations* (pp. 51–86). New York: Plenum Press.

Münsterberg, H. (1909). *Psychotherapy*. New York: Moffat Yard.

Murray, H. A. (1938). *Explorations in personality: A clinical and experimental study of fifty men of college age*. New York: Oxford University Press.

Overmier, J. B., & Seligman, M. E. P. (1967). Effects of inescapable shock upon subsequent escape and avoidance learning. *Journal of Comparative and Physiological Psychology, 63*, 23–33.

Pagels, H. R. (1982). *The cosmic code: Quantum physics as the language of nature*. New York: Simon & Schuster.

Pavlov, I. P. (1927). *Conditioned reflexes: An investigation of the physiological activity of the cerebral cortex* (G. V. Anrep, Trans.). New York: Oxford University Press.

Rabinowitz, V. C., Sechzer, J. A., Denmark, F. L., & Wilkins, C. (1992). *Gender bias in research on depression*. Paper presented at the meeting of the International Council of Psychologists, Amsterdam, The Netherlands.

Roback, A. A. (1952). *History of American psychology*. New York: Library Publishers.

Salzinger, K. (1975). Behavior theory models of abnormal behavior. In M. Kietzman, S. Sutton, & J. Zubin (Eds.), *Experimental approaches to psychopathology* (pp. 213–244). San Diego, CA: Academic Press.

Salzinger, K. (1980). The behavioral mechanism to explain abnormal behavior. *Annals of the New York Academy of Sciences, 340*, 66–87.

Salzinger, K. (1984). The immediacy hypothesis in a theory of schizophrenia. In W. D. Spaulding & J. K. Cole (Eds.), *Theories of schizophrenia and psychosis* (pp. 231–282). Lincoln: University of Nebraska Press.

Salzinger, K. (1986). Diagnosis: Distinguishing among behaviors. In T. Millon & J. Klerman (Eds.), *Contemporary issues in psychopathology* (pp. 115–134). New York: Guilford Press.

Salzinger, K. (1992). Connections: A search for bridges between behavior and the nervous system. *Annals of the New York Academy of Sciences, 658*, 276–286.

Salzinger, K., Feldman, R. S., Cowan, J. E., & Salzinger, S. (1965). Operant conditioning of verbal behavior of two young speech-deficient boys. In L. Krasner & L. P. Ullman (Eds.), *Research in behavior modification: New developments and their clinical implications*. New York: Holt, Rinehart & Winston.

Salzinger, K., & Pisoni, S. (1958). Reinforcement of affect responses of schizophrenics during the clinical interview. *Journal of Abnormal and Social Psychology, 57*, 84–90.

Salzinger, K., & Pisoni, S. (1960). Reinforcement of verbal affect responses of normal subjects during the interview. *Journal of Abnormal and Social Psychology, 60*, 127–130.

Salzinger, K., & Pisoni, S. (1961). Some parameters of the conditioning of verbal affect responses of schizophrenic subjects. *Journal of Abnormal and Social Psychology, 63*, 511–516.

Salzinger, K., & Portnoy, S. (1964). Verbal conditioning in interviews: Application to chronic schizophrenics and relationship to prognosis for acute schizophrenics. *Journal of Psychiatric Research, 2*, 1–9.

Salzinger, K., Portnoy, S., & Feldman, R. S. (1964a). Experimental manipulation of continuous speech in schizophrenic patients. *Journal of Abnormal and Social Psychology, 68*, 508–516.

Salzinger, K., Portnoy, S., & Feldman, R. S. (1964b). Verbal behavior of schizophrenic and normal subjects. *Annals of the New York Academy of Sciences, 105*, 845–860.

Salzinger, K., Portnoy, S., & Feldman, R. S. (1966). Verbal behavior in schizophrenics and some comments toward a theory of schizophrenia. In P. Hoch & J. Zubin (Eds.), *Psychopathology of schizophrenia.* New York: Grune & Stratton.

Salzinger, K., Portnoy, S., & Feldman, R. S. (1978). Communicability deficit in schizophrenics resulting from a more general deficit. In S. Schwartz (Ed.), *Language and cognition in schizophrenia.* Hillsdale, NJ: Erlbaum.

Salzinger, K., Portnoy, S., Pisoni, D. B., & Feldman, R. S. (1970). The immediacy hypothesis and response-produced stimuli in schizophrenic speech. *Journal of Abnormal Psychology, 76*, 258–264.

Sanderson, W. C., & Barlow, D. H. (1991). Research strategies in clinical psychology. In E. Walker (Ed.), *Clinical psychology: Historical and research foundations* (pp. 37–49). New York: Plenum Press.

Sechzer, J. A. (1977). The neonatal split-brain kitten: A laboratory analogue of minimal brain dysfunction. In J. D. Maser & M. E. P. Seligman (Eds.), *Psychopathology: Experimental models* (pp. 308–333). New York: Freeman.

Seligman, M. E. P. (1975). *Helplessness: On depression, development and death.* New York: Freeman.

Seligman, M. E. P., & Maier, S. F. (1967). Failure to escape traumatic shock. *Journal of Experimental Psychology, 74*, 1–9.

Sidman, M. (1952). A note on functional relations obtained from group data. *Psychological Bulletin, 49*, 263–269.

Sidman, M. (1960). *Tactics of scientific research.* New York: Basic Books.

Skinner, B. F. (1934, January). Has Gertrude Stein a secret? *Atlantic Monthly.*

Solomons, L. M., & Stein, G. (1896). Studies from the Psychological Laboratory of Harvard University. II. Normal motor automatism. *Psychological Review, 3*, 492–512.

Spaulding, W. D., & Cole, J. K. (Eds.) (1984). *Theories of schizophrenia and psychosis.* Lincoln: University of Nebraska Press.

Spohn, H. E. (1984). Discussion. In W. D. Spaulding & J. K. Cole (Eds.), *Theories of schizophrenia and psychosis* (pp. 345–359). Lincoln: University of Nebraska Press.

Sutton, S. (1973). Fact and artifact in the psychology of schizophrenia. In M. Hammer, K. Salzinger, & S. Sutton (Eds.), *Psychopathology: Contributions from the social, behavioral, and biological sciences*. New York: Wiley.

Taylor, W. L. (1953). Cloze procedure: A new tool for measuring readability. *Journalism Quarterly, 30*, 415–433.

Whitman, R. D., Milberg, W. P., & Maher, B. A. (1983). Experimental psychopathology. In C. E. Walker (Ed.), *The handbook of clinical psychology* (Vol. 1, pp. 56–74). Homewood, IL: Dow Jones–Irwin.

Zubin, J. (1975). A biometric approach to diagnosis and evaluation of therapeutic intervention in schizophrenia. In G. Usdin (Ed.), *Overview of the psychotherapies*. New York: Brunner/Mazel.

Zubin, J., Eron, L. E., & Schumer, F. (1965). *An experimental approach to projective techniques*. New York: Wiley.

HANS H. STRUPP

PSYCHOTHERARY RESEARCH

RESEARCH

EVOLUTION AND CURRENT TRENDS

HANS H. STRUPP

H ans H. Strupp is currently Distinguished Professor of Psychology at Vanderbilt University. He received his PhD from George Washington University in 1954. He is also a graduate of the Washington School of Psychiatry and a Diplomate in Clinical Psychology, American Board of Professional Psychology. Following two research positions (with the Department of the Air Force and the Department of the Army), he was appointed associate professor in the departments of psychiatry and psychology at the University of North Carolina (UNC) at Chapel Hill and was promoted to full professor in 1962. He also served as Director of Psychological Services in the department of psychiatry at UNC at Chapel Hill. In 1966, he joined the faculty of Vanderbilt University. In 1976, he became Distinguished Professor. From 1967 to 1976 Strupp was director of clinical psychology training at Vanderbilt.

Strupp's publications, which number over 300 articles and several books, have been largely devoted to psychotherapy research, psychoanalytic psychology, the training of psychotherapists and clinical psychologists, and related scientific and professional issues. He began his research career with a series of empirical studies of psychotherapeutic techniques. His attention was soon drawn to analyses of the psychotherapeutic process. He became particularly impressed with complications in patient–therapist transactions resulting from patients' negative attitudes, hostility, and other impediments to progress in therapy. The topic of negative complementarity, that is, therapists' difficulties in dealing effectively with patients' negative attitudes, became the leitmotiv of the Vanderbilt group of researchers who became members of Strupp's research team. In addition to publishing a number of theoretical papers, Strupp became interested in the study of negative effects of psychotherapy, a project whose findings were published, in collaboration with Suzanne Hadley and Beverly Gomes-Schwartz, in a book titled *Psychotherapy for Better or Worse* (1977). With Jeffrey Binder, Strupp authored a treatment manual, published in book form as *Psychotherapy in a New Key* (1984). The book became the centerpiece of a 5-year project on time-limited dynamic psychotherapy that was designed to study the effects of a specialized training program on process and outcome (the Vanderbilt II project). The project was one of the first empirical investigations on the effects of therapist training and is still in progress.

Strupp is coeditor of the journal *Psychotherapy Research* and advisory editor to numerous professional journals. He is a fellow of APA and has served as president of APA's Division of Clinical Psychology and as president of the Society for Psychotherapy Research. He is the recipient of the Distinguished Professional Achievement Award of the American Board of Professional Psychology, the Distinguished Scientific Contribution Award of the Division of Psychology, Distinguished Career Contribution Award of the Society for Psychotherapy Research, and Distinguished Professional Contributions to Knowledge Award of the American Psychological Association (APA). The University of Ulm (Federal Republic of Germany) conferred on him the honorary degree of Doctor of Medicine. He was a previous contributor, in 1982, to APA's Master Lecture Series.

He continues to be interested in the problem of change in psychotherapy, both long term and time limited—how change comes about and factors leading to the maintenance of change or its absence. The focus of his research is the patient–therapist relationship and its vicissitudes.

HANS H. STRUPP

PSYCHOTHERAPY RESEARCH

EVOLUTION AND CURRENT TRENDS

M odern psychotherapy, which had its modest beginnings toward the end of the 19th century, has become today an enormously complex and popular enterprise that has sometimes been called a billion-dollar industry threatening to go out of control. It has achieved prominence in western countries and particularly in the United States, which has shown a particular affinity for treatments that promise relief from emotional disturbances and from more diffuse "problems in living." At the same time, empirical research on various aspects of psychotherapy has become a prominent feature, as shown by a burgeoning literature that has gradually influenced theory and practice. In this chapter, I briefly trace the history of psychotherapy research and exemplify it by reference to a program of research which I, together with collaborators, have undertaken since the early 1950s. Thus, I have participated in a history to which, in some measure, I have contributed. I wish to show that psychotherapy research has grown in breadth and depth and that it has achieved a level of sophistication that only a few decades ago would have been unthinkable. In short, psychotherapy research

Parts of this chapter have been adapted from "A Brief History of Psychotherapy Research" by H. H. Strupp and K. Howard, in *History of Psychotherapy: A Century of Change*, 1992, edited by D. Freedheim. Copyright 1992 by the American Psychological Association.

today is an established branch of clinical research, meriting substantial financial support by such governmental agencies as the National Institute of Mental Health (NIMH). Researchers formed the international Society of Psychotherapy Research (SPR) in 1968, and it now has over 1,000 members from 27 countries.

The Emergence of Psychotherapy Research

From its inception, modern psychotherapy, much like the practice of medicine, has been considered a practical art. However, as soon as Freud, toward the end of the 19th century, had advanced bold claims for a uniquely effective psychological treatment he had labeled *psychoanalysis*, he was forced to answer skeptics who demanded to be shown hard empirical evidence. Freud's answer (1916/1963) took two forms. On the one hand, he appealed to his own clinical findings as well as to those of his collaborators, asserting that the case-study method, on which they had placed primary reliance, was fully adequate to satisfy the challenges. Thus, Freud contended that anyone who had been properly trained in the practice of psychoanalysis would obtain results comparable with his own, and he believed that his case histories had adequately documented and replicated his assertions. The evidence, as far as he was concerned, was conclusive. His argument further implied that only trained psychoanalysts could be objective and impartial observers.

Second, Freud voiced a skeptical attitude toward "statistics" (which he equated with the rudimentary procedures of behavioral research as it existed in the early 1900s). He asserted that the clinical material available to the investigator was so diverse and heterogeneous as to make meaningful comparisons all but impossible. In addition, he had the following harsh words for critics who disparaged his treatment results:

> A therapeutic novelty is either received with delirious enthusiasm—as, for instance, when Koch introduced his first tuberculin against tuberculosis to the public—or it is treated with abysmal distrust—like Jenner's vaccination, which was in fact a blessing and which even to-day has its irreconcilable opponents. There was obviously a prejudice against psycho-analysis. If one had cured a severe case, one might hear people say: "That proves nothing. He would have recovered on his own account by this time." And when a woman patient, who had already passed through four cycles of depression and mania, came to be treated by me during an interval after an attack of melancholia and three weeks later started on a phase of mania, all the members of her family—and a high medical authority, too, who was called in for consultation—were convinced that the

fresh attack could only be the result of my attempted analysis. Nothing can be done against prejudices... The most sensible thing to do is to wait, and to leave such prejudices to the eroding effects of time. One day the same people begin to think about the same things in quite a different way from before; why they did not think so earlier remains a dark mystery. (Freud, 1916/1963, pp. 461–462)

Despite Freud's rejoinders, the critics' basic question, "Does the treatment work?" did not disappear. On the contrary, it has continued to occupy a position of central interest and—at least in the judgments of its critics—has not yet received a satisfactory response despite the accumulation of a sizable body of empirical research. The birth of psychotherapy research may be said to have occurred as soon as the question of its effectiveness and efficacy was first broached. Also, treatment centers associated with psychoanalytic training institutes (first in Berlin, later in London, and then in Chicago and Topeka) began to collect systematic data on treatment results around 1920, disregarding Freud's strictures (Bergin & Lambert, 1978, chapter 5). These studies may be regarded as the precursors of modern psychotherapy research.

Does Psychotherapy Work?

As we have stated, Freud was convinced of the scientific and clinical value of his method of treatment. Not only did he claim superior treatment outcomes, but he argued at length that the modus operandi of psychoanalytic therapy was now well understood and that little remained to be learned (Freud, 1937/1964). Posterity has strongly disagreed with this assessment, and the voluminous literature on psychotherapy research provides eloquent testimony that the process and the outcome of therapeutic interventions embody important clinical and scientific questions, many of which have not yet been adequately answered. I begin by delineating the domains of inquiry that occupy the modern psychotherapy researcher (see also the three editions of the *Handbook of Psychotherapy and Behavior Change*; Bergin & Garfield, 1971; Garfield & Bergin, 1978, 1986).

The period from 1920 to 1940 occasioned the first stirrings of scientific investigations in psychotherapy. Between 1940 and 1960, researchers initiated empirical investigations to illuminate the process of psychotherapy and its outcomes. From about 1960 to the present, a rapidly growing literature includes a host of studies that have shed important light on the basic questions that set the agenda for the future. As will be seen, methodology and research strategies have undergone developments, and the sophistication of researchers who, typically, are also skilled practitioners has significantly increased.

Following the early efforts of analytic institutes and clinics to document their treatment results, studies of psychotherapeutic outcomes of eclectic (nonpsychoanalytic) treatments gradually made their appearance in the 1930s (Bergin & Lambert, 1978, chapter 5). The patient samples were typically small, the diagnoses were vague, and the treatments were not described in great detail. By contrast, the studies of psychoanalytic treatment, deficient as they were in many respects, adopted rather stringent criteria for evaluating outcomes (Fenichel, 1930).

As an interesting historical sidelight, the practice by psychoanalytic training centers to report treatment outcomes was discontinued in the 1940s. Perhaps one of the reasons for the changed policy was the judgment that the outcomes were not as impressive as had been hoped and the fact that data were often used by critics as ammunition for wholesale attacks on psychoanalysis. A large-scale effort by collaborating analysts, the so-called fact-gathering study mounted in the 1940s, was notably slow in being published (Hamburg et al., 1967) and, in many respects, was judged disappointing. The analysts' most ambitious entry into process and outcome research was the groundbreaking Menninger Psychotherapy Project that spanned a period of 30 years, beginning around 1950. It was one of the most carefully designed and well-executed investigations of its kind and still stands as an impressive monument.

The modern era of outcome research is generally dated to Eysenck's (1952) broadside attack on all forms of psychotherapy. Although his results in some sense supported the efficacy of psychotherapy, his conclusion—to abandon the training of psychotherapists—was very damning. The field responded with a variety of attacks on the database, the methodology, and Eysenck's motives. On the positive side, there occurred an explosion of research activity. Bergin and Lambert (1978) reanalyzed Eysenck's data and showed that alternate conclusions could have been reached, on the basis of different codings of the original data. In fact, what Eysenck's data purported to show was that 67% of emotionally disturbed people who do not seek individual psychotherapy are improved in 2 years—the results of a myriad of therapeutic events (except formal psychotherapy). In contrast, 67% of those who did seek psychotherapy were improved in about 2 months (Howard, Kopta, Krause, & Orlinsky, 1986; McNeilly & Howard, 1991). This was a clear demonstration of the efficacy of psychotherapy, but Eysenck's conclusion, that the effect of psychotherapy does not exceed the spontaneous remission rate, is still widely quoted.

Some 30 years later, Smith, Glass, and Miller (1980) presented a so-called meta-analysis of the psychotherapy research literature, from which they concluded that psychotherapy was indeed very effective. They reported a mean "effect size" for psychotherapy of .85 (p. 87), which they interpreted to mean that the average treated person would have an outcome equal to or better than 80% of the average of untreated persons. The field was elated by this statistical–scientific fact, and the efficacy of psychotherapy seemed firmly established. Few psychotherapy researchers challenged Smith, Glass, and Miller's reasoning, although many challenged their study selection and methodology. To balance their conclusion, however, it seems fair to point out that 50% of the untreated group would have had an outcome equal to or better than the average untreated person (i.e., in a normal distribution half the subjects will fall at or above the mean). In other words, psychotherapy added 30% to this statistical criterion. Moreover, their findings indicated that 20% of treated persons presumably would have had an outcome equal to or less than the average untreated person. On the whole, however, there seems little sense in attempting to answer such a global question as Does psychotherapy work? One might just as usefully ask physicians, Does surgery work? Needed are specifications of the conditions that describe more stringently the treatments, patients, therapists, nature of the disorders, and so on.

Common Versus Unique Factors

From the inception of psychoanalysis, Freud (1916/1963) was at pains to differentiate the nature of its therapeutic influence from suggestion, which he regarded as the moving force in hypnotherapy. Having declared that the modus operandi of psychoanalytic therapy was unique, it became incumbent on him and his followers to demonstrate that it differed radically from other psychological therapies. If, on the other hand, this claim could not be sustained, then psychoanalysis, despite its supposedly unique technical features (especially analysis of the transference), was merely another variant of a psychological treatment, perhaps not very different from hypnosis, for which Freud had developed considerable disdain. The crux of the difference was the purportedly differential use of suggestion in the two forms of therapy.

As other approaches and systems of psychotherapy made their appearance in this century, beginning prominently in the 1940s with Rogers's (1951) nondirective or client-centered therapy, each claimed uniqueness, both in terms of advocated techniques and purported psychological mechanisms. Behavior therapy extolled principles of learning (Emmelkamp, 1986, chapter 9) and cognitive behavior therapy invoked reorganization of beliefs (Hollon & Beck, 1986, chapter 10).

The developing controversy had other far-reaching implications. If, as the growing research literature has strongly suggested, generic (or common) relationship factors in all forms of psychotherapy (e.g., empathic understanding, respect, caring, genuineness, and warmth) carry most of the weight, other purportedly unique (technical) features of a system may be relatively inconsequential. Thus, the seeming uniqueness of each system simply might be semantic or stylistic or reflect prevailing fashions. The view that common factors may be of overriding importance in all forms of psychotherapy has been persuasively argued by Frank (1973, 1974, 1982) and has found widespread acceptance. If correct, it would cast serious doubt on the accuracy of Freud's original assertion concerning the unique therapeutic action of psychoanalysis. Similar strictures would apply to other systems and techniques claiming unique effectiveness.

The controversy between unique and common factors in therapeutic influence has had other implications. With respect to the training of therapists, it has been argued that if professionals essentially use "common factors" in their work, what is unique about their expertise? And, furthermore, might not naturally talented and intuitive persons, without prolonged and thorough training, be able to function as effectively in the therapist role? (See the later discussion of the Vanderbilt I study.) Thus, therapists have been challenged to demonstrate precisely the nature of their professional expertise. This challenge has become more pressing as the market for therapeutic services has grown immensely and large numbers of "service providers," many of whom have limited training and experience, have created a highly competitive atmosphere. Thus, the major mental health professions (psychiatry, clinical psychology, and psychiatric social work) have endeavored to protect practitioners who are properly licensed. The latter, as well as researchers, have understandably taken a defensive position, pointing to such areas as professional commitment and responsibility, technical skill (e.g., in the therapeutic management of difficult patients, who tend to be the rule rather than the exception), and adherence to codes of ethics that protect clients from harm (Strupp, Butler, & Rosser, 1988). Nonetheless, there remain considerable lacunae in the field's ability to define the nature of competence and professional expertise.

The Emergence of Techniques for Studying Process and Outcome

The problem of how therapeutic change occurs in psychoanalysis and in all other forms of psychotherapy remains the central issue of concern to the scientist. What are the parameters? Why does change occur under some conditions but not under others? Who are the patients who will benefit? What causes a symptom or a pattern of maladaptive behavior to yield to therapeutic intervention? Does prolonged and intensive therapy produce more pervasive changes (i.e., in the patient's personality makeup or character structure) than short-term or more "superficial" treatments?

Advances in methodology were greatly hastened by the advent of electronic recording techniques and the slowly growing willingness of patients and therapists to subject their transactions to rigorous scrutiny. Beginning in the 1940s, Carl Rogers and his students collected sound recordings of therapy sessions, using them as a basis for intensive studies of therapeutic technique and the patient–therapist relationship. Predictably, there were many objections to such "invasions" of the privacy of therapy, a possibility against which Freud had already inveighed, asserting flatly that psychoanalysis did not tolerate the presence of third parties. Objections to recordings, however, eventually diminished, with the result that sound recordings have become common, particularly in training and research. In recent years, filming and videotaping of therapy have become widely accepted and are now tolerated quite well by most clients and therapists.[1]

Having thus gained access to the primary behavioral data of psychotherapy, it became possible for external observers to scrutinize the communications between patient and therapist. Thus, *process analyses* of psychotherapy came into being. These research efforts were sustained by the belief that the *outcomes* of psychotherapy could be illuminated, perhaps even explained, by intensive study of the transactions between patients and therapists. Thus, it became essential to develop adequate methodological tools and to forge links between process and outcome. The dual thrust of process and outcome research has been the hallmark of psychotherapy research to this day, together with the realization that the two must necessarily complement each other.

APA Conferences (1958, 1961, and 1966)

In response to a growing need for systematic research, the first major conference on research in psychotherapy (Rubinstein & Parloff, 1959) was convened in Washington, DC, in 1958. Planning and programming were carried out by an ad hoc committee of the Division of Clinical Psychology of the American Psychological Association (APA), and the financial support was provided by the NIMH. There were 37 invited conference participants (psychologists and psychiatrists) representing the major psychotherapy research groups in the United States. The major goal was to "afford an opportunity for taking stock of the present status of research in psychotherapy and thus provide information for and stimulus to further research" (Rubinstein & Parloff, 1959, p. v). The confer-

---

[1]Beginning in the 1950s, even conservative psychoanalysts foresaw the value of filming analytic interviews. Franz Alexander spearheaded an effort to create a film studio–consulting room in Chicago. The aim was to film an entire psychoanalysis. For some time the project languished because, despite the availability of a willing patient, no willing analyst could be found. Some years later, after David Shakow had built a similar facility at the NIMH in Bethesda, MD, Paul Bergman filmed an entire psychoanalysis. Hundreds of hours were stored in metal containers, under controlled climatic conditions. Subsequently, small samples of these interactions were studied intensively by such investigators as Dittmann (1962). Eventually, because of space and storage problems, the films were destroyed, many sessions remaining unstudied.

ence was organized around three research themes: (a) problems of experimental controls, (b) methods for assessment of change, and (c) the therapist–patient relationship.

The second conference, paralleling the first in structure and format, was held in Chapel Hill, North Carolina, in 1961 (Strupp & Luborsky, 1962). It was aimed at examining several large projects that had been completed since the 1958 meeting and at considering new research developments and problems in three areas: (a) the measurement of personality change in psychotherapy; (b) the psychotherapist's contribution to the treatment process; and (c) the definition, measurement, and analysis of such variables as transference, resistance, and so on.

A third (and final) conference was held in Chicago in 1966 (Shlien, Hunt, Matarazzo, & Savage, 1968). It examined psychotherapy research as a practical art and centered on (a) behavior therapy; (b) therapist–patient interaction; and (c) as an innovation, psychopharmacology in relation to psychotherapy.

The three conferences, in addition to facilitating exchanges of ideas, pointed up the need for investigators to pool their resources and to consider the design of research projects that might be executed on a collaborative basis. Precedents for such ventures were, of course, available in biomedical research but had been conspicuously absent in psychotherapy.

Exploring the Feasibility of Collaborative Research

After the Chicago conference, a small group of investigators became articulate about the need for collaboration. Furthermore, the recently formed Clinical Research Branch of NIMH (see the next section) took an active interest in the possibilities of large-scale collaborative research in the area. To this end, an informal committee of researchers (chaired by Joseph D. Matarazzo) was formed, which in turn recruited me and Allen Bergin to take responsibility for a major feasibility study that was eventually supported by NIMH. Following a comprehensive and critical review of the literature (Strupp & Bergin, 1969), individual interviews with some 36 experts (researchers, clinicians, methodologists, and other scientists representing a broad spectrum of interests and commitments) were held. A number of recommendations emerged from this exploration, the major one being that large-scale collaborative studies of psychotherapy did not appear feasible at the time (Bergin & Strupp, 1972). In 1977, however, NIMH reevaluated the situation, concluding that a collaborative study could and should be undertaken. Accordingly, the NIMH Treatment of Depression Collaborative Research Program was initiated. It became the largest psychotherapy study of its kind.

NIMH Treatment of Depression Collaborative Research Program

In 1977, the staff of the NIMH Psychotherapy and Behavioral Intervention Section initiated the NIMH Treatment of Depression Collaborative Research Program. The decision was based, in part, on progress that had been made in the treatment of outpatient depression, the fact that new methods had been developed for more systematic diagnosis and characterization of specific subgroups of depressed patients, and that promising new psychotherapeutic approaches had appeared. Under the direction of Morris Parloff and Irene Elkin, a multisite controlled clinical trial was initiated to study the relative efficacy of two forms of psychotherapy (cognitive behavior therapy [CB] and interpersonal psychotherapy [IPT]) and one form of pharmacological intervention (imipramine) (Elkin, Parloff, Hadley, & Autry, 1985). The study entailed random assignment of 250 patients to 16 to 20 sessions of CB, IPT, imipramine, or placebo. The last two conditions were administered in the context of "clinical management," described as a "generally supportive atmosphere" (p. 311). Therapists were trained according to standardized procedures, and all therapies were based on specially prepared treatment manuals. All therapy sessions were videotaped to allow for checks on the competence of the delivery of each therapy as well as to permit studies of the therapeutic process. Extensive assessments were made before the beginning of treatment; at several points during treatment; at termination; and at 6-, 12-, and 18-month follow-up periods.

Several articles describing the results have been published (Elkin et al., 1989; Imber et al., 1990), but additional analyses of the data remain to be completed. It is impossible to provide a brief summary of the results emerging from such a large-scale and complex investigation. In general, it may be said that patients in all treatment conditions showed significant improvement but that differences attributable to the different treatment modalities were relatively slight.

The Role of the NIMH

By 1966, the Clinical Research Branch (CRB) of the Division of Extramural Research Programs had taken shape. One of the major functions of the CRB was to serve as the central administrative unit for grants and fellowships dealing particularly with the psychosocial therapies. In 1969, NIMH created the Psychotherapy and Behavioral Intervention Section within the CRB. A. Hussain (Sein) Tuma was the first chief of this section.

During Tuma's tenure as chief, some of his contributions to the field of psychotherapy research included (a) organizing the first NIMH conference on behavior therapy and behavioral modification, (b) supporting the feasibility study of possibilities for collaborative efforts (mentioned earlier), and (c) conducting workshops on critical theoretical and design issues in psychotherapy research (e.g., Fiske et al., 1970).

Society for Psychotherapy Research

As already reported, the 1966 Psychotherapy Research Conference was held in Chicago and, as was true of the preceding conferences, was by invitation. David Orlinsky and Kenneth Howard concluded that the field had grown to a point where a broader forum was needed, that is, one that included new investigators such as themselves. It also appeared unlikely that NIMH would continue to support research conferences. Accordingly, Howard and Orlinsky (1972), along with Nathaniel Raskin and Ferdinand van der Veen, decided to invite all interested investigators to attend a preconference meeting before the 1966 Annual Convention of the APA. Enough interest was shown to plan a 1967 "interest group" meeting in Chicago, with the support of the Institute for Juvenile Research and Psychologists Interested in the Advancement of Psychotherapy (PIAP—the precursor of Division 29 of the APA). The first meeting of what became the international, multidisciplinary Society for Psychotherapy Research (SPR) was held in Chicago in 1968. The SPR has grown impressively in size and stature and has become the major voice for psychotherapy research throughout the world.

The Vanderbilt Projects

In the early 1950s, the psychotherapy research literature could point to relatively sparse accomplishments. Noteworthy was the previously mentioned Eysenck (1952) article that attracted considerable attention, and there were other studies devoted to treatment outcomes. A collection of papers edited by Rogers and Dymond (1954) was perhaps the first compilation of systematic research devoted to process and outcome conducted in a single setting, the Counseling Center at the University of Chicago. Another series of studies by Fiedler (1950a, 1950b, 1951) supported the view that experienced therapists, irrespective of their theoretical orientation, establish therapeutic relationships whose "atmosphere" showed greater resemblance to each other than was true of novices. However, very few empirical studies focusing on therapists' techniques and personality had been conducted.

Beginning in 1953, I initiated a series of empirical studies (Strupp, 1955a, 1955b, 1955c) to shed light on the therapist's contribution to the treatment process. Results revealed systematic relationships between therapists' personal reactions to a hostile male patient depicted in a filmed interview and the quality of the respondents' hypothetical communications, diagnostic impressions, and treatment plans (Strupp, 1958, 1960b). Specifically, the studies adduced evidence that therapists' negative attitudes toward a patient, which were frequent and occurred almost instantly, tended to be associated with unempathic communications and unfavorable clinical judgments, whereas the opposite was true of therapists who felt more positively toward the patient. This early research provided the first empirical evidence for what later became the leitmotiv of the Vanderbilt research group, namely, the underestimated pervasive problem encountered by therapists in managing hostility in the patient–therapist relationship.

More broadly, this early work led to the formulation of the therapist's contribution to the treatment as both personal and technical. Personal attributes (e.g., maturity, warmth, and acceptance) were seen as enabling the therapist to create the kind of interpersonal relationship in which constructive personality change could take place; knowledge of psychodynamic principles and techniques would then permit the therapist, in and through this relationship, to initiate the kinds of emotional unlearning and learning experiences that are considered necessary to the alleviation or resolution of neurotic difficulties. The latter would be impossible without the former; the former, by itself, would not be sufficient.

Further exploration of salient aspects of the therapist's behavior and its consequences on the development of the therapeutic relationship as well as its outcome were pursued in a project dealing with patients' retrospective accounts of their therapy experience (Strupp, Fox, & Lessler, 1969). Results showed that patients' positive attitudes toward the therapist were closely associated with success in therapy, irrespective of how success was measured. Successful patients described their therapists as warm, attentive, interested, understanding, and respectful. They also perceived the therapist as experienced and active in the therapeutic situation. In short, the composite picture of the "good" therapist drawn by the respondents was more "human" than the stereotype of the impersonal, detached analyst, an image that psychodynamic therapists still tended to follow. The quality of the patient–therapist relationship again emerged as the fulcrum of therapeutic change, and many of the improvements reported by patients were cast in interpersonal terms.

The collaboration with Allen Bergin in the NIMH-sponsored project designed to explore the feasibility of large-scale studies of process and outcome in psychotherapy (Bergin & Strupp, 1972) had called forceful attention to questions about the relative contributions to treatment outcomes of nonspecific (common or interpersonal) and specific (technique) variables, a topic that had begun to receive considerable attention in the research literature. Although Bergin and I had concluded that large-scale collaborative studies did not appear feasible at the time, we outlined a number of projects whose pursuit we believed would contribute materially to scientific progress. I elected to pursue the topic of specific and nonspecific factors in what came to be known as the Vanderbilt I study.

From a theoretical perspective, I published a number of articles (Strupp, 1959, 1960a, 1969, 1970, 1972a, 1972b, 1973) whose primary objective was to shed further light on the therapist's contribution to the treatment process and on the kinds of learning experiences patients underwent in successful treatment. A few years later, Strupp, Hadley, and Gomes-Schwartz (1977) addressed the problem of negative effects in psychotherapy from a clinical and theoretical perspective. In addition, work had been progressing on the development of several process measures, beginning in the 1950s with a system for analyzing therapists' communications (Strupp 1957a, 1957b). Two additional instruments, the Vanderbilt Psychotherapy Process Scale (VPPS) and the Vanderbilt Negative Indicators Scale (VNIS; Suh, O'Malley, & Strupp, 1986) were subsequently created to aid in the quantitative study of patient–therapist interactions in psychodynamic psychotherapy.

Vanderbilt I

In the Vanderbilt I study, beginning in the early 1970s, the Vanderbilt team endeavored to assess empirically the relative contribution of nonspecific and specific factors to therapeutic outcomes. The design called for systematic comparisons between the performance of trained psychotherapists and a group of college professors who lacked formal training in psychotherapy but who were selected for their caring and warmth in human relationships. In a nutshell, we (Strupp & Hadley, 1979) discovered that technical and interpersonal factors cannot be readily partitioned and that the nature of the psychotherapeutic influence is considerably more complex than had been assumed. We also adduced evidence to help us pinpoint more sharply where to look for the answers.

The absence of hypothesized group differences between trained therapists and college professors was a highly provocative finding that required further explanation. In particular, we realized that group comparisons often obscure important but subtle differences. To deal with this problem, we carried out intensive process studies to shed light on the factors differentiating successful from unsuccessful outcomes (Gomes-Schwartz, 1978; Hartley & Strupp, 1983; Sachs, 1983; Strupp 1980a, 1980b, 1980c, 1980d). We observed the following:

1. The group data had obscured the finding that professional therapists were often more effective than lay therapists with patients showing such characteristics as high motivation for psychotherapy, ability to rapidly form a good working alliance, and relative absence of longstanding maladaptive patterns of relating to others.

2. Neither group was notably effective in treating patients with more severe characterological problems, manifested by pronounced hostility, pervasive mistrust, negativism, inflexibility, and the like.

3. The quality of the patient–therapist working alliance seemed to be formed rather quickly (by the end of the third session) and was shown to be an important predictor of outcome in a time-limited context (approximately 25 sessions). In addition, we obtained evidence that reasonably good predictions of process can be made from the first session, particularly judgments relating to the patient's motivation for therapy. Most important, we found evidence that an initially negative or ambivalent therapeutic alliance was rarely altered in the course of the therapies under study. Thus, we encountered again the previously mentioned leitmotiv, that is, therapists' difficulties in managing hostility— both patients' and their own—and the devastating effect of this problem on outcome.

4. Professional therapists generally failed to adapt their therapeutic approach or techniques to the specific characteristics and problems of individual patients, and they did not formulate specific therapeutic goals that were then systematically pursued. On the whole, we found substantial evidence that when the therapist maintains a fairly rigid approach, the quality of the therapeutic relationship was determined to a very important degree by *patient* characteristics, that is, the patient's ability to relate comfortably to, and work productively within, the therapist-offered conditions.

5. Professional therapists, although well versed in the concepts of transference and countertransference, nonetheless often reacted negatively and countertherapeutically to a patient's hostility.

Strupp (1980a, 1980b, 1980c, 1980d) intensively studied eight cases from the Vanderbilt I data bank in which four therapists had each treated a good- and a poor-outcome case. The third session of these eight cases was later subjected to a fine-grained (utterance-by-utterance) interpersonal process analysis using the Structural Analysis of Social Behavior (SASB; Henry, Schacht, & Strupp, 1986). Results indicated that although the therapists used similar techniques in their good- versus poor-outcome cases, the therapies differed markedly in the quality of the interpersonal processes that emerged. Furthermore, although technique varied substantially across the four therapists being studied, the actual interpersonal processes differentiating high-change and low-change outcomes were markedly similar across dyads. In the poor-outcome cases, therapists engaged in a surprising amount of subtly controlling blame of the patient (which was usually responded to by the patient in complementary fashion, namely, with hostile submission). Finally, therapist and patient complex communications ("mixed messages" containing simultaneous affiliative and disaffiliative components) were relatively common in poor-outcome cases but virtually absent with the same therapist in their good-outcome cases. The foregoing research-informed case studies represent what Soldz (1989) has termed a promising new genre, an approach we have continued to cultivate.

Example: A male college student who was suffering from a moderately severe depression seemed intent from the start on provoking his male therapist. The latter, while ostensibly trying to empathize with the patient who complained that people in his life were rejecting him, was being drawn into an argument with the patient. The latter had asked a young woman for a date, but she laughed at him. The therapist chose to deal with the issue by actively confronting the patient, which clearly diminished further the patient's self-esteem. The therapist said, "What do you do to catch people's attention? You must be doing something . . . usually people don't notice. You sit there and look mad." The patient responded with a challenge: "There is nothing to feel cheery about." Pursuing the attack, the therapist observed, "People don't like you. I haven't heard anything that might get them to act differently" (Strupp, 1980b).

The Era of Therapy Manuals

One of the difficulties facing psychotherapy researchers before about 1980 was the absence of clear descriptions of the independent variable, the nature of the treatment under study. Behaviorally oriented researchers had begun to set the stage for treatment manuals by carefully delineating their "treatment packages" so as to further an understanding of the treatment and to permit replication. The problem was more complex in the case of the psychodynamic psychotherapies, which traditionally had been described only in broad outlines. The scene changed radically as psychodynamic therapies rapidly became the subject of manualization (e.g., Klerman, Rounsaville, Chevron, Neu, & Weissman, 1984; Luborsky, 1984; Strupp & Binder, 1984). Although they were moving the field in the direction of greater specification, psychodynamically based treatment manuals still remained relatively general. Nonetheless, they became the standard in government-funded psychotherapy research. Together with treatment manuals, instruments were created to measure the degree to which therapists "adhered" to a particular approach (e.g., Rounsaville, O'Malley, Foley, & Weissman, 1988).

Manuals that were based on psychodynamic principles brought about a number of improvements. Specifically, they provided (a) descriptions of technical concepts in a language closer to the experiences of actual practice, (b) specific and concrete models for organizing clinical material around a focal theme, (c) clearer definitions of the therapeutic processes, (d) better descriptions of the therapist's role, and (e) extensive verbatim illustrations of the therapist at work. Although treatment manuals have elucidated technical concepts more effectively than previous texts, they still have not captured conceptually the blending of technical adherence and other skills that constitute therapeutic expertise. However, they have highlighted the problem of conceptualizing therapist skillfulness (Schaffer, 1982, 1983).

Time-limited dynamic psychotherapy (TLDP) was developed by Strupp and Binder (1984) as an approach to individual psychotherapy that emphasizes analysis of the patient–therapist relationship (transference and countertransference) as the central task for the psychotherapist. It is based on psychoanalytic conceptions (Gill, 1982; Schlesinger, 1982) as well as on formulations by interpersonal theorists (Anchin & Kiesler, 1982; Epstein & Feiner, 1979; Levenson, 1972; Sullivan, 1953). TLDP attempts to specify principles and strategies geared to the assessment and management of potential problems in the therapeutic relationship. Interpersonal problems that emerge in therapy are assumed to be similar in form and content to the chronic maladaptive interpersonal patterns that underlie the patient's difficulties in living, often expressed as symptoms such as anxiety and depression.

Fuller discussions of our approach are found in Strupp and Binder (1984) and Binder and Strupp (1991). For the present purposes, it suffices to mention that patients' resistances to the therapeutic work are seen as manifestations of their difficulties in establishing a meaningful, collaborative, and successful relationship with the therapist. These difficulties are not fundamentally different from the patient's problems in establishing satisfying relationships in their lives. Transference, in our view, refers to the tendency to reenact problematic interpersonal scenarios within the therapy. Accordingly, the therapist's task consists of identifying the problematic interpersonal patterns (called *cyclical maladaptive patterns*) as they evolve in the therapeutic relationship and helping the patient to understand, rather than act out, the problematic interpersonal scenarios. Therapeutic change was thus hypothesized to occur as a result of the patient's developing *awareness* of his or her self-defeating patterns and his or her *experience* of a different outcome within the therapeutic relationship itself.

Manuals appeared to be particularly useful in time-limited approaches to psychotherapy, in which therapists, patients, and society at large have shown increasing interest. Indeed, it may be said that time-limited or short forms of psychotherapy constitute the wave of the future. In part, this development occurred as a function of determined attempts by an increasingly cost-conscious society to shorten long-term and intensive forms of psychotherapy whose cost was considered excessive. Efforts to shorten psychotherapy had begun in the early 1920s (Ferenczi & Rank, 1925), were resumed in the 1940s (Alexander & French, 1946), and began to occupy center stage in the 1980s (Crits-Christoph & Barber, 1991).

A central feature of all short-term or time-limited forms of psychotherapy has been the delineation of a circumscribed area of work, variously called *dynamic focus* (Malan, 1963, 1976), *core-conflictual re-*

lationship theme (Luborsky, 1977) *cyclical maladaptive pattern* (see earlier discussion), and the like. This development was consonant with the objective of behavioral and cognitive forms of therapy that, from their beginning, had posited specific goals and developed technical procedures for achieving them. The latter encompassed limited, circumscribed, skill-deficiency problems that have been shown to respond well to structured treatments (Lambert, 1991, p. 9).

Although treatment manuals achieved greater specification of a particular treatment, they assumed that therapists who adhered to a particular manual were doing so skillfully. Both in longer and shorter forms of psychotherapy there has been a dearth of research on such questions as how to define the skills required for adequate performance, how skills are acquired, and how skillful performance can be measured.

Vanderbilt II

As a result of our research in Vanderbilt I and broader developments within psychotherapy research, issues of training and competence had become a major interest of the Vanderbilt team. Thus, following the development of our TLDP manual, we wished to explore in greater detail and depth the extent to which therapists acquire the skills stipulated by the manual. We therefore undertook pilot work to explore the feasibility of a study that was specifically focused on the training of therapists. The major objective of what became a long-term study (Vanderbilt II) was to examine as closely as possible the effects of specialized training on therapist performance and on the therapeutic process in time-limited dynamic psychotherapy. Specifically, the study was an attempt to enhance therapists' performance by specialized training that would sensitize them to hostile interactions and give them tools for more effectively managing hostility.

We recruited eight psychiatrists and eight clinical psychologists who had completed graduate training in dynamic psychotherapy and had from 4 to 9 years of postgraduate experience without emphasis on time limits. Our main objectives were to provide a full-year's training in TLDP and to carry out systematic comparisons of the therapists' performances before and after training. The comparisons were based on the interactions between each therapist and comparable patients (2 before, 2 after, and 1 during training), each of whom was treated in 25 hours of weekly psychotherapy. The database, therefore, consisted of 80 patients and their therapists. Extensive assessments were obtained before and during therapy as well as at termination and at 1- and 2-year follow-ups. A long-term follow-up study 4 to 5 years after termination is in progress.

In Phase I of the study, each therapist treated two carefully selected patients in accordance with the therapist's "usual" practices (except for audiotape recording of all sessions, videotaping of the 3rd and 16th session, and extensive assessments). During Phase II (the training period), each therapist treated a so-called training case under supervision. In the final phase (Phase III), each therapist again treated two patients, comparable with those in Phase I. In Phase III, therapists were encouraged—although not required—to use TLDP principles and techniques in accordance with their clinical judgment.

To administer the TLDP training program in a reasonably parsimonious fashion, we formed four groups of four therapists. Each group was led by a senior therapist (the authors of the manual), each of whom was assisted by a more junior clinician. Groups met for 2 hours each week for a full year (approximately 100 hours). The supervision was preceded by a didactic portion, in which therapists studied the TLDP manual and were given lectures by the team leaders.

Supervision itself was conducted along fairly traditional lines, with detailed emphasis on TLDP principles and techniques as well as on the management of hostile and negativistic patient–therapist interactions whose signal importance had been highlighted in our previous research. We observed the following:

1. Results clearly showed that the training program was successful in teaching our manualized form of psychotherapy to independently judged criteria of adherence. The pre–post training comparisons (with therapists serving as their own controls) were very encouraging, that is, therapists showed the predicted increments in the use of specific TLDP techniques (Henry, Strupp, Butler, Schacht, & Binder, 1993). There was further evidence that training also improved their general interviewing style. These results were consonant with the findings obtained by other investigators (e.g., Luborsky, McLellan, Woody, O'Brien, & Auerbach, 1985; Rounsaville et al., 1988).

With respect to the relationship between technical adherence and outcome (Henry, Strupp, et al., 1993; Henry, Strupp, Schacht, Binder, & Butler, in press), significantly better posttraining outcomes occurred, as judged by the treating therapists, but this was not reflected in the ratings of the independent clinicians and in the patients' self-reports. This relationship between TLDP training and improved outcome was, however, not immediately apparent in direct pre–post comparisons of all dyads, but instead appeared more clearly in the comparisons of the training groups.

2. The pronounced subgroup differences appeared to be attributable to differences in the conduct of the training program. An informal analysis of the sound-recorded training sessions suggested that the subgroup with the lower adherence (Group B) engaged in discussions of therapeutic processes and psychodynamics at higher levels of abstraction (more or less akin to traditional supervision), whereas the group with the higher adherence (Group A) focused more consistently on microevents in the patient–therapist transactions. Furthermore, the leader of Group A was more active in the supervision sessions, focusing more

specifically and directively on TLDP principles and techniques. Although the leader of Group B followed very similar precepts, his approach might be characterized as more open-ended or laissez-faire. We also noted that in Group A there were greater improvements in the patients' cyclical maladaptive patterns.

3. We obtained another finding of potentially great importance that may have diminished our chances of demonstrating stronger relationships between technical adherence and treatment outcome. Corroborating the results of a study by Henry et al. (1986), we found that therapists whose introject emerged as self-controlling and self-blaming showed the highest technical adherence to TLDP. Moreover, when we examined treatment outcomes as a function of the therapist's introject, we found that self-controlling and self-blaming therapists had outcomes that were significantly poorer than those of therapists having different patterns. Finally, therapists with self-indicting introjects were judged to display in their therapy sessions the least warmth and friendliness, and their patients showed the highest level of hostility. Thus, it appeared that therapists who were most vulnerable to certain types of problematic processes were the ones most likely to manifest greater technical adherence to the new training protocol. These findings also suggested a puzzling interaction that worked against a demonstration that specialized training enhances treatment outcomes.

4. Concomitant with the finding that training increased the activity level of our therapists, we also adduced evidence that therapists frequently tended to apply their recently learned techniques in a forced and mechanical manner, suggesting that *adherence* to particular aspects of a protocol and *skillful* performance were far from synonymous. Finer distinctions may also have to be made between particular components of a training program and overall skill.

5. The changes in the perceptions of the same therapists by their pre- and posttraining patients were likewise intriguing. On the one hand, posttraining patients described their therapists as more genuine and at ease in the relationship; on the other hand, with higher technical adherence, patients often experienced their therapists as more impatient, and the patients often had greater difficulty in making themselves understood.

These and other seemingly contradictory changes in process suggested that altering therapists' interpersonal behaviors as one means of improving their technical skills is a complex and demanding process that calls for a new—and perhaps fairly radical—reconceptualization of training procedures (see the next section). In particular, it became clear that training therapists in manualized therapies to criteria of technical adherence does not by itself specify and control "the therapist variable" to the extent that had been anticipated. Although a number of benefits had apparently accrued to therapists as the result of specific training, we continued to be confronted by a finding of major importance, namely, the pronounced inability of therapists to avoid countertherapeutic processes with difficult patients. Indeed, this recurrent finding emerged again as the hallmark of the Vanderbilt research group's efforts.

Further Comments on the Vanderbilt Leitmotiv: Negative Complementarity

At the beginning of this chapter, we referred to the serendipitous finding that therapists often developed strong negative attitudes toward a filmed patient with whom they had been asked to "interact." The patient was an angry, hostile, and provocative individual who often elicited markedly negative (complementary) reactions from many viewers whose attitudes crystallized rapidly, perhaps in a few minutes. More important, the therapists' negative attitudes were also reflected in their "communications" (i.e., written statements) to the patient as well as in their diagnostic impressions, treatment plans, and prognostic judgments. Strupp (1960a) speculated that there may be a circular relationship involving a therapist's attitude toward a patient, the therapists' clinical judgments, and the quality of the patient–therapist communications.

Subsequently, we repeatedly found, both in the Vanderbilt I and the Vanderbilt II studies, that angry, hostile, and negativistic patients tended to elicit negative responses from their therapists who, in turn, had marked difficulties in dealing with these manifestations of negative transference. In short, empirical research confirmed that the problem of managing negative transference, particularly with more difficult patients (e.g., those with a borderline personality disorder) is one of the most critical challenges facing the practicing therapist. Furthermore, the work raised serious questions as to whether traditional therapist training programs adequately equip therapists to defuse these attacks and turn them to therapeutic advantage. The therapist's personal analysis therapy, as advocated in psychoanalytic training, is clearly not a panacea for dealing with the problem.

Closely related to the foregoing issue was the frequent occurrence of accusatory and pejorative communications (Wile, 1984) that difficult patients tended to elicit from their therapists. In our experience, the vicious circle that may thus be created usually originates with the patient, more rarely with the therapist. Because of their early interpersonal life experiences, patients have been "programmed" to induce a significant other (including prominently the therapist) to play a particular, often rejecting, part in their problematic interpersonal scenarios, thereby potentially vitiating the therapeutic effort. Therapists are thus in great danger of getting embroiled in such scenarios and responding with pejorative or rejecting communications.

Typical of the latter were disaffiliative and complex mixed messages that were simultaneously supportive and critical or demeaning (see earlier discussion). Thus, it emerged that whereas the absence of poor process does not ensure a good therapeutic outcome, the presence of even small amounts of poor process was almost always linked to poor outcome. Therefore, the therapist's ability to limit participation in a (negative) complementary role and doing so consistently appears to be one of the important touchstones of therapeutic competence. It is a paradox that for therapists to be understanding and empathic—and therefore potentially effective—they must be willing to become participants in the patient's troublesome interpersonal scenarios. Equally important, however, they must be capable of extricating themselves from the patient's neurotic net. They can do so primarily by engaging in communications that have neutral or positive complementarity as well as by empathic metacommunications about the transactions in the therapeutic relationships. This ability to oscillate constructively between the roles of a participant (empathic listener) and effective metacommunicator may well be the centerpiece of the dynamic therapist's expertise. In our experience, this complex skill is by no means as common as might be expected; in fact, it seems to be relatively rare.

Overall, our data strongly suggested that the meaningfulness of efficacy research will be enhanced if we can acquire a deeper understanding of exactly what happens in the therapeutic process when therapists attempt to apply particular therapeutic techniques. As we discovered, there is no straight-line function between technical adherence, interpersonal process, and patient and therapist characteristics. These variables interact in complex ways to shape treatment outcomes. To extract the greatest possible meanings directly relevant to treatment efficacy and future training programs, it is now necessary to search for and to describe in much greater detail and penetration dyads sharing common process and outcome features. Our current research addresses this question by examining specific transactions in cases with divergent outcomes treated by the same therapist. We have placed great hope in and become impressed with the heuristic value of intensive, research-informed analyses of contrasting single-case patient–therapist dyads. Finally, we have begun to deal more critically with issues of training, particularly the problems surrounding the acquisition of therapeutic expertise.

Further Observations on Therapists' Training

In our training program, we followed time-honored practices. We reviewed general psychodynamic strategies but focused consistently on microevents in the therapeutic process to enhance our therapists' ability to detect and constructively respond to transference enactments. In so doing, we took advantage of the professional training and the clinical experience our therapists had brought with them. They also had varying amounts of personal therapy that undoubtedly had raised their awareness of transference and countertransference issues; personal therapy may also have contributed to a better understanding of their "blind spots" and their personal problems. All therapists had been recommended by their former trainers and supervisors on the basis of interest, competence, and caring. By following the invitation to participate in our research and training program, they had undertaken a very substantial responsibility (a 3-year commitment) that entailed a significant amount of work (typically 2-hour weekly evening meetings) beyond their regular clinical duties. On the other hand, they were under no explicit obligation to consistently implement TLDP principles and techniques in the project cases after training.

We had made the tacit assumption that all therapists started from similar baselines of competence and motivation, that they were fairly comparable in their ability to profit from TLDP training, and that they were learning at a similar rate and speed. We had further assumed that patient variables (other than "difficulty") would not play a significant role and could be left uncontrolled. In brief, in the overall design of our study, we treated therapists as interchangeable units, thus courting the danger of what Kiesler (1966) has termed the *uniformity myth*.

Although the therapists' adherence to TLDP technical guidelines in the posttraining phase increased, we had no independent measure of the extent to which TLDP was being practiced *skillfully*. Indeed, as previously noted, therapists frequently used TLDP techniques in an awkward, mechanical, and forced manner. It was as if they wanted to demonstrate that they had "mastered" the techniques we had attempted to teach, but their effort often did not result in a smooth and well-integrated performance. At times, the therapists' attempts to apply TLDP principles and techniques gave rise to *adverse* reactions on the patients' part.

In short, we discovered what educators in other domains of skill (e.g., other professions, sports) have known, namely, that attempts to modify a smoothly functioning albeit imperfect performance may for a time result in a more awkward, forced, and poorly timed one (Henry, Schacht, Strupp, Butler, & Binder, 1993). Such disruptions may be temporary until a new plateau is reached; however, we had no data to explore whether the therapists' awkwardness eventually gave way to more secure expertise, whether they continued to practice TLDP, or whether their performance reverted to the status quo.

Is adherence to a treatment manual an adequate index of a therapist's newly acquired expertise? There is reason to believe that treatment manuals may not adequately capture the blending of a particular approach with other skills that encompass a therapist's expertise. Also unresolved are questions relating to the *impact* (or *effect*) of a particular TLDP intervention. As with psychotherapy process research in general, it is difficult to determine the effect from a patient's immediate response to, say, an interpretation dealing with a "disguised allusion to the transference" (Gill, 1982). Should we accept as a criterion the patient's *immediate* response to the therapist's intervention or should we search for effects later in the same hour or further on? Although no satisfactory algorithms are available, it seems reasonably certain that the patient's *immediate* response to a therapist intervention must be viewed with considerable skepticism. Nor can studies of broader "episodes" or "events" answer the question in an unequivocal manner, partly because we do not know how to demarcate them. The immediate response may be a convenient measure, but it is clearly of limited value.

In other words, we do not know to what extent a manualized approach results in measurable improvements of a therapist's skillfulness and expertise. Eventually, the therapist may feel comfortable with a new approach and recognize its value, but the changes may be quite subtle and hence not amenable to measurement by available instruments. Nor should one expect dramatic changes in treatment outcomes that, as we know, are so profoundly affected by patient variables and the idiosyncrasies of the patient–therapist interaction.

Acquisition of Therapeutic Skills

Traditionally, training programs have placed great stress on the mastery of clinical theory, which in largely unspecified ways is expected to give rise to technical competence (Binder, in press). Technical skills are thought to be honed through readings, lectures, supervision of the trainee's actual work, and, to a lesser extent, observing highly experienced colleagues at work. In the language of cognitive psychology, the therapist must have both *declarative* knowledge (i.e., principles, concepts, and understanding of configurations) and *procedural* knowledge (i.e., decisions and actions that result in a successful performance; Chase & Simon, 1973; Chi, Glaser, & Farr, 1988).

In psychodynamic training programs, it has generally been assumed that declarative knowledge is sufficient to activate procedural knowledge. Declarative knowledge has been thought to hold the key to what is important to know, although it frequently fails to inform the student when or how to use it (Binder, in press). The latter must be taught through specific instruction. Bransford and Vye (1988) have described a gradual process by which the teacher's "implicitly communicated knowledge" is "internalized" by the learner. Inexperienced therapists (like other novices) tend to rely rigidly on technical rules that, in practice, may actually interfere with full attention to the patient's communications. The process of acquiring new skills may also involve an extended period of disorganization and awkwardness.

In discussing the application of cognitive psychology principles to therapy training, Binder (in press) emphasized the relationship between instructional techniques and the student's ability subsequently to access information. It appears that the following conditions exert primary influence on the depth of comprehension and accessibility of acquired knowledge.

1. The knowledge to be learned must be explicitly linked or made relevant to a problem to be solved (Chi et al., 1988).

2. The knowledge must be acquired through *active* involvement of the learner in a manner that encourages both memorization and comprehension of the material. Learners must be encouraged to view the material from a variety of perspectives and develop meaningful elaborations about it. In addition, the material must be presented in a manner that elicits a process of linking the new material with previous knowledge (Bransford et al., 1982).

3. The knowledge must be acquired in a context as similar as possible to the conditions of actual practice so that the learner learns to recognize features of problems as they appear in reality. The learner is also encouraged to practice selecting relevant from irrelevant material in the context of problem solving (Rock & Bransford, 1990).

A structured teaching format that is designed around these three conditions is called *anchored instruction* (Bransford, Franks, Vye, & Sherwood, 1989; Michael, 1989; Risko et al., 1989; Rock, 1990; Rock & Williams, 1991). Material is presented in narrative form on video recordings (tape or disc formats). Anchored instruction then provides the student with the opportunity to actively engage in solving authentic problems in a realistic context. It facilitates learning not only of facts and procedures but also of the conditions in which they are useful. Learners have the opportunity to practice separating relevant from irrelevant information and formulating relevant information into a problem statement. After the recorded material is viewed, the learner is presented with a problem that involves a principle or concept to be learned. The learner must combine reading about the to-be-learned material with searching the video material for relevant information. This process is iterated for learning new principles and concepts, often with the same video material.

In summary, our training program had been designed to teach *both* declarative and procedural knowledge, but the links between the two were perhaps not sufficiently stressed during training. To the extent that we failed to teach procedural knowledge, we may have contributed to the acquisition of "inert" knowledge, that is, abstract (declarative) knowledge that our therapists were unable to access and use at the proper time.

Outlook

Psychotherapy has always been a very practical undertaking, emerging from the clinician's desire to help a suffering human being in the most

effective, economical, efficient, and humane way. Accordingly, psychotherapeutic techniques have, in Einstein's phrase, been "free inventions
of the human spirit" rather than blueprints created in the armchair or
the laboratory. The clinician's first question has always been, How can
I help? Almost simultaneously, practitioners have devised theories to
explain why a treatment works. Of course, a treatment or a set of therapeutic procedures may work when the theory is wrong; or the theory
may be reasonable but the techniques may be inefficient or ineffective.
The point is that the individual practitioner has no sure way of answering
these questions because one must necessarily rely on the clinical method,
that is, on the naturalistic observation of a few cases. Furthermore, the
history of science amply demonstrates that humanity's capacity for self-
deception is so great that misconceptions (e.g., the geocentric view of
the universe) may persist for centuries.

As modern psychotherapy gained momentum around the turn of
the 19th century and as its practitioners grew in number, questions were
raised about the quality of outcome, the nature of the problems to which
psychotherapy might be applied, and the relative effectiveness of different techniques. From slow beginnings in the 1940s, research in psychotherapy has grown in size and quality. It plays a significant part in
developments in contemporary behavioral and clinical science and as
such exemplifies the application of modern scientific methodology to
the solution of important clinical and theoretical problems. There are
numerous indications that research in this area is coming of age and
that several developments warrant greater optimism about the future
than was common among researchers only a decade or two ago (Bergin
& Strupp, 1972).

The quality of research has markedly increased. The main requirements of good research—to describe with increasing precision the nature of the therapeutic interventions, the kinds of patients whom a
particular form of therapy is designed to benefit, and the changes expected from these interventions—are being taken much more seriously.
Journal editors and granting agencies, as well as researchers themselves,
demand greater specificity that is rapidly becoming the hallmark of well-
designed studies. Although definitive studies are still difficult to find,
researchers have developed a surer grasp of the design requirements
of good research in the area, and they are better able to avoid studies
leading predictably to dead ends. If progress in science means, in part,
to become increasingly aware of the sources of one's ignorance, together
with an ability to ask better questions, psychotherapy research has made
significant advances. Persisting problems relate less to questions of what
needs to be done than to the logistics of doing it (e.g., recruiting adequate
samples of a patient population, obtaining the cooperation of clinic
staffs, dealing with the enormously time-consuming and labor-intensive
tasks faced by studies about the process of therapy).

Research in psychotherapy is expensive, but the cost is far less than that of research in the physical and biomedical sciences. Although governmental support of research in psychotherapy has not kept pace with inflation and social needs, well-designed research continues to have a fair chance of being supported (NIMH being by far the leading funding source).

The desideratum of specificity has enormous practical implications because it will lead to more focused therapeutic strategies and provide sharper answers to the question of what psychotherapy can do for particular patients, at what cost, and over what periods of time. Other important areas of growth that can only be briefly mentioned include (a) greater rapprochement between researchers, therapists, and theoreticians, reflecting a trend toward eclecticism; (b) clarification of what constitutes a good therapeutic outcome; (c) refinement of diagnostic categories to aid in treatment planning; (d) explorations of what briefer or time-limited forms of psychotherapy can contribute as well as specification of the limitations of such treatment; (e) development of more clearly defined techniques for the treatment of particular patient problems (e.g., biofeedback techniques for the treatment of tension headaches and insomnia, brief dynamic psychotherapy for the resolution of "focal" problems, the treatment of sexual dysfunctions by behavioral techniques); (f) improvements in the training of psychotherapists; and (g) a greater understanding of factors leading to negative effects.

In conclusion, I wish to offer a comment on the future relationships between practicing therapists and researchers. In the past, therapists have tended to regard researchers as unwelcome intruders who disrupted the sanctity of the patient–therapist relationship, produced findings of peripheral or trivial interest to the practitioner, and robbed a living human relationship of its excitement and vitality. To be sure, every scientific effort seeks to order, simplify, condense, and control. It is also true that practitioners cannot directly apply statistical trends (such as averages) in their everyday dealings with patients; they must deal with the inevitable idiosyncrasies of every patient–therapist interaction. The greater contribution of psychotherapy research may ultimately lie on a different plane: Researchers of the future, who must also be well-trained clinicians, must learn to work more closely with practicing therapists on vital issues encountered in everyday clinical work, subject these issues to empirical analysis and test, and provide clinicians with information they can use more readily. What is envisaged is a form of action research, originally proposed by Lewin (1947), in which research is brought to bear on a practical (clinical) problem; research findings are then applied in the clinical setting; and their utility is again tested by means of research. Thus, there results a continuous and productive feedback loop in which practice inspires research, and research provides information that is relevant to practice. For example, researchers may recommend to a clinic, on the basis of available research data relating to optimal matches between therapists and patients, that particular patients be assigned to particular therapists. The outcome of these dyads may then be studied and compared with contrasting assignments; on the basis of these results, subsequent assignment procedures may then be modified in the light of new information, at which point the process is repeated. This approach might also have important implications for the selection and training of young therapists. Obviously, it would not replace more sustained research efforts along traditional lines, but it would be one means of bringing about a closer working alliance between therapists and researchers.

As responsible professionals, therapists must learn to think critically and scrutinize continually the quality of their professional activities and the "therapeutic product." This has always been the hallmark of a mature profession (Peterson, 1976). As steps are taken in this direction, it is predictable that psychotherapy will become a better and more mature profession, meriting society's confidence and respect. Last, but not least, psychotherapy will become a profession that is based on solid scientific knowledge.

Future Directions

Psychotherapy is a service offered by professionals drawn from a variety of disciplines (medicine, nursing, psychology, and social work). It is a treatment system that is influenced by the values and norms of (a) each discipline; (b) the public (e.g., patients, families, schools, and courts); and (c) mental health policy makers (e.g., governmental agencies and insurers). Each of these constituencies has unique requirements regarding the kinds of psychotherapy research information that would be useful. Moreover, from the point of view of an investigator, clinical practitioners, a fourth constituency, and yet another set of values and norms. How is psychotherapy research going to serve these varied constituencies in the future?

1. As psychologists, our training leads us to an application of the experimental approach (the true experiment) in order to specify the causal mechanisms of change. In this context, we must develop theoretical propositions and subject these to rigorous empirical tests. Our discipline trains us in this methodology and our colleagues (e.g., personality, social, cognitive, and physiological psychologists), reviewers, and review committees hold this methodology in the highest esteem. This has led us to focus on a clearer specification and monitoring of our main independent variable, the treatment conditions (e.g., through the development of treatment manuals and integrity checks). The future should witness an even stronger trend in this direction, especially with the emergence of a more phenomenologically oriented cognitive psy-

chology. However, we should not overlook the fact that psychotherapy proceeds in the context of a human relationship; therefore, patient qualities, therapist qualities, and their interactions in a given dyad play an important role that is perhaps greater than that of techniques per se.

2. The vast majority of people in need of psychotherapy do not come to the attention of any mental health professional. More research attention should be turned to (a) prevention and outreach programs, (b) rehabilitation (e.g., relapse prevention), and (c) the development of psychotherapeutic applications to a broader array of disorders (e.g., substance abuse). We also need to be more active in the development and evaluation of new therapeutic approaches. Moreover, if we are to present a better image to the public and destigmatize the use of our services, more attention should be given to evaluations of training programs and to certification of competence.

3. Psychotherapists operate in the public interest as a service. We must develop a fuller understanding of how this service is financed and distributed, how people are trained to deliver this service, how patients find their way into the system, and the impact of this service on the productive functioning of our patients. The delivery of our services has been significantly influenced by the decisions of policy makers (e.g., session limits, fee limits, and selection of providers). We must provide these policy makers with the best information on which to base their decisions. Hence, we must leave the "laboratory" for more real-world naturalistic investigations, and we must attend to the outcome criteria (e.g., workdays lost, turnover, cost-effectiveness, and cost-efficiency) that concern these policy makers. We can no longer ignore this important constituency. Also, we must provide information regarding the ways in which our services may be of use, in a manner that can be communicated to the public, so that they can become effective advocates of our profession.

4. To make research more relevant to clinicians, we have to disaggregate our results to focus on relevant patient parameters—either individual patients or groups of patients who are clinically (meaningfully) alike in some important way. No clinician will be convinced that a particular treatment is superior for all patients (main effects). Indeed, an important component of clinical work entails making decisions about the appropriateness of an intervention for a particular patient. (As an analogous example, even though, in the treatment of pneumonia, penicillin is more effective than aspirin, a doctor would not give penicillin to a patient who is allergic to the drug.) We need to develop statistical procedures for identifying the joint characteristics of patients, therapists, techniques, and settings that provide acceptable outcomes and those that require the development of new therapeutic approaches. In addition, we should explicitly recognize the advances of psychopharmacological interventions and include these, where suitable and feasible, in our research designs.

The existence of these four constituencies creates a healthy tension between naturalistic (discovery) and experimental (confirmatory) research methodologies. The field of psychotherapy research is charged by this tension and is characterized by excitement and innovation. There is plenty of work to be done by a growing complement of highly trained, productive professionals. The fundamental short-term goal of psychotherapy research is to provide the necessary information for determining to which of a specified set of treatments future patients are to be assigned. The ultimate goal is to refine the best treatments available, namely, to make them more nearly optimal for all patients.

References

Alexander, F., & French, T. M. (1946). *Psychoanalytic therapy: Principles and applications*. New York: Ronald Press.

Anchin, J. C., & Kiesler, D. J. (Eds.). (1982). *Handbook of interpersonal psychotherapy*. Elmsford, NY: Pergamon Press.

Bergin, A. E., & Garfield, S. L. (Eds.). (1971). *Handbook of psychotherapy and behavior change: An empirical analysis*. New York: Wiley.

Bergin, A. E., & Lambert, M. J. (1978). The evaluation of therapeutic outcomes. In S. L. Garfield & A. E. Bergin (Eds.), *Handbook of psychotherapy and behavior change: An empirical analysis* (pp. 139–190). New York: Wiley.

Bergin, A. E., & Strupp, H. H. (1972). *Changing frontiers in the science of psychotherapy*. Chicago: Aldine-Atherton.

Binder, J. L. (in press). Is it time to improve psychotherapy training? *Clinical Psychology Review*.

Binder, J. L., & Strupp, H. H. (1991). The Vanderbilt approach to time-limited dynamic psychotherapy. In P. Crits-Christoph & J. P. Barber (Eds.), *Handbook of short-term dynamic psychotherapy* (pp. 137–161). New York: Basic Books.

Bransford, J. D., Franks, J. J., Vye, N. J., & Sherwood, R. D. (1989). New approaches to instruction: Because wisdom can't be told. In S. Vosniadou & A. Ortony (Eds.), *Similarity and analogical reasoning* (pp. 470–497). New York: Cambridge University Press.

Bransford, J. D., Stein, B. S., Vye, N. J., Franks, J. J., Auble, P. M., Mezynsky, K. J., & Perfetto, G. A. (1982). Differences in approaches to learning: An overview. *Journal of Experimental Psychology: General, 11*, 390–398.

Bransford, J. D., & Vye, N. J. (1988). *Research on cognition and its implications for instruction: An overview*. Unpublished manuscript, Vanderbilt University, Nashville, TN.

Chase, W. G., & Simon, H. A. (1973). Perception in chess. *Cognitive Psychology, 4*, 55–81.

Chi, M. T. H., Glaser, R., & Farr, M. J. (1988). *The nature of expertise*. Hillsdale, NJ: Erlbaum

Crits-Christoph, P., & Barber, J. P. (Eds.). (1991). *Handbook of short-term dynamic psychotherapy*. New York: Basic Books.

Dittmann, A. T. (1962). The relationship between body movements and moods in interviews. *Journal of Consulting Psychology, 26*, 480.

Elkin, I., Parloff, M., Hadley, S., & Autry, J. (1985). NIMH Treatment of Depression Collaborative Research Program: Background and research plan. *Archives of General Psychiatry, 42,* 305–316.

Elkin, I., Shea, M. T., Watkins, J. T., Imber, S. D., Sotsky, S. M., Collins, J. F., Glass, D. R., Pilkonis, P. A., Leber, W. R., Docherty, J. P., Fiester, S. J., & Parloff, M. B. (1989). NIMH Treatment of Depression Collaborative Research Program: General effectiveness of treatments. *Archives of General Psychiatry, 46,* 971–983.

Emmelkamp, P. M. G. (1986). Behavior therapy with adults. In S. L. Garfield & A. E. Bergin (Eds.), *Handbook of psychotherapy and behavior change* (3rd ed., pp. 385–442). New York: Wiley.

Epstein, L., & Feiner, A. H. (Eds.). (1979). *Countertransference.* Northvale, NJ: Jason Aronson.

Eysenck, H. J. (1952). The effects of psychotherapy: An evaluation. *Journal of Consulting Psychology, 16,* 319–324.

Fenichel, O. (1930). Statistischer Bericht über die therapeutische Tätigkeit, 1920–1930 [Statistical report on the therapeutic activities, 1920–1930]. In *Zehn Jahre Berliner Psychoanalytisches Institut* [Ten years of the Berlin Psychoanalytic Institute], (pp. 13–19). Vienna: International Psychoanalytischer Verlag.

Ferenczi, S., & Rank, O. (1925). *Development of psychoanalysis* (C. Newton, Trans.). New York: Nervous and Mental Disease Publishing Company.

Fiedler, F. (1950a). A comparison of therapeutic relationships in psychoanalytic, nondirective, and Adlerian therapy. *Journal of Consulting Psychology, 14,* 436–445.

Fiedler, F. (1950b). The concept of an ideal therapeutic relationship. *Journal of Consulting Psychology, 14,* 239–245.

Fiedler, F. (1951). Factor analyses of psychoanalytic, nondirective, and Adlerian therapeutic relationships. *Journal of Consulting Psychology, 15,* 32–38.

Fiske, D. W., Hunt, H. F., Luborsky, L., Orne, M. T., Parloff, M. D., Reiser, M. F., & Tuma, A. H. (1970). Planning of research on effectiveness of psychotherapy. *Archives of General Psychiatry, 22,* 22–32.

Frank, J. D. (1973). *Persuasion and healing: A comparative study of psychotherapy* (2nd ed.). Baltimore: Johns Hopkins University Press.

Frank, J. D. (1974). Therapeutic components of psychotherapy. *Journal of Nervous and Mental Disease, 159,* 325–342.

Frank, J. D. (1982). Therapeutic components shared by all psychotherapies. In J. H. Harvey & M. M. Parks (Eds.), *Psychotherapy research and behavior change* (Vol. 1, The Master Lecture Series, pp. 5–37). Washington, DC: American Psychological Association.

Freud, S. (1963). Analytic therapy. In J. Strachey (Ed. & Trans.), *The standard edition of the complete psychological works of Sigmund Freud* (Vol. 16, pp. 448–463). London: Hogarth Press. (Original work published 1916).

Freud, S. (1964). Analysis terminable and interminable. In J. Strachey (Ed. & Trans.), *The standard edition of the complete psychological works of Sigmund Freud* (Vol. 23, pp. 216–253). London: Hogarth Press. (Original work published 1937)

Garfield, S. L., & Bergin, A. E. (Eds.). (1978). *Handbook of psychotherapy and behavior change: An empirical analysis* (2nd ed.). New York: Wiley.

Garfield, S. L., & Bergin, A. E. (Eds.). (1986). Introduction and historical overview. In S. L. Garfield & A. E. Bergin (Eds.), *Handbook of psychotherapy and behavior change* (3rd ed., pp. 3–22). New York: Wiley.

Gill, M. M. (1982). *Analysis of transference I: Theory and technique.* Madison, CT: International Universities Press.

Gomes-Schwartz, B. (1978). Effective ingredients in psychotherapy: Predictions of outcome from process variables. *Journal of Consulting and Clinical Psychology, 46,* 1023–1035.

Hamburg, D. A., Bibring, G. L., Fisher, C., Stanton, A. H., Wallerstein, R. S., Weinstock, H. I., & Haggard, E. (1967). Report of ad hoc committee on central fact-gathering data of the American Psychoanalytic Association. *Journal of the American Psychoanalytic Association, 15,* 841–861.

Hartley, D. E., & Strupp, H. H. (1983). The therapeutic alliance: Its relationship to outcome in brief psychotherapy. In J. Masling (Ed.), *Empirical studies of psychoanalytical theories* (Vol. 1, pp. 1–37). Hilldale, NJ: Analytic Press.

Henry, W. P., Schacht, T. E., & Strupp, H. H. (1986). Structural analysis of social behavior: Application to a study of interpersonal process in differential psychotherapeutic outcome. *Journal of Consulting and Clinical Psychology, 54,* 27–31.

Henry, W. P., Schacht, T. E., Strupp, H. H., Butler, S. F., & Binder, J. L. (1993). The effects of training in time-limited dynamic psychotherapy: Mediators of therapists' response to training. *Journal of Consulting and Clinical Psychology, 61,* 441–447.

Henry, W. P., Strupp, H. H., Butler, S. F., Schacht, T. E., & Binder, J. L. (1993). The effects of training in time-limited dynamic psychotherapy: Changes in therapist behavior. *Journal of Consulting and Clinical Psychology, 61,* 434–440.

Henry, W. P., Strupp, H. H., Schacht, T. E., Binder, J. L., & Butler, S. F. (in press). The effects of training in time-limited dynamic psychotherapy: IV. Changes in therapeutic outcome. *Journal of Consulting and Clinical Psychology.*

Hollon, S. D., & Beck, A. T. (1986). Research on cognitive therapies. In S. L. Garfield & A. E. Bergin (Eds.), *Handbook of psychotherapy and behavior change* (3rd ed., pp. 443–482). New York: Wiley.

Howard, K. I., Kopta, S. M., Krause, M. S., & Orlinsky, D. E. (1986). The dose–effect relationship in psychotherapy. *American Psychologist, 41,* 159–164.

Howard, K. I., & Orlinsky, D. E. (1972). Psychotherapeutic processes. *Annual Review of Psychology, 23,* 615–668.

Imber, S. D., Pilkonis, P. A., Sotsky, S. M., Watkins, J. T., Shea, M. T., Elkin, I., Collins, J. F., Leber, W. R., & Glass, D. R. (1990). Mode-specific effects among three treatments for depression. *Journal of Consulting and Clinical Psychology, 58,* 352–359.

Kiesler, D. J. (1966). Some myths of psychotherapy research and the search for a paradigm. *Psychological Bulletin, 65,* 110–136.

Klerman, G. L., Rounsaville, B., Chevron, E., Neu, C., & Weissman, M. M. (1984). *Interpersonal psychotherapy of depression.* New York: Basic Books.

Lambert, M. J. (1991). Introduction to psychotherapy research. In L. E. Beutler & M. Crago (Eds.), *Psychotherapy research.* Washington, DC: American Psychological Association.

Levenson, E. A. (1972). *The fallacy of understanding: An inquiry into the changing structure of psychoanalysis.* New York: Basic Books.

Lewin, K. (1947). Frontiers in group dynamics: II. Channels of group life: Social planning and action research. *Human Relations, 1*, 143–153.

Luborsky, L. (1977). Measuring a pervasive psychic structure in psychotherapy: The core conflictual relationship theme. In N. Freedman & S. Grand (Eds.), *Communicative structures and psychic structures*. New York: Plenum Press.

Luborsky, L. (1984). *Principles of psychoanalytic psychotherapy: A manual for supportive–expressive treatment*. New York: Basic Books.

Luborsky, L., McLellan, A. T., Woody, G. E., O'Brien, C. P., & Auerbach, A. (1985). Therapist success and its determinants. *Archives of General Psychiatry, 42*, 602–611.

Malan, D. H. (1963). *A study of brief psychotherapy*. New York: Plenum Press.

Malan, D. H. (1976). *Toward the validation of dynamic psychotherapy: A replication*. New York: Plenum Press.

McNeilly, C. L., & Howard, K. I. (1991). The effects of psychotherapy: A reevaluation based on dosage. *Psychotherapy Research, 1*, 74–78.

Michael, A. L. (1989). *The transition from language theory to therapy: Test of two instructional models*. Unpublished doctoral dissertation, Vanderbilt University, Nashville, TN.

Peterson, D. R. (1976). Is psychology a profession? *American Psychologist, 31*, 553–560.

Risko, V. J., Kinzer, C. K., Goodman, J., McLarty, K., Dupree, A., & Martin, H. (1989). *Effects of macrocontexts on reading comprehension, composition of stories, and vocabulary development*. Paper presented at the meeting of the American Educational Research Association, San Francisco.

Rock, D. L. (1990). *Pattern recognition in psychological assessment: Nature of differences between notive, intermediate, and expert psychotherapists*. Unpublished manuscript, Vanderbilt University, Nashville, TN.

Rock, D. L., & Bransford, J. D. (1990). *An empirical evaluation of three components of the tetrahedon model of clinical judgment*. Manuscript submitted for publication.

Rock, D. L., & Williams, S. M. (1991). *Anchored instruction: Suggestions for research on therapist learning*. Manuscript submitted for publication.

Rogers, C. R. (1951). *Client-centered therapy*. Boston: Houghton Mifflin.

Rogers, C. R., & Dymond, R. F. (Eds.). (1954). *Psychotherapy and personality change*. Chicago: University of Chicago Press.

Rounsaville, B. J., O'Malley, S., Foley, S., & Weissman, M. M. (1988). Role of manual-guided training in the conduct and efficacy of interpersonal psychotherapy for depression. *Journal of Consulting and Clinical Psychology, 56*, 681–688.

Rubinstein, E. A., & Parloff, M. B. (Eds.). (1959). *Research in psychotherapy* (Vol. 1). Washington, DC: American Psychological Association.

Sachs, J. S. (1983). Negative factors in brief psychotherapy: An empirical assessment. *Journal of Consulting and Clinical Psychology, 51*, 557–564.

Schaffer, N. D. (1982). Multidimensional measures of therapist behavior as predictors of outcome. *Psychological Bulletin, 92*, 670–681.

Schaffer, N. D. (1983). Methodological issues of measuring the skillfulness of therapeutic techniques. *Psychotherapy: Theory, Research and Practice, 20*, 486–493.

Schlesinger, H. (1982). Resistance as a process. In P. Wachtel (Ed.), *Resistance in psychodynamic and behavioral therapies*. New York: Plenum Press.

Shlien, J. M., Hunt, H. F., Matarazzo, J. D., & Savage, C. (Eds.). (1968). *Research in psychotherapy* (Vol. 3). Washington, DC: American Psychological Association.

Smith, M. L., Glass, G. V., & Miller, T. I. (1980). *The benefits of psychotherapy*. Baltimore: Johns Hopkins University Press.

Soldz, S. (1989). The therapeutic interaction. In R. A. Wells & V. J. Giannetti (Eds.), *Handbook of the brief psychotherapies* (pp. 27–53). New York: Plenum Press.

Strupp, H. H. (1955a). An objective comparison of Rogerian and psychoanalytic techniques. *Journal of Consulting Psychology, 19*, 1–7.

Strupp, H. H. (1955b). Psychotherapeutic technique, professional affiliation, and experience level. *Journal of Consulting Psychology, 19*, 97–102.

Strupp, H. H. (1955c). The effect of the psychotherapist's personal analysis upon his techniques. *Journal of Consulting Psychology, 19*, 197–204.

Strupp, H. H. (1957a). A multidimensional analysis of techniques in brief psychotherapy. *Psychiatry, 20*, 387–397.

Strupp, H. H. (1957b). A multidimensional system for analyzing psychotherapeutic techniques. *Psychiatry, 20*, 293–306.

Strupp, H. H. (1958). The psychotherapist's contribution to the treatment process: An experimental investigation. *Behavioral Science, 3*, 34–67.

Strupp, H. H. (1959). Toward an analysis of the therapist's contribution to the treatment process. *Psychiatry, 22*, 349–362.

Strupp, H. H. (1960a). Nature of psychotherapist's contribution to treatment process: Some research results and speculations. *AMA Archives of General Psychiatry, 3*, 219–231.

Strupp, H. H. (1960b). *Psychotherapists in action: Explorations of the therapist's contribution to the treatment process*. New York: Grune & Stratton.

Strupp, H. H. (1969). Toward a specification of teaching and learning in psychotherapy. *Archives of General Psychiatry, 21*, 203–212.

Strupp, H. H. (1970). Specific vs. nonspecific factors in psychotherapy and the problem of control. *Archives of General Psychiatry, 23*, 393–401.

Strupp, H. H. (1972a). Needed: A reformulation of the psychotherapeutic influence. *International Journal of Psychiatry, 10*, 114–120.

Strupp, H. H. (1972b). On the technology of psychotherapy. *Archives of General Psychiatry, 26*, 270–278.

Strupp, H. H. (1973). On the basic ingredients of psychotherapy. *Journal of Consulting and Clinical Psychology, 41*, 1–8.

Strupp, H. H. (1980a). Success and failure in time-limited psychotherapy: A systematic comparison of two cases (Comparison 1). *Archives of General Psychiatry, 37*, 595–603.

Strupp, H. H. (1980b). Success and failure in time-limited psychotherapy: A systematic comparison of two cases (Comparison 2). *Archives of General Psychiatry, 37*, 708–716.

Strupp, H. H. (1980c). Success and failure in time-limited psychotherapy: With special reference to the performance of a lay counselor (Comparison 3). *Archives of General Psychiatry, 37*, 831–841.

Strupp, H. H. (1980d). Success and failure in time-limited psychotherapy: Further evidence (Comparison 4). *Archives of General Psychiatry, 37*, 947–954.

Strupp, H. H., & Bergin, A. E. (1969). Some empirical and conceptual bases for coordinated research in psychotherapy: A critical review of issues, trends and evidence. *International Journal of Psychiatry, 7*, 18–90.

Strupp, H. H., & Binder, J. L. (1984). *Psychotherapy in a new key: A guide to time-limited dynamic psychotherapy*. New York: Basic Books.

Strupp, H. H., Butler, S. F., & Rosser, C. L. (1988). Training in psychodynamic psychotherapy. *Journal of Consulting and Clinical Psychology, 56*, 689–695.

Strupp, H. H., Fox, R. E., & Lessler, K. (1969). *Patients view their psychotherapy*. Baltimore: Johns Hopkins University Press.

Strupp, H. H., & Hadley, S. W. (1979). Specific versus nonspecific factors in psychotherapy: A controlled study of outcome. *Archives of General Psychiatry, 36*, 1125–1136.

Strupp, H. H., Hadley, S. W., & Gomes-Schwartz, B. (1977). *Psychotherapy for better or worse: An analysis of the problem of negative effects*. Northvale, NJ: Jason Aronson.

Strupp, H. H., & Howard, K. I. (1992). A brief history of psychotherapy research. In D. Freedheim (Ed.), *History of psychotherapy: A century of change* (pp. 309–334). Washington, DC: American Psychological Association.

Strupp, H. H., & Luborsky, L. (Eds.). (1962). *Research in psychotherapy* (Vol. 2). Washington, DC: American Psychological Association.

Suh, C. S., O'Malley, S. S., & Strupp, H. H. (1986). The Vanderbilt process measures: The Psychotherapy Process Scale (VPPS) and the Negative Indicators Scale (V-NIS). In L. S. Greenberg & W. M. Pinsof (Eds.), *The psychotherapeutic process: A research handbook* (pp. 285–324). New York: Guilford Press.

Sullivan, H. S. (1953). *The interpersonal theory of psychiatry*. New York: Norton.

Wile, D. B. (1984). Kohut, Kernberg, and accusatory interpretations. *Psychotherapy, 21*, 353–364.

EARN CONTINUING EDUCATION CREDITS THROUGH HOME STUDY PROGRAMS BASED ON THE APA MASTER LECTURES

The Master Lectures, presented each year at the APA Convention, can be used to earn Continuing Education (CE) Credits through the successful completion of a test developed to accompany most volumes of this series. The following Home Study Programs are available:

1993—"PSYCHOLOGY AND THE LAW"

1992—"A CENTENNIAL CELEBRATION—FROM THEN TO NOW: PSYCHOLOGY APPLIED"

1991—"PSYCHOPHARMACOLOGY"

1990—"PSYCHOLOGICAL PERSPECTIVES ON HUMAN DIVERSITY IN AMERICA"

1989—"PSYCHOLOGICAL ASPECTS OF SERIOUS ILLNESS"

1988—"THE ADULT YEARS: CONTINUITY AND CHANGE"

1987—"NEUROPSYCHOLOGY AND BRAIN FUNCTION"

For more information about the Home Study Programs, detach and mail the form below (please print, type or use pre-printed label), or telephone 202/336-5991, 9 a.m.–5 p.m. EST/EDT.

- ✂

Please send me more information about APA's Home Study Programs for Continuing Education Credit.

Name: _____

Address: _____

_____

_____

    (City)   (State)   (Zip code)

Daytime phone: _____ / _____
              Area Code

Mail this form to the following address:

Continuing Education Home Study Programs
American Psychological Association
750 First Street, NE
Washington, DC 20002
202/336-5991